# the GOD of Abraham, Isaac & Jacob

by Theodore H. Epp

Director
Back to the Bible Broadcast

Back to the Bible
Lincoln, Nebraska 68501

38,000 printed to date—1981
(5-0684—3M—121)
ISBN 0-8474-1286-5

Printed in the United States of America

# Foreword

In the title *The God of Abraham, Isaac and Jacob*, the emphasis is on the word "God." The men involved were important only as they permitted God to reveal Himself through their lives. In these three men we see the long-suffering and patience of God in molding men into what He wants them to be. When God begins to do a work in a man's life, He does not stop until that work is finished. This is never more clearly seen than in the lives of Abraham, Isaac and Jacob.

The biographical studies of these three men are not left on the parched pages of history. They are brought home pointedly to the 20th-century Christian. These men were not perfect. They were mightily used of God, but they also had great weaknesses. The present-day believer will be encouraged to realize that if God could do such a work in the lives of these men, He can work mightily in his life also.

Abraham, Isaac and Jacob were distinctively different. Abraham had an obedient faith, Isaac had a passive faith, and Jacob had a restless faith. Somewhere in the lives of these three men every believer will find himself. From the pages of this book you will gain a new appreciation of how God is able to take what the world considers foolish and use it to put to shame what the world considers wise. You will thrill at the ways of God as you see how He works out His sovereign plan through human vessels. The study of the lives of these three men will give you a greater concept of who God is and what He wants to do through your life.

As Theodore Epp prepared these messages—first for radio, then for book form—his main burden was that believers might realize that the God of Abraham, Isaac and Jacob is their God also. Mr. Epp, through the urging of the

Spirit in his own life, was especially concerned that all of us might realize that this same God—unchanged—is just as powerful and great in meeting our needs as He was in meeting the needs of Abraham, Isaac and Jacob. It is wonderful to be able to say, "This same God is our God." It is even more wonderful to be able to say, "This same God is *my* God."

May this book cause you to exclaim in worship, "How fathomless the depths of God's resources, wisdom, and knowledge! How unsearchable His decisions, and how mysterious His methods! For who has ever understood the thoughts of the Lord, or has ever been His adviser? Or who has ever advanced God anything to have Him pay him back? For from Him everything comes, through Him everything lives, and for Him everything exists. Glory to Him forever! Amen" (Rom. 11:33-36, *Wms.*).

—*The Publishers*

# CONTENTS

Chapter 1

# The God of Abraham, Isaac and Jacob

It is not enough just to know information about the Bible. We must relate the Word of God to our lives. Even more than that—we must relate the Eternal God to our lives.

The Scriptures speak of the God of Abraham, the God of Isaac, and the God of Jacob. Is He really your God too? Perhaps you wonder how you can relate the God of Abraham, Isaac and Jacob to your life. It will become obvious to you, however, as we see what the Scriptures have to say about God and His relationship with Abraham, Isaac and Jacob.

God told Moses, "I am the God of thy father, the God of Abraham, the God of Isaac, and the God of Jacob" (Ex. 3:6). When Moses heard this he "hid his face; for he was afraid to look upon God." Exodus 3:6 is not the only place in Scripture where God is referred to as the God of Abraham, Isaac and Jacob. In the New Testament, Christ Himself referred to this description of God when He said to the Sadducees, "But as touching the resurrection of the dead, have ye not read that which was spoken unto you by God, saying, I am the God of Abraham, and the God of Isaac, and the God of Jacob? God is not the God of the dead, but of the living" (Matt. 22:31,32). Notice especially Christ's statement that "God is not the God of the dead, but of the living." This same Almighty God is living today. Through faith in Him, every person can be delivered from condemnation and can have God residing in his life to produce fruit by His Spirit (John 5:24; 15:5).

Not only is God still living, but His Word is living also. Hebrews 4:12 says, "For the Word that God speaks is alive and active: it cuts more keenly than any two-edged sword: it strikes through to the place where soul and spirit meet, to the innermost intimacies of a man's being: it exposes the very thoughts and motives of a man's heart" (*Phillips*). If there were no other proof of the inspiration of the Scriptures, this is sufficient—the Word of God lives. The longer I study the Bible and dig deeper into it, the more it does for my heart. One of the multitude of blessings I have received from the Word of God is the realization that the God of Abraham, Isaac and Jacob is the same God I serve. You, too, will be greatly encouraged as we study the living Word and see that this same God can be your God too.

As we consider man's creation and his fall into sin, we are taken back to Genesis—the book of origins, or beginnings. Most everything, except God Himself, can be traced back to the Book of Genesis. This book gives us the beginning of the universe, life, man, covenants, marriage, sin, redemption, death, nations, governments, music, art, literature, agriculture, mechanics, cities, languages, etc.

As to the origin of man, he was created to be a companion to God. This is a significant truth to remember throughout our study of the God of Abraham, Isaac and Jacob. We must never forget God's original intention for man—that of relationship and fellowship with Himself. Genesis 1:26,27 tells us, "And God said, Let us make man in our image, after our likeness: and let them have dominion over the fish of the sea, and over the fowl of the air, and over the cattle, and over all the earth, and over every creeping thing that creepeth upon the earth. So God created man in his own image, in the image of God created he him; male and female created he them." Thus we see that man is the offspring of God. As such, he is related to God in different ways.

## Related by Creation

Man is directly related to God by creation because he was created by God. Because God made man, He alone perfectly understands man. So also God is the only One who can perfectly govern man because He knows every detail about every man.

When we look upon ourselves as fallen men, we find it hard to understand how there has ever been a close relationship between man and God. Sin broke this relationship, and even after the relationship is restored it is strained by sin. As we consider God's purpose in creating man and then see how man has been alienated from God, we are caused to wonder how there could ever be a true fellowship with God again. It is only logical for each of us to ask, How can I really have fellowship with such a holy God, who was the God of Abraham, the God of Isaac, and the God of Jacob? But there is a way that we can have fellowship with God even as these great patriarchs of the faith had.

## Related by Authority

There is an intimate fellowship we can have with God because He, in His sovereign power, governs us. In fact, man cannot live apart from God. Colossians 1:16,17 tells us, "For it was through him that everything was made, whether spiritual or material, seen or unseen. Through him, and for him, also, were created power and dominion, ownership and authority. In fact, every single thing was created through, and for, him. He is both the first principle and the upholding principle of the whole scheme of creation" (*Phillips*). God is not only the Creator but He is also the upholding principle of the whole creation. As we consider man's degeneracy in contrast to the holiness of God, we are forced to ask, Is there any hope? Can man—can I—actually have an intimate relationship with God?

As we trace man's history after his fall into sin, it looks more and more doubtful that a harmonious relationship between God and man could ever exist again. The third chapter of Genesis records man's fall into sin; the fourth chapter tells of the first recorded murder; chapters 6-8 describe the terrible destruction of the universal flood; and chapter 11 relates man's attempt to build the Tower of Babel in defiance of God. But God is not dead. And because He is living and because He is God, He had a plan for restoring man's fellowship with Himself.

Concerning Christ, we are told in Colossians that "he is the head of the body which is the Church. Life from nothing began through him, and life from the dead began through him, and he is, therefore, justly called the Lord of all. It was in him that the full nature of God chose to live, and through him God planned to reconcile in his own person, as it were, everything on earth and everything in Heaven by virtue of the sacrifice of the cross. This reconciliation assumes, of course, that you maintain a firm position in the faith, and do not allow yourselves to be shifted away from the hope of the gospel, which you have heard, and which, indeed, the whole world is now having an opportunity of hearing. I myself have been made a minister of the same gospel" (1:18-20,23, *Phillips*).

Christ originated physical life through His creative powers. Man now has physical life, but because of his fall into sin he is spiritually dead. But just as Christ was able to produce life from nothing, so also He is able to bring life out of death. Therefore, He is "justly called the Lord of all." Through Christ every person is made reconcilable to God. Because of what He did on the cross, every person can be reconciled to God by receiving Jesus Christ as his personal Saviour.

There is no room for any wavering of faith here. There was a wavering of faith in Genesis 3 when the Devil, through the serpent, said to Eve, "Yea, hath God said, Ye shall not eat of every tree of the garden?" (v. 1). Later, in verse 4, the Devil told her, "Ye shall not surely die." This was the opposite of what the Lord had told Adam and Eve: "But of the tree of the knowledge of good and evil, thou shalt not eat of it: for in the day that thou eatest thereof thou shalt surely die" (Gen. 2:17). Satan is the great slanderer and liar. Jesus Himself said of him, "He is a liar, and the father of it" (John 8:44). Truly one begins to wonder if there is any hope for man. Because of a lack of faith, Adam and Eve disobeyed God. But at the cross, faith and obedience are joined together–resulting in a wonderful restoration of man's relationship to God. Our greatest need is to trust and obey.

The requirement to trust and obey is so simple and yet so profound. It is the very heart of true Christian religion. In fact, we can call it the "law of faith." In using the word "law," I am not referring to the Old Testament Law but to a principle that is always true, such as the law of gravity. The law of faith is the basis on which God can work out His will in man, and man can demonstrate through his life the salvation he has received from God.

That faith is the basis on which God works will also be seen as we study the lives of Abraham, Isaac and Jacob. The fundamental truth is that man can only realize his own God-created life by trusting God and walking in His way by true obedience. Thus, as we move into the life stories of these men, we will see through God's revelation that He is seeking to restore men to obedience by restoring them to the main principle of human life–that of faith in Himself. God is the God of the living, and it is only through faith in Him that man can be restored to his true relationship with God.

## Kinds of Faith

God was willing to call Himself the God of all three of the men we are considering–Abraham, Isaac and Jacob. He was willing to be called the God of these three men even though they were very different in character and had a great variance in their faith response to God. Abraham's faith was an obedient faith, whereas Isaac's faith was a passive faith. Jacob, on the other hand, had a restless faith. As we study the patriarchs, it is not until we observe Joseph's life that we see the perfection of faith, or the resting faith.

Somewhere in these three principal characters of the Old Testament, I am sure you will find demonstrated the kind of faith you have. You will see yourself described in Abraham if you have a great and obedient faith. You will find God doing great things for you in spite of the fact that He will take you through many trials. Or perhaps you see yourself with a faith like Isaac's. He had a passive faith and did not do great, outstanding things as the world measures them. If yours is a restless faith, and if you are unable to wait for God to work, you will find yourself described in Jacob. Or perhaps your faith is like that of Joseph, who had a resting faith, or a perfected faith.

In Hebrews 4:9-11 we are told, "There still exists, therefore, a full and complete rest for the people of God. And he who experiences his rest is resting from his own work as fully as God from his. Let us then be eager to know this rest for ourselves, and let us beware that no one misses it through falling into the same kind of unbelief as those we have mentioned" (*Phillips*). In other words, when we believe God as He is revealed through His Word, we will find the full and complete rest that He has for His people.

Faith has different forms of expression. Abraham's faith always took the form of unquestioned obedience. Abraham made many mistakes but he had an obedient faith that did not question God. Isaac was different. His faith took the form of passive expression. God spoke to him merely to ratify what He had already said to Abraham. There was nothing especially new given to Isaac. Rather than an acting faith, his faith was more the kind that accepted without resisting. He was submissive to his father and to God, but he performed no great acts of adventuring faith himself. Yet God chooses to be called "the God of Isaac" as well as "the God of Abraham."

Jacob was altogether different from Abraham and Isaac. His faith took the expression of restlessness—he could not wait on God. The communications from God always came to Jacob after a period of spiritual wandering, and their purpose was to restore his fellowship with God.

Even though the faith of all three of these men took different forms of expression, we must recognize that at least they all did exercise faith. Abraham's was an obedient faith; Isaac's was a passive faith; and Jacob's was a restless faith. Yet there was faith. God was able to work in remaking these men because they were men of faith. They were able to find their way back into conscious relationship with God because of their faith. So again we see that faith is the basis on which God works out His will in man. Also, it is through faith that man is enabled to realize the will of God.

In Romans 12:1,2 we see the relationship between an obedient faith and discovering the will of God. Paul wrote: "I beseech you therefore, brethren, by the mercies of God, that ye present your bodies a living sacrifice, holy, acceptable unto God, which is your reasonable service. And be not conformed to this world: but be ye transformed by the renewing of your mind, that ye may prove what is that good, and acceptable, and perfect, will of God."

When we have an obedient faith we will present our bodies and renew our minds as we are instructed. The result will be our discovering or proving what is God's good, acceptable and perfect will. God will reveal His will to us when we are obedient to Him. As we are obedient in one step, God will show us the next step. From the lives of Abraham, Isaac and Jacob we will see the importance of living by faith one step at a time. Man can only find himself and realize the true meaning of his own life as he places his confidence in God and obeys Him with unquestioning loyalty.

You, too, can establish a conscious relationship with God by obedient faith. You will not be able to salvage the years you have wasted, but you can go forward with God from this point if you will serve Him through an obedient faith. If you have sinned and have not yet confessed that sin to God, you should do so now so you can move forward with Him. The Word of God promises that "if we confess our sins, he is faithful and just to forgive us our sins, and to cleanse us from all unrighteousness" (I John 1:9).

Remember that the God who identifies Himself as the God of Abraham, Isaac and Jacob also identifies Himself as your God and my God. However, in order to have this vital relationship and fellowship with Him, we must have an obedient faith that takes God at His word and acts accordingly. Notice the promises in II Corinthians 6:17,18: "Wherefore come out from among them, and be ye separate, saith the Lord, and touch not the unclean thing; and I will receive you, And will be a Father unto you, and ye shall be my sons and daughters, saith the Lord Almighty." When we are obedient to God in doing what He says, He promises three things: "I will receive you, And will be a Father unto you, and ye shall be my sons and daughters." The same truth is emphasized in Revelation 21:7: "He that overcometh shall inherit all things; and I will be his God, and he shall be my son." All of this results from an obedient faith.

The lives of Abraham, Isaac and Jacob show the significance of the phrase, "The just shall live by faith" (Rom. 1:17). This statement was first recorded in Habakkuk 2:4, and in addition to Romans 1:17 it is mentioned in Galatians 3:11 and Hebrews 10:38. It is an irrefutable scriptural principle that those who are justified are to live on the basis of faith. That this principle underlies our entire relationship with God is seen from Hebrews 11:6: "But without faith it is impossible to please him: for he that cometh to God must believe that he is, and that he is a rewarder of them that diligently seek him." This means there is hope for you. You can have God's blessing on your life and experience intimate fellowship with Him if you will exercise your faith in Him and take Him at His word.

## The Response to God's Communications

God's communications to Abraham, Isaac and Jacob were distinctively different. He communicated differently with each man. Why? Because He knows man. He knows all the details about your life and mine, and He knows how to deal with us.

There were seven divine communications with Abraham, each initiating a significant move forward. Every time God appeared to Abraham there was a giant forward step involved. Abraham responded with an obedient faith—he obeyed God.

There were only two divine communications to Isaac. The purpose of these was to ratify what had already been told to Abraham. There was no special call given to Isaac nor any specific action asked of him. Isaac was not discontent, however, for he accepted these things obediently and waited upon God.

There were five divine communications with Jacob, and in each of them God arrested Jacob's activity and changed the order of his life. Jacob was usually doing something out of the way—either running ahead of God or backsliding—and God came to him, halted him in his ways and redirected his life. Jacob had a restless faith. Nevertheless, he became obedient.

## God Communicates With Abraham

As we consider each of these men in more detail, we notice that the first communication to Abraham was a call to leave his country and to set his face toward a new land with new conditions of life. God told Abraham (whose name was Abram at the time), "Get thee out of thy country, and from thy kindred, and from thy father's house, unto a land that I will shew thee" (Gen. 12:1). This is all the information Abraham had about the land he was to seek. Abraham moved slowly at first in incomplete action, but after a time he came to the land of Canaan.

After Abraham had come to the land, God communicated a second time with him and said, "I will make of thee a great nation, and I will bless thee, and make thy name great; and thou shalt be a blessing: And I will bless them that bless thee, and curse him that curseth thee: and in thee shall all families of the earth be blessed" (vv. 2,3). In addition to promising Abraham a land, God promised him a seed (descendants) and a blessing. But at this time it was only a promise. All Abraham could do was wait on God in faith.

God's third communication with Abraham resulted in the land being given to him directly, but under very interesting and remarkable circumstances of faith. There was a quarrel between his herdsmen and the herdsmen of Lot. Knowing it would be better for them to live in different places, Abraham gave Lot his choice of the land. After Lot and his herdsmen had departed from Abraham, God said to Abraham, "Lift up now thine eyes, and look from the place where thou art northward, and southward, and eastward, and westward: For all the land which thou seest, to thee will I give it, and to thy seed for ever. And I will make thy seed as the dust of the earth: so that if a man can number the dust of the earth, then shall thy seed also be numbered. Arise, walk through the land in the length of it and in the breadth of it; for I will give it unto thee" (13:14-17).

In His fourth communication with Abraham, God promised him a seed which would become a great nation. Up until now He had simply said, "Unto thy seed." There had been no further details given. Abraham asked God, "Lord God, what wilt thou give me, seeing I go childless, and the steward of my house is this Eliezer of Damascus? And Abram said, Behold, to me thou hast given no seed: and, lo, one born in my house is mine heir" (15:2,3). God graciously answered Abraham, saying, "This shall not be thine heir; but he that shall come forth out of thine own bowels shall be thine heir" (v. 4). God had now become more specific to Abraham regarding his seed.

In the fifth communication with Abraham, God reiterated His solemn covenant with Abraham and gave circumcision as the sign of the covenant. God's covenant with Abraham was an unconditional one and could not be broken.

God's sixth communication with Abraham was a final and direct promise of the birth of a son in the following year. God told Abraham, "I will certainly return unto thee according to the time of life, and, lo, Sarah thy wife shall have a son" (18:10).

The seventh and final communication of God with Abraham was when God tested Abraham's faith regarding the offering of his son, Isaac. Genesis 22 deals with this crucial time in Abraham's life.

In these seven communications God led Abraham through circumstances that became more and more trying. Because Abraham followed by faith, God was able to lead him on to higher experiences and larger possessions that were not just associated with the earth. Anything that Abraham sacrificed so that he might enjoy the fellowship of God was reduced to nothingness in view of what he received. He was loaded daily with God's benefits. He forsook a home, but he received a country. He cut himself off from the past, but he entered into the present with all God's provisions and into the future with all God's promises. He forfeited an inheritance of his forefathers, but he received eternal treasures. He lived in a tent in the wilderness instead of a roofed house in Ur, but he gained for himself a city whose builder and maker was God. It is always so.

The only reason God deprives man is that He might make room for something better. All of this is given to us in God's Word that we may benefit from the experiences of others. First Corinthians 10:11 reminds us that "these things happened unto them for ensamples: and they are written for our admonition, upon whom the ends of the world are come."

## God Communicates With Isaac

In contrast to Abraham, Isaac led a very simple life—unassuming and uneventful. In the quietness of his life, Isaac had two communications from God. In the first, God revealed to him that the covenant made with Abraham should continue in him. No action was called for on Isaac's part. The only requirement necessary was a faith in God to do what He had promised. Genesis 26:1-5 tells us about this communication with Isaac. God commanded him not to go down into Egypt but to dwell in the land of Canaan. God promised Isaac, "I will make thy seed to multiply as the stars of heaven, and will give unto thy seed all these countries; and in thy seed shall all the nations of the earth be blessed" (v. 4).

God communicated with Isaac the second time for the purpose of ratifying the same covenant. The Lord appeared to Isaac and said, "I am the God of Abraham thy father: fear not, for I am with thee, and will bless thee, and multiply thy seed for my servant Abraham's sake" (v. 24).

Thus we see that Isaac was a quiet type of person—restful and passive. His life was not characterized by actions of magnificence nor by great daring triumphs. God never broke in on Isaac's life with the thick darkness of trial that Abraham passed through or with the alarming struggle at Peniel that Jacob experienced. Although Isaac had a quiet and simple life, he, too, was included in the covenant and received covenant privileges. Isaac, the well digger, was necessary in God's great plan and economy.

It is important to remember that we are all needed in God's great plan. It is not necessary for everyone to be a trailblazer or pioneer of faith as Abraham was. There are those whom God calls for this type of work, and I am thankful He called us to venture out as pioneers of faith regarding the Back to the Bible Broadcast. But God has not called everyone to do this type of work.

### God Communicates With Jacob

Neither should everyone be like Jacob, a man with a restless spirit who was never securely anchored in God until he was crippled at Peniel. God dealt with Jacob in an entirely different manner because Jacob was an entirely different type of person. The greatest aspect of Jacob's life is that he was a man who believed God. Nevertheless, he was a man of restless activity because he had a restless faith. The five communications of God with him were all for the purpose of checking him, correcting his methods and keeping him in the pathway of the divine will. Whereas God dealt with Abraham so that he might move forward in new adventures of faith, God had to deal with Jacob in order to correct him.

God first communicated with Jacob after he had left home for a new country. Jacob had to leave home because of his trickery and deceit. He had connived with his mother to obtain the blessing which God had meant for him to have anyhow. Although Jacob believed it was in the purpose of God for him to receive the blessing, he was unable to wait on God. Thus he connived and deceived until it was necessary for him to flee from the wrath of his brother Esau. At the encouragement of his parents, Jacob fled to his uncle, Laban—his mother's brother.

On the first night of Jacob's flight, he was lying under the stars with a rock for his pillow when God appeared to him with great tenderness. God knew Jacob's heart and He knew how to bridge the gulf between Jacob's materialistic desires and spiritual realities. God did not come to Jacob scoldingly, even though Jacob had done wrong. However, Jacob suffered for his disobedience because he had to be away from his home and his loving mother for 20 years. The fact is, he never saw his mother again. Jacob experienced all of this because of his carnality.

Nevertheless, when God appeared to Jacob in a vision of a ladder with angels ascending and descending, He confirmed to Jacob the same covenant that He had made with Abraham and had confirmed with Isaac. Genesis 28:10-15 records this significant time in Jacob's life, which we will be examining later in greater detail.

The second time God appeared to Jacob was after Jacob's 20 years of heartbreaking experience with Laban and after Jacob had become rich in earthly goods. Lest Jacob should become satisfied with his present success in an alien land, God appeared to him and commanded him to return. The Lord said to Jacob, "Return unto the land of thy fathers, and to thy kindred; and I will be with thee" (31:3). Other than the command to return to the place where he had met God, there was nothing especially new that was revealed to Jacob in God's appearance to him. Jacob obeyed God and made preparation to return to the land of his fathers.

The methods Jacob used in returning revealed his self-reliance and independent spirit. First, Jacob fled from his father-in-law with his family. Then we see Jacob's independent attitude in his praying about meeting Esau. He committed the whole thing to God, but he did not wait for God to perform it. Therefore, there followed a third communication from the Lord. God set Himself against Jacob's independence, and in the mystery of that long night He revealed Himself to Jacob as the Conquering One. The account of Jacob's wrestling with God at the place Jacob later called "Peniel" is given in Genesis 32:24-32. At this time Jacob's name was changed to "Israel" (v. 28). In God's wrestling with Jacob we see God as One who breaks in order to make; as One who cripples in order that He might place a crown. The Scriptures do not give us details of all that went on that night when God revealed Himself as the Conquering One. I am rather glad that He did not give us all the details because even this shows what a wonderful, loving God our God is. He does not expose all of our mistakes to others. The Scriptures only briefly record Jacob's struggle with God and the results that followed.

Once Jacob was back in the land, he immediately compromised with the circumstances that surrounded him. The result was sin and sorrow in his household. So God had to communicate with him again. This fourth time God came to him for the purpose of restoration, commanding him, "Arise, go up to Beth-el, and dwell there: and make there an altar unto God, that appeared unto thee when thou fleddest from the face of Esau thy brother" (35:1).

God's fifth communication was made with Jacob after Jacob obeyed the command to return to Bethel. This time the purpose of God's communication was to further ratify the covenant which He had made with Abraham and had confirmed to Isaac. This crucial appearance of God to Jacob is recorded in Genesis 35:9-13. There is evidence there was another communication of God with Jacob, which was connected with his sons, but we will examine that later in our study.

God's communications with Jacob came at the close of movements in Jacob's life. They were the kind of movements which made it necessary for God to stop Jacob in his way and redirect his life to the proper place and proper action in order for spiritual progress to result. Even though God communicated with Jacob these five times, Jacob's life continued to be of a very restless nature.

Again we see that the one great principle by which God is able to work with man is the principle of faith. It is not faith in man himself—not an independence which runs ahead of God. It is a faith that rests in God. When this is the case, God is able to act. Such faith may express itself in different ways. When God finds obedient faith He leads forward quickly, as we have seen in Abraham's life. Where there is a passive faith, God comforts and strengthens as He did in Isaac's life. But where there is a restless faith, such as Jacob had, God checks and corrects toward the ultimate realization of His goal.

## Joseph's Faith

Although God does not speak of Himself as the God of Joseph, in the life of Joseph we have a further revelation of how God works with individuals. In Joseph we see faith resting in God. We might think of this as the perfection of faith as described in Hebrews 4:9-11, which we have noted previously. There is a rest for the people of God today who place their faith solidly in God. When this is done there is a resting from self-works, even as God rested from His work of creation. So the writer of Hebrews said, "Let us then be eager to know this rest for ourselves, and let us beware that no one misses it through falling into the same kind of unbelief as those we have mentioned" (v. 11, *Phillips*).

Joseph's life shows how God overruled all the failures of man in order to bring about His ultimate good for man. Joseph's faith is the most beautiful picture of the mature Christian who has learned to rely on God and to trust Him to the uttermost. Joseph's great, triumphant faith was revealed in the command he gave concerning his body which he wanted taken back to the land which God had promised to Abraham, Isaac and Jacob (Gen. 50:24-26).

## Practical Lessons From Abraham's Life

It is easy for us to think that Abraham was so far superior to anything we could be that there is very little we can apply from his life to ours. However, we must remember that his greatness stemmed from the fact that he dared to believe God and was obedient to Him. We ought to be this kind of believer also. When we are, each of us will be able to say, "I can do all things through Christ which strengtheneth me" (Phil. 4:13).

In considering the practical lessons from the life of Abraham, we see that he was a pioneer in the life of faith. Remember that he had no Bible like you and I have. He could not go to this wonderful Book to find something from God as we are able to do. His communications with God were on a different basis. Abraham heard the Word from God Himself and became the pioneer in the life of faith. At first we might think that because Abraham's communication was directly from God, he had a more privileged position than we. But think of how much better it is to have God's inerrant Word in printed form so we can read it as often as we want to. Abraham had to rely on his memory, but we have God's recorded Word to refer to. Thus, there is no excuse for our not being strong in faith. Because we have God's recorded Word, it is not necessary for Him to communicate with us as He did with Abraham.

Abraham's faith in God resulted in many wonderful works of obedience. In his life of faith there are many basic principles set forth. As we examine his life in further detail, we will see that it is essential for us to follow these principles if we are to live a faith life today.

In Abraham we also see what we might call the "full life" of faith. We see him going forth, trusting in divine guidance, believing the divine promises, receiving divine assurance, inheriting the divine blessings and undergoing severe testings. Although there were occasional failures, for the most part Abraham lived victoriously for God. God saw his faith and accounted righteousness to him. The Apostle Paul later wrote of Abraham: "He staggered not at the promise of God through unbelief; but was strong in faith, giving glory to God; And being fully persuaded that, what he had promised, he was able also to perform. And therefore it was imputed to him for righteousness" (Rom. 4:20-22). Abraham's walk of faith was so precious in God's sight that Abraham is called "the Friend of God" (James 2:23).

Perhaps you say that it is impossible for you to attain the heights of Abraham's life of faith. But remember, these men we are studying about were people who had natures like you and I have. They became intimate with God because they trusted Him. God will become intimate with you, too, if you will trust Him. Yes, He was the God of Abraham, but He is your God too. For every believer faith is the working principle. It is the principle by which we receive life, walk in dependency on the Lord and mature spiritually. The kind of faith referred to is not the kind that simply agrees to several facts, but it is the kind of faith that is based on the facts and produces action. This is real faith.

## Three Distinct Phases

Abraham's life can easily be divided into three distinct parts. First, there is the awakening of faith. This phase of his life extended from his call in Ur of the Chaldees to his settlement in the land of Canaan—a period of about six years. The Scripture which records this time in Abraham's life is Genesis 11:31—13:18. It was during this time that Abraham became settled in his faith.

Second, there is the disciplining of faith. This part of Abraham's life extended from his settlement in Canaan to the birth of his son Isaac. This is a period of about 25 years and is recorded in Genesis 14:1–21:21.

The third division of Abraham's life has to do with the perfecting of faith. This time extended from the birth of Isaac to Abraham's death. This covers a period of about 75 years and is recorded in Genesis 21:22–25:18.

Notice the progress in these divisions of Abraham's life. He progressed from the awakening of faith to the disciplining of faith to the perfecting of faith.

In Isaac and Jacob, as well as in Joseph—whom we will study briefly—we see men of different temperaments, but faith remains the one and only principle by which God worked in their lives, even as He worked in Abraham's. God always deals with His children on the basis of faith. This is His method of dealing with all mankind, from regeneration to glorification. This is clearly seen from the lives of these men in the Book of Genesis.

The God of Abraham, Isaac and Jacob is also our God. First Corinthians 8:6 tells us, "But to us there is but one God, the Father, of whom are all things, and we in him; and one Lord Jesus Christ, by whom are all things, and we by him." There is but one God, and He is our God. John 1:12 also emphasizes that God is the Father of those who believe when it says, "But as many as received him, to them gave he power to become the sons of God, even to them that believe on his name." Thus, through faith, the God of Abraham becomes our God too. Revelation 21:7 promises: "He that overcometh shall inherit all things; and I will be his God, and he shall be my son." Those who have overcome by faith are the children of God and He is their Father.

What it really means for the God of Abraham, Isaac and Jacob to be your God too will be clearly seen as we study the lives of these men in detail.

Chapter 2

# Abraham's Call

Abraham was chosen or elected on the basis of the sovereignty of God. He had no Bible so he was not able to receive his call through God's written Word. God sought a man, and on the basis of His sovereign will and purpose He chose Abraham.

As to calling or electing we are reminded of Peter's words: "Elect according to the foreknowledge of God the Father" (I Pet. 1:2). Abraham was not chosen because of any merits in his life. His was a supernatural call based on God's own purpose and will. When God calls according to His own purpose and will it is always a call for the good. Abraham had no choice in the matter. God did not ask, "Abraham, would you like to be the man that I can use?" Instead, God said in effect, "Abraham, I want you to come out of your country. . . ."

In considering the choice involved, consider Adam, who was created and placed on earth to begin the human race. Adam had no choice in this. God simply created him and placed him on earth to be the progenitor of mankind.

In contrast, however, consider Noah and his sons. They had the privilege of choosing whether they wanted to be saved from the flood or not. God gave that privilege to everyone, but only Noah, his sons and their wives made the choice to escape the flood. They were saved through the flood for the new beginning after the destruction of a corrupt race.

On the other hand, Abraham was called to begin a special, chosen nation through which salvation would eventually come to all mankind. There was much involved in this great call. God staked His whole plan of redemption on the possibility of a man being willing, by his faith and obedience, to become the bridgehead for delivering an erring world. But did God take a chance? We must not forget Peter's words: "Elect [chosen] according to the foreknowledge of God the Father." The purpose of God's choosing a man was that through that man there would be a family which would become a nation, and that nation would produce the Saviour of the world. Thus with infinite patience and loving care, God shaped and disciplined His man until he reached the pinnacle of spiritual experience, which won for him the distinction of being called "the Friend of God." In addition to this significant description, Abraham is also called "the father of all them that believe" (Rom. 4:11).

All of this came about because God elected Abraham as the person through whom all of these things should be performed. To elect is to choose. Those of the election are those who have been chosen. Election is according to the foreknowledge of God and is wholly of grace apart from any human merit whatever. Election proceeds from the divine volition; that is, God makes the decision based on His thinking and planning. Election is, therefore, the sovereign act of God in grace whereby certain ones are chosen from among mankind for God Himself. Jesus said, "Ye have not chosen me, but I have chosen you" (John 15:16). It is through such a choice that certain persons are chosen for distinctive service for God. Thus it was with Abraham who became "the Friend of God" and "the father of all them that believe."

Have you ever thought about the fact that you and I have the gospel today because Abraham and others who were chosen of God were faithful? God has chosen to work through men; therefore, the future of God's work rests on what He is able to motivate men to do. In Old Testament times the work of God depended on men such as Abraham,

Isaac and Jacob. In New Testament times Jesus Christ made His future program dependent on the apostles. He spent time with these men and properly trained them for the work they had to do. Later, Paul was able to write: "Now therefore ye are no more strangers and foreigners, but fellowcitizens with the saints, and of the household of God; And are built upon the foundation of the apostles and prophets, Jesus Christ himself being the chief corner stone" (Eph. 2:19,20).

Not only was faithfulness required of the patriarchs and the disciples, but it is also required of us because God has committed to us the ministry of reconciliation. Paul wrote: "God was in Christ, reconciling the world unto himself, not imputing their trespasses unto them; and hath committed unto us the word of reconciliation. Now then we are ambassadors for Christ, as though God did beseech you by us: we pray you in Christ's stead, be ye reconciled to God" (II Cor. 5:19,20). There is no choice in the matter. We are the sovereign appointees of God to represent Him to others. Abraham was faithful. The disciples were faithful. Are we faithful?

## An Age of Idolatry

The Lord's call to Abraham is recorded in Genesis 12 where we read: "Now the Lord had said unto Abram, Get thee out of thy country, and from thy kindred, and from thy father's house, unto a land that I will shew thee" (v. 1). The time of Abraham's call is significant. Genesis 11:1-9 records the confusion of tongues at Babel. Here the peoples of the earth were dispersed and various languages came into being. The last part of chapter 11 gives a genealogy and then tells of Abraham's departure from Ur of the Chaldees and his arrival at Haran. Verse 1 of chapter 12 says the Lord "had" spoken to Abraham. This indicates that this took place before Abraham left Ur of the Chaldees for Canaan. Thus we see that Abraham's call came sometime after the destruction of Babel but before he left Ur of the Chaldees for the land that God said He would show him.

Shem was still living at this time, and it is possible that Abraham was born even before Noah died. Abraham grew up in an age of idolatry, as evidenced by what took place at the Tower of Babel. The condition of men's hearts at this time is explained in Romans 1 where Paul wrote: "Because that, when they knew God, they glorified him not as God, neither were thankful; but became vain in their imaginations, and their foolish heart was darkened. Professing themselves to be wise, they became fools, And changed the glory of the uncorruptible God into an image made like to corruptible man, and to birds, and fourfooted beasts, and creeping things" (vv. 21-23).

Man knew God but rejected Him and, as a result, started on the downward path of corruption. Noah and his sons knew God, as did Nimrod, who was born at a later time. However, Nimrod and his followers did not glorify God nor were they thankful, but they became vain in their imaginations. They thought they were wise, but in reality they were fools. They built a great tower and started a new pagan religion, which is the basis of all pagan religions today. Its tentacles are even reaching into the Church Age and producing a desire for an ecumenical church.

It was in the midst of these conditions that God called Abraham. In fact, it is evident from Joshua 24:2,3 that Abraham was an idol worshiper before God called him. Joshua reminded the Israelites, "Thus saith the Lord God of Israel, Your fathers dwelt on the other side of the flood [river] in old time, even Terah, the father of Abraham, and the father of Nachor: and they served other gods. And I took your father Abraham from the other side of the flood [river], and led him throughout all the land of Canaan, and multiplied his seed, and gave him Isaac." So Abraham's family was included in the idolatry of the age.

God dealt in judgment at Babel when He scattered the people and confused their language, but God dealt in mercy and grace as He called Abraham. Abraham did not receive God's call because he merited God's esteem. Rather, in God's foreknowledge He knew Abraham and chose him for a special purpose. God's election must always be traced to God's will and purpose. It is all of grace for it is by God's sovereign choice. This is made clear in Romans 11:5, which refers to God's choice of the nation, Israel. Here Paul said, "Even so then at this present time also there is a remnant according to the election of grace."

It is the same with our salvation. If it were not for God's grace we would be doomed to an eternity in hell. But notice what God has done because of His grace: "But God, who is rich in mercy, for his great love wherewith he loved us, Even when we were dead in sins, hath quickened us together with Christ, (by grace ye are saved;) And hath raised us up together, and made us sit together in heavenly places in Christ Jesus" (Eph. 2:4-6). God did not do this for us because we merited it—it was while we were yet sinners that Christ died for us. It is important that we realize that our salvation is all of grace.

Abraham was not chosen because he was a special kind of person nor because he had a high IQ nor because he had great faith. It was totally of the grace of God that He called Abraham out of idolatry, and it is only of the grace of God that we have been called out to salvation. As referred to previously, God's call to Abraham came while he was still in Ur of the Chaldees. Stephen's message recorded in Acts 7 verifies this. Stephen said, "Men, brethren, and fathers, hearken; The God of glory appeared unto our father Abraham, when he was in Mesopotamia, before he dwelt in Charran [Haran], And said unto him, Get thee out of thy country, and from thy kindred, and come into the land which I shall shew thee. Then came he out of the land of the Chaldaeans, and dwelt in Charran [Haran]: and from thence, when his father was dead, he removed him into this land, wherein ye now dwell" (vv. 2-4). Acts 7

### Obedience With Reservations

Abraham's call demanded absolute confidence in God and total obedience to Him. But God did not force Abraham to respond to the call. Abraham had a free will and had the right to refuse or to obey. Abraham could also make the decision whether to obey with reservations or to obey explicitly.

At first Abraham chose to obey with reservations. God had commanded Abraham not only to leave his country and his kindred but also his father's house. However, in Genesis 11 it is recorded that "Terah took Abram his son and Lot the son of Haran his son's son, and Sarai his daughter in law, his son Abram's wife; and they went forth with them from Ur of the Chaldees, to go into the land of Canaan; and they came unto Haran, and dwelt there" (v. 31). Why Terah went to Haran with Abraham, we do not know. Perhaps Abraham counseled with his father and his father may have decided, "Why don't we all go?" Whatever the reason, we know that Terah was with Abraham when they came to Haran and stopped there.

Abraham was not completely obeying God's call at this time. There were four important parts of God's call to Abraham, which was a call to total separation. First, Abraham was called to "get thee out of thy country" (12:1). This was a call for separation from an idolatrous country. Second, God called Abraham to get away "from thy kindred." In other words, God was saying, "Abraham, leave your natural ties and by faith tie yourself to Me." Third, Abraham was commanded to get away from "thy father's house." Abraham was to leave his place of comfort and rest and also his position of heirship. He was to give up any possibility of inheriting anything from his father. He was to leave his father and acknowledge another Father. Fourth, God commanded Abraham to go "unto a land that I will shew thee." God did not even tell Abraham where the land was or what it was like. God was saying to Abraham in effect, "It is a land you cannot find by yourself, but I will reveal it to you."

## The Christian's Call

Our call is like Abraham's call—it is a call to complete separation. The Christian's citizenship is in heaven even though he is still living in the world. Our hearts are not to be set on the treasures of earth but on the riches of heaven. When the rich, young ruler came to Jesus and asked, "What shall I do to inherit eternal life?" Jesus said, "Sell all that thou hast, and distribute unto the poor, and thou shalt have treasure in heaven: and come, follow me." But when the young ruler heard this "he was very sorrowful: for he was very rich" (Luke 18:18,22,23). The ruler's heart was so strongly attached to his riches that he was unable to sever the ties and follow Jesus Christ.

The Christian is a pilgrim on this earth—his home is in heaven. His heart is not to be set on earthly possessions because his inheritance is in heaven. What is your attitude toward the world and earthly possessions? Is your attention focused on the incorruptible, undefiled inheritance that fades not away and is reserved in heaven for you (I Pet. 1:4)?

Hebrews 11 tells us more of the pilgrim nature of Abraham's faith when it says, "By faith he sojourned in the land of promise, as in a strange country, dwelling in tabernacles with Isaac and Jacob, the heirs with him of the same promise: For he looked for a city which hath foundations, whose builder and maker is God" (vv. 9,10). Abraham was a rich man and could have lived in a mansion, but he chose to live in a tent.

This does not mean that you and I should leave our houses and live in tents, but it shows what our attitude ought to be toward the things of this earth. Abraham was *in* this world but he was not *of* this world. In him we see the starting point of the life of faith—separation. There must be a separation from the world if we are going to have a faith life that pleases God.

To be separated from the world does not mean that you need to become a hermit. You do not need to hide in a cave or avoid people in order to have a life that is separated unto God.

The reason we need to be separated from the world in order to have a faith that pleases God is that two cannot walk together unless they are agreed. Even though Christ was *in* this world He was not *of* the world, and neither are we to be. Our citizenship is in heaven and we are only ambassadors here representing Jesus Christ. A question each of us should ask ourselves is, Do I live and act as an ambassador of Christ?

Abraham had to make the decision between an earthly inheritance and an inheritance that God would give him. We, too, have the same decision to make. Jesus Himself said, "No man can serve two masters: for either he will hate the one, and love the other; or else he will hold to the one, and despise the other. Ye cannot serve God and mammon [wealth]" (Matt. 6:24). Elijah also presented a choice to the worshipers of Baal when he said, "How long halt ye between two opinions? if the Lord be God, follow him: but if Baal, then follow him" (I Kings 18:21). There is absolutely no room for compromise. The Communists know that only hard-core men will be disciplined enough to advance the cause of Communism. God, too, chooses hard-core men who are disciplined enough to keep their eyes on Him regardless of the obstacles. He chose Gideon with his 300 disciplined and dedicated men to conquer the Midianites and their allies (Judg. 7:7-25). They were 300 men who were devoted to the God of Israel.

As mentioned previously, our being separated to God does not mean we must lead monastery lives. Jesus was a man among men. He ate with sinners, yet He separated Himself from the activities of the sinners. We are helped to see what it means to be separated from the world when we see how Christ prayed for His disciples. Jesus prayed to the Father and said, "I have given them thy word; and the world hath hated them, because they are not of the world, even as I am not of the world. I pray not that thou shouldest take them out of the world, but that thou shouldest keep them from the evil [one]. They are not of the world, even as I am not of the world. Sanctify them through thy truth: thy word is truth. As thou hast sent me into the world, even so have I also sent them into the world" (John 17:14-18).

## Friendship With the World

In the letter of I John we see the seriousness of loving the world. John wrote: "Love not the world, neither the things that are in the world. If any man love the world, the love of the Father is not in him. For all that is in the world, the lust of the flesh, and the lust of the eyes, and the pride of life, is not of the Father, but is of the world. And the world passeth away, and the lust thereof: but he that doeth the will of God abideth for ever" (2:15-17).

Those who say they do not have time to serve the Lord or to tell others about Him are indicating their love is for the world and not for God. Those who know Jesus Christ as Saviour will someday answer to Christ for what they have done for Him during this life. Second Corinthians 5:10 says, "For we must all appear before the judgment seat of Christ; that every one may receive the things done in his body, according to that he hath done, whether it be good or bad."

Notice what James said about a friendship with the world: "Ye adulterers and adulteresses, know ye not that the friendship of the world is enmity with God? whosoever therefore will be a friend of the world is the enemy of God" (4:4). Nothing could be clearer than this. Each person is easily able to see which class he fits into—a friend of God or a friend of the world. It is impossible to be a friend of both.

We can only overcome the world by our faith in God. First John 5:4,5 says, "For whatsoever is born of God overcometh the world: and this is the victory that overcometh the world, even our faith. Who is he that overcometh the world, but he that believeth that Jesus is the Son of God?" All goes back to faith as the basis.

## A Call for Sacrifice

Abraham's call involved a great sacrifice on his part. He was to leave his country, relatives and immediate family. So also the Christian's call today is not to be taken lightly. God is calling for a sacrifice from us too. Jesus said, "He that loveth father or mother more than me is not worthy of me:

and he that loveth son or daughter more than me is not worthy of me. And he that taketh not his cross, and followeth after me, is not worthy of me. He that findeth his life shall lose it: and he that loseth his life for my sake shall find it" (Matt. 10:37-39). Sometimes you hear a person say, "I am looking for reality." Of course, the question is, What kind of reality? The person who concentrates all of his attention on this life and its physical satisfactions may find them at the expense of his spiritual life. Thus, he who finds his life may lose it.

The same thought is set forth in Luke 14:26,27: "If any man come to me, and hate not his father, and mother, and wife, and children, and brethren, and sisters, yea, and his own life also, he cannot be my disciple. And whosoever doth not bear his cross, and come after me, cannot be my disciple." When our affection for our family is compared to our affection for the Lord, the contrast should be so great that the affection for our loved ones seems as hate in comparison to our great love for the Lord. In other words, we are to so love the Lord that everything else in the world—even our families—will become secondary. The word "cross" always speaks of death to something, and in this case it is death to the flesh (the old man).

The Apostle Paul exhorted Christians: "Present your bodies a living sacrifice, holy, acceptable unto God, which is your reasonable service. And be not conformed to this world: but be ye transformed by the renewing of your mind, that ye may prove what is that good, and acceptable, and perfect, will of God" (Rom. 12:1,2). The word "transformed" is literally "transfigured." Christians are to live a different kind of life—they are to be a living sacrifice.

### Rewards for Obedience

A call to be a missionary is much like Abraham's call. It is necessary to leave home, possessions, relatives, worldly ambitions, and to go to another country to which God has led. But one can never outgive God. Though Abraham was called to give up much, he was promised much more. In fact, God gave Abraham a sevenfold promise which we will examine in detail later. The important thing to remember is that God always promises blessings when we obey and follow Him.

Hebrews 13:5 says, "Let your conversation be without covetousness; and be content with such things as ye have: for he hath said, I will never leave thee, nor forsake thee." Much the same thing was said to the people of Israel: "Be strong and of a good courage, fear not, nor be afraid of them: for the Lord thy God, he it is that doth go with thee; he will not fail thee, nor forsake thee" (Deut. 31:6). The psalmist spoke of the same thing when he said, "For the Lord God is a sun and shield: the Lord will give grace and glory: no good thing will he withhold from them that walk uprightly" (Ps. 84:11). The psalmist also said, "Trust in the Lord, and do good; so shalt thou dwell in the land, and verily thou shalt be fed" (37:3). God promised to bless Israel and He promises to bless us when we trust and obey. God's call for us today is that we might be separated unto Him.

Chapter 3

# Abraham's Response

There were four specific things that God had called Abraham to do. He was to separate himself from his country, from his relatives, from his father's house, and he was to set out for a land which God would show him.

Abraham obeyed the first command for he left his country which was a place of paganism. However, Abraham only partially obeyed the commands to leave his relatives and his father's house. Genesis 11:31 says, "And Terah took Abram his son and Lot the son of Haran his son's son, and Sarai his daughter in law, his son Abram's wife; and they went forth with them from Ur of the Chaldees, to go into the land of Canaan; and they came unto Haran, and dwelt there." Abraham had not completely obeyed God's commands to leave his relatives and immediate family. God did not lead Abraham into the land and fulfill the fourth part of the call until Abraham had completely obeyed the previous commands.

Abraham stayed at Haran for at least five years and perhaps for as long as 15 years. It was a delay in God's program for him. Abraham was not to dwell at Haran but was to go to the land God had promised to show him. Because Abraham was not completely in God's will at Haran, these were fruitless years for him.

The child of God is to be fruitful. Jesus said, "Ye have not chosen me, but I have chosen you, and ordained you, that ye should go and bring forth fruit, and that your fruit should remain: that whatsoever ye shall ask of the Father in my name, he may give it you" (John 15:16). Abraham was not in the center of God's will at Haran so he was not bearing fruit.

The trip from Ur of the Chaldees to Haran was not exceedingly hard because they were able to travel northwest along the Euphrates River. Along the river there was grass for their livestock. However, from Haran to the land of Canaan was quite a different type of trip. They would have to leave the Euphrates River and strike out across the desert. This was a real test and was too much for Terah and his family. Besides, God was not going to take Abraham into the land until he separated from his father. The years Abraham spent at Haran were wasted years of waiting.

Many Christians today start off like Abraham. They launch out with great enthusiasm to follow the Lord, perhaps as a result of a crisis experience, but then later grind to a standstill in their Christian walk. Has this happened to you? Remember, the key issue for Abraham was separation. It is the same for us. This age of materialism has gripped even the Christians. We cannot expect God to lead us into fruitfulness unless we become separated from the things of the world. Each Christian must make the decision for himself, even as Abraham had to make the decision for himself. Once we break from the things of the world, we will see that the treasures of God far more than take the place of the things of this world.

### The Flesh

God's call to Abraham to leave his country was comparable to leaving the world behind. This he had done. God's call to him to leave his kindred and family was comparable to leaving the flesh. There is a difference between the world and the flesh. The word "flesh" is also referred to as "the old man," which is the believer's old nature. Abraham's immediate family was steeped in paganism and certainly represented the things of the old nature. Abraham faithfully obeyed God and left his country (the world), but he took with him his family (the flesh).

In the same manner, Christians today are often willing to separate from the world but may not be willing to leave the desires of the flesh behind. Leaving the world and the flesh behind, of course, is a step that can only be taken after one has received Jesus Christ as Saviour and has become a child of God. For victory, blessing and fruitbearing there must be a total separation not only from the world but also from the ways of the old nature.

In Stephen's message, which resulted in his martyrdom, he referred to God's call to Abraham. He said of Abraham, "Then came he out of the land of the Chaldaeans, and dwelt in Charran [Haran]: and from thence, when his father was dead, he removed him into this land, wherein ye now dwell" (Acts 7:4). When did Abraham leave Haran? "When his father was dead." God had to take away that which bound Abraham to Haran, the place of fruitlessness. Abraham had to be separated from the bondage of the flesh.

God has also made provision for us to be separated from the old man; that is, the old nature. Romans 6:6 says, "Knowing this, that our old man is crucified with him, that the body of sin might be destroyed, that henceforth we should not serve sin." The words "is crucified" should read "was crucified." The provision for us to be separated from the old man was made when Jesus Christ died. By His death on the cross He not only made provision to pay the penalty for our sins but He also made provision that we, in Him, should die to sin. Thus in verse 11 of the same chapter we are told, "Likewise reckon ye also yourselves to be dead indeed unto sin, but alive unto God through Jesus Christ our Lord." We are to reckon as a fact what is a fact—that in Christ we have died to sin.

Paul said, "God forbid that I should glory, save in the cross of our Lord Jesus Christ, by whom the world is crucified unto me, and I unto the world" (Gal. 6:14). When Christ died, God saw us—in Christ—dying to sin, the old nature. This is what has taken place, so we must reckon on it and appropriate this truth by applying it to our lives. For each of us there must be a burial service in Haran—the place of fruitlessness. Once the believer realizes that he has died with Christ, he must apply it to himself—he must have a funeral service. This is important because there must be an act or a decision in order to appropriate what Christ has done for us.

Genesis 12:4,5 tells us, "Abram departed, as the Lord had spoken unto him; and Lot went with him: and Abram was seventy and five years old when he departed out of Haran. And Abram took Sarai his wife, and Lot his brother's son, and all their substance that they had gathered, and the souls that they had gotten in Haran; and they went forth to go into the land of Canaan; and into the land of Canaan they came." Abraham finally departed from Haran. Flesh was finally renounced. He could now go forward; the funeral service had taken place. He had appropriated his death to the flesh, but this was not the last battle he had with the flesh.

## Mortifying the Flesh

Christians need to recognize they have died to the old man and have been made alive in Christ. Once the death has taken place, there is more that follows regarding mortifying the flesh. Romans 8:13 says, "For if ye live after the flesh, ye shall die: but if ye through the Spirit do mortify the deeds of the body, ye shall live." It is important to realize that the believer's death to the old man was once and for all. It is in the past for the Christian because he died with Christ. However, we need to apply this fact every day to our lives. To "mortify" means to "put to death." This is to be a continuous process for the Christian. He dies once, but he is to continuously appropriate the results of that death with Christ and put to death the flesh. The believer is enabled to appropriate these benefits through the ministry of the Holy Spirit.

When Abraham separated from his family in Haran, he did it in one act. However, later there had to be other acts of separation to God. These involved such events as his separating from Lot, the sacrificing of his son, and the burial of his wife. All of these things that Abraham experienced were used to further set him apart for the Lord. This is sanctification—the daily process of being further separated unto God. Christ put it in these words: "If any man will come after me, let him deny himself, and take up his cross daily, and follow me" (Luke 9:23).

After his wasted years in Haran, Abraham entered the land of Canaan. Observe the grace of God in that Abraham's disobedience was never brought up again. In Hebrews 11 we are told, "By faith Abraham, when he was called to go out into a place which he should after receive for an inheritance, obeyed; and he went out, not knowing whither he went" (v. 8). When God rehearsed the incident in the New Testament the wasted time in Haran was not mentioned. Hebrews 11:8 also shows us the absoluteness of Abraham's faith in that "he went out, not knowing whither he went." Faith never knows where it is being led, or it would not be faith. Faith is a confidence in God as the One who is leading. This is not a reckless thing. True faith is content to travel under sealed orders; that is, under God's orders. Faith boldly ventures out for God and leaves the results to Him.

In the days of Abraham, to start out for a land one had never seen was as great a venture of faith as astronauts going to the moon today. It took a great deal of faith for Abraham to leave Ur of the Chaldees and go to a strange land. Like Abraham, we Christians are pilgrims on this earth and by faith we are traveling to a land we have never seen.

Abraham only partially obeyed at first and did not go directly to the land God wanted to show him. There were the years of wasted time in Haran, which to Abraham meant lost time and lost rewards. As Abraham left Haran he still had no clear directive about the land to which he was going. God had not even so much as described the land as "a land of milk and honey," as He did later for the Israelites in Egypt. Abraham had nothing to rely on except God's clear command to go. By faith he was to walk a step at a time.

God seldom accompanies His commands with reasons or explanations, but He always accompanies them with wonderful promises. Do you trust God? When you know God wants you to do something, can you step out for Him and claim His promises even though He hasn't given you reasons why He wants you to do it?

### Commands and Promises

Notice in Genesis 12:1-3 how the promises of God correspond to His commands. First, Abraham was to leave his country—but God promised to make of Him a great nation. Second, Abraham was to leave his kindred—all earthly blessings—but God promised to bless him. Third, he was to leave his father's house—his name, his prestige, his inheritance—but God promised to make his name great and to make him a blessing to others. As a result of Abraham's obedience to these commands, today he is known as the "father" of the Israelites (Acts 7:2) and "the father of all them that believe" (Rom. 4:11).

That Abraham was to be a means of blessing is seen in Genesis 12:3: "And I will bless them that bless thee, and curse him that curseth thee: and in thee shall all families of the earth be blessed." These were the commands and promises given to Abraham. It was left to be seen whether he could rely on the promises and step out by faith for God.

Whenever something is given up because God has commanded it, His rewards are immeasurable. This is clearly seen in the New Testament passage, Mark 10:28-30: "Then Peter burst out, 'But look, we have left everything and followed you!' 'I promise you,' returned Jesus, 'nobody leaves home or brothers or sisters or mother or father or children or property for my sake and the gospel's without getting back a hundred times over, now in this present life, homes and brothers and sisters, mothers and children and land—though not without persecution—and in the next world eternal life' " (*Phillips*). See the promises? In the light of these words of Jesus, you can believe God for everything He has in store for you.

### Complete Separation

Abraham finally left Haran and forsook everything. Speaking of Abraham and those who were with him, Hebrews 11:15,16 says, "And truly, if they had been mindful of that country from whence they came out, they might have had opportunity to have returned. But now they desire a better country, that is, an heavenly: wherefore God is not ashamed to be called their God: for he hath prepared for them a city." Abraham's separation from Haran was complete. Genesis 12:5 records that "Abram took Sarai his wife, and Lot his brother's son, and all their substance that they had gathered, and the souls that they had gotten in Haran; and they went forth to go into the land of Canaan; and into the land of Canaan they came."

Once Abraham was in the land, he did not stop to possess it but merely passed through it. He did not stop because God did not order him to stop. Genesis 12:6 says, "And Abram passed through the land unto the place of Sichem, unto the plain of Moreh. And the Canaanite was then in the land." As to Abraham's inheritance in the land, Acts 7:5 says that "he [God] gave him none inheritance in it, no, not so much as to set his foot on: yet he promised that he would give it to him for a possession, and to his seed after him, when as yet he had no child." At this time, therefore, Abraham was not occupying the land, but merely passing through it. The Scriptures comment that "the Canaanite was then in the land" (Gen. 12:6). The Canaanites posed a problem and were the source of future conflict.

Our separation is similar. God calls for an all-out separation which often results in conflict. There will be persecution and problems, but we must remember the words of Jesus: "In the world ye shall have tribulation: but be of good cheer; I have overcome the world" (John 16:33). In times of conflict it will be especially helpful to remember also the words of the Apostle Paul as recorded in Ephesians 6:12,13: "For we wrestle not against flesh and blood, but against principalities, against powers, against the rulers of the darkness of this world, against spiritual wickedness in high places. Wherefore take unto you the whole armour of God, that ye may be able to withstand in the evil day, and having done all, to stand."

God's first communication with Abraham had taken place in Ur of the Chaldees. God's second communication with Abraham took place after Abraham had entered the land of Canaan. This second communication is recorded in Genesis 12:7: "And the Lord appeared unto Abram, and said, Unto thy seed will I give this land." This communication with Abraham came after he had obeyed God's earlier commands to leave his country, his kindred and his father's house. God's first communication with Abraham was a call; the second was a promise. At first God had only told Abraham to go to a land that He would show him, but now God promised to give the land to Abraham's seed. However, Abraham did not know this until he had actually reached the land. By faith he had to walk a step at a time. This is a spiritual principle because God works this way in every believer's life. First, God only said that He would *show* Abraham the land. Now, after Abraham's obedience, God promises to *give* the land to his seed. God's progressive promises come after progressive obedience.

### Communion and Worship

Up to this point in Abraham's life, God had simply communicated to him what He wanted him to do. However, at the time of God's second communication with Abraham we see that God reveals Himself for communion and worship. After God promised to give the land to Abraham's seed, we are told that "there builded he an altar unto the Lord, who appeared unto him" (12:7). An altar is the place of communion with God.

In every believer's life there must be first an obedience to faith and then communion and worship. First John 1:6,7 tells us of this fellowship when it says, "If we say that we have fellowship with him, and walk in darkness, we lie, and do not the truth: But if we walk in the light, as he is in the light, we have fellowship one with another, and the blood of Jesus Christ his Son cleanseth us from all sin."

After Abraham built an altar unto the Lord, "he removed from thence unto a mountain on the east of Beth-el, and pitched his tent, having Beth-el on the west, and Hai on the east: and there he builded an altar unto the Lord, and called upon the name of the Lord" (Gen. 12:8). The place names of Bethel and Hai make Abraham's act a significant one. "Beth-el" means "house of God" and "Hai" means "a heap of ruins." This symbolizes the sphere of life for the believer. The old creation—the old ruins—are on the one side, but the house of God is on the other. We are *in* the world but we are not *of* the world. Although in the world, we are to be constantly experiencing the reality of His abiding presence. Because the battle lines are clearly drawn, we should not be surprised when the world hates us. Jesus said, "If ye were of the world, the world would love his own: but because ye are not of the world, but I have chosen you out of the world, therefore the world hateth you. Remember the word that I said unto you, The servant is not greater than his lord. If they have persecuted me, they will also persecute you; if they have kept my saying, they will keep your's also" (John 15:19,20).

When Abraham moved to a mountain east of Bethel, we are told that he did three things: pitched his tent, built an altar and called upon the name of the Lord. Each of these acts was highly significant and symbolic of Abraham's life.

The tent symbolized Abraham's dependence on God. Hebrews 11:9,10 says of Abraham that "by faith he sojourned in the land of promise, as in a strange country, dwelling in tabernacles [tents] with Isaac and Jacob, the heirs with him of the same promise: For he looked for a city which hath foundations, whose builder and maker is God." Every child of God is a pilgrim in this world and is to have his eyes fixed on his home in heaven.

The altar that Abraham built indicated his dependence on God and his worship of God. Note the order. First, the believer is to take his place as a stranger and pilgrim on earth; then comes true acceptance and worship. This is not referring to an acceptance as far as salvation is concerned, which comes by faith in Christ Jesus. This is acceptance in the realm of being a child true to God.

It is revealing to trace Abraham's life as it is connected with the tent and the altar. We will also see that this has meaning for us as we live for the Lord in the 20th century.

In what we commonly call "The Lord's Prayer," we say, "Hallowed be thy name. Thy kingdom come" (Matt. 6:9,10). This has to do with the altar—not a literal altar such as Abraham built, but our relationship to and worship of God. We want His name to be holy, which means that we are not seeking a holy place for ourselves. We want His kingdom to come; that is, we want Him to rule supreme. To sincerely pray this means that we are not trying to build a little kingdom for ourselves. The phrase "Thy will be done" (v. 10) shows that we want God's will, not ours, to be done. This is worship. This is a vital relationship with God.

## Attitude Toward Possessions

The prayer in Matthew 6 goes on to say, "Give us this day our daily bread" (v. 11). Can you honestly pray this prayer? Perhaps you have a freezer full of meat and many groceries stocked away. In addition to that you probably have a checking account. In these circumstances it would be impossible to claim that you are hungry. How, then, can you honestly pray for the Lord to give you your daily bread?

It is possible if we have the right attitude toward the things of this world. It depends on whether we have the attitude of a tent-life, realizing that we are just pilgrims in this world. Of greatest importance to the Christian is his devotional life—his dependence on God. Crucial to his devotional life are Bible study, meditation, prayer and worship. Next to the devotional life in importance comes our attitude toward things such as our property, home, car, clothes and furniture. How attached are you to your possessions? Could you let them go without murmuring? Or, if you should lose them, would you feel deeply discouraged and think that God had forsaken you?

Perhaps a way for us to see where our treasures really are is to ask ourselves the question, What are we spending much of our time for? Is it for things for our homes? Is your house a place to live and worship God, or are you so attached to it that all of your labor is to provide things for it so it will look as nice or nicer than someone else's?

Perhaps in the past you have fought the battle of material things, but this does not mean the struggle is over. No matter how long you have been a Christian, Satan will try to get your mind centered on material things instead of the goodness of God. I have had to face this same thing in my life. Once it involved the matter of furnishing a new office. Was I to take along the same furniture from the old office, or was I to have new furniture purchased? I had to come to grips with the problem and honestly face God about this matter. Of course, there is nothing wrong with having new furniture, but there can be a wrong attitude toward the furniture. We have to keep checking ourselves spiritually and reminding ourselves that we are only pilgrims here in this world. Do we have the attitude of a pilgrim, or does it seem that this life is all we are living for?

The wonderful Chinese Christian, Watchman Nee, has written:

"The life of a Christian is the life of the altar and the tent. God requires of His children that in His presence they have an altar and that on the earth they have a tent. An altar calls for a tent, and a tent in turn demands an altar. It is impossible to have an altar without a tent, and likewise impossible to have a tent without a return to the altar. The altar and the tent are interrelated; the two cannot be divorced.

"And for what purpose is the burnt offering placed on the altar? To be wholly burnt. Many of us think we offer ourselves to God to do this or that for Him, whereas what He is wanting of us is not our work, but ourselves. What the altar signifies is not doing for God, but being for God. Unlike the sacrifice of the Old Testament, which in one act was finally burnt, the sacrifice of the New Testament is 'a living sacrifice.' The meaning of the altar is the offering up of the life to God to be ever consumed, yet ever living: to be ever living, yet ever consumed. God wants these lives of ours consecrated to Him that throughout their entire course they may be ceaselessly being consumed for Him.

## The Life of the Tent

"Actually he [Abraham] lived in a tent before, but not until he had built the altar does the Word of God bring the tent into view.

"What is a tent? A tent is not a settled abode, it is moveable. Through the altar God deals with ourselves; through the tent God deals with our possessions. At the altar Abraham had offered up his all to God. Was he thereafter stripped of everything? No! Abraham still possessed cattle and sheep and many other things; but he had become a tent-dweller. In other words, what was not consumed on the altar became attached to the tent.

"Abraham's life was a life of the altar. A day came when even his only begotten son was offered upon it. But what did God do with Isaac? He restored him to Abraham. What you place on the altar God accepts. The altar claims your all, and while God restores certain things from the altar, they can no longer be regarded as your own.

"We need to remember that we have a life to live before God, and we have also a life to live in the world. In the world we still have need of many material things. We need clothing, and food and a dwelling-place. We may use them, but we must not be governed by them. We can have them, or we can let them go; they can be given, and they can be taken away. This is the principle of tent-life.

## The Second Altar

"The altar had led to the tent, and now [Gen. 12:8] the tent leads again to the altar. If our possessions are not held loosely on the principle of the tent, they will cause us to take root, and there will never be a second altar. When we have consecrated our all to God, He lets us use certain things in the tent. At any time God may say, 'I want this thing.' If we cling to it and say, 'This is mine,' then in heart we have forsaken the altar and cannot say to God that our life is being lived for Him.

### The Recovery of the Altar and the Tent

"Abraham had his failures. In his history there was a forsaking of the altar and the tent. But there was recovery. Recovery is a matter of returning to the altar and the tent" (*The Life of the Altar and the Tent*).

Chapter 4

# Abraham's Faith Severely Tested

The believer must be tested if it is to be known whether he has real faith or not. The New Testament tells us, "That the trial of your faith, being much more precious than of gold that perisheth, though it be tried with fire, might be found unto praise and honour and glory at the appearing of Jesus Christ" (I Pet. 1:7). When we say that faith must be tried, we do not mean that it has to be tried for God to know whether it is true faith or not. He knows without question the innermost secrets of our hearts. His purpose in testing our faith is so that we might be able to see and understand the kind of faith we have.

After Abraham pitched his tent, built an altar and called upon the name of the Lord, the Scriptures say that "Abram journeyed, going on still toward the south" (Gen. 12:9). Instead of staying where he had his altar—his contact with God—Abraham went farther south. He went away from the altar and made provisions for the flesh.

Have you not also found that failures arise when you neglect the altar? The altar is representative of our communion and fellowship with God. Do you have an altar? It is common to refer to the "family altar." By this is meant a time when a family reads the Word of God and prays together. But do you also have an individual altar—a time alone with God in reading and prayer? You desperately need this time with God, and to omit it is to invite all kinds of trials and failures into your life. I do not think it is exaggerating to say that 85 percent of the failures and trials that Christians have can be traced to the fact that their altar relationship with God is not right. They have moved away from the time of fellowship with Him.

### The Trial of Circumstances

Genesis 12 continues by saying, "And there was a famine in the land: and Abram went down into Egypt to sojourn there; for the famine was grievous in the land" (v. 10). Having left the altar, at once a trial comes to Abraham—famine. To escape this trial of circumstances, Abraham went down to Egypt. Famine was often a disciplinary testing of God's people in the land. It occurred not only during Abraham's lifetime but also many other times in Israel's history, such as during the time of Ruth.

When Abraham's trial came, he went down to Egypt. Egypt is always spoken of as "down" and is a symbol of the world as far as the believer is concerned. Those who lost spiritual power in the land God had promised them often resorted to Egypt. There, they endeavored to substitute the resources of Egypt for their spiritual power.

Isaiah 31:1 says, "Woe to them that go down to Egypt for help; and stay on horses, and trust in chariots, because they are many; and in horsemen, because they are very strong; but they look not unto the Holy One of Israel, neither seek the Lord!" God warned Israel that an alliance with Egypt was really a reliance on the arm of the flesh and would bring nothing but failure.

Had God failed Abraham? By no means. But it was His way of testing Abraham's faith. This test proved to Abraham that his faith was not yet strong. God allowed the famine to come in order to test Abraham. This test forced Abraham to choose whether he would rely on the arm of the flesh or on the arm of God. Abraham did what we so often do. He sought relief from the difficulty rather than profiting from the trial. How many times has God permitted us to be tried and, rather than seeking God's wisdom to find out why we were being tried, we sought only to relieve the difficulty?

James referred to our many trials when he said, "My brethren, count it all joy when ye fall into divers temptations" (1:2). In this same chapter James said, "If any of you lack wisdom, let him ask of God, that giveth to all men liberally, and upbraideth not; and it shall be given him" (v. 5). This has to do with seeking the Lord's wisdom to discover why He is allowing us to suffer. If Abraham had waited on God to be shown the reason for His testing, he possibly never would have gone into Egypt. Had he not gone into Egypt, he would not have become involved in many other troubles. Therefore, it is essential that we do not seek to avoid God's testing, but wait upon Him to find out the reason for it.

There is no record that Abraham asked God's counsel about going down into Egypt. It was because he did not seek God's counsel that Abraham got into trouble. He looked more to the blessing than to the Blesser. He trusted God for his eternal interest, but he was afraid to trust Him to supply his temporal needs. So also, our faith must not rest on God's gifts, but on God Himself. We should not look at the famine, but at God's faithfulness.

## Fear and Insecurity

God's Word tells us that "whatsoever is not of faith is sin" (Rom. 14:23). Abraham's lack of faith led him into more sin. He soon began to worry and fear. We are told, "And it came to pass, when he was come near to enter into Egypt, that he said unto Sarai his wife, Behold now, I know that thou art a fair woman to look upon: Therefore it shall come to pass, when the Egyptians shall see thee, that they shall say, This is his wife: and they will kill me, but they will save thee alive. Say, I pray thee, thou art my sister: that it may be well with me for thy sake; and my soul shall live because of thee" (Gen. 12:11-13). Abraham had lost his peace and had begun to worry. He was afraid they would take his life. Courage goes when faith fails. Because of his lack of faith, he also lost his feeling of security.

Do you have doubts about your salvation? There may be some good reasons why you do. First, you should make sure that you have made the decision to receive Christ as Saviour. Once you have made certain of this decision, you need thereafter only check whether you have left the altar—the place of fellowship with God. The lack of fellowship with God often makes you feel insecure. Perhaps you are trusting God to save you for eternity but you are not willing to trust Him to keep you day by day.

### Selfishness

Not only did Abraham's lack of faith lead to fear and insecurity, but it also led to selfishness. He was more concerned about his safety than he was about the honor and chastity of his wife. It is true that in Abraham's day a wife was not respected as highly as she should have been, but a believing man like Abraham should have looked upon his wife as more than just property. Temporarily, Abraham turned away from God and began to center everything on himself.

### Hypocrisy

Abraham's lack of faith also led to hypocrisy—he pretended to be what he was not. He pretended to be Sarah's brother when, in actuality, he was her husband. It is true that Sarah was his half sister, and some might argue on this basis that Abraham was only telling a half lie. However, God does not accept anything that is only half truth. Half truth is untruth.

In verses 14-16 of Genesis 12 we have recorded what actually took place: "And it came to pass, that, when Abram was come into Egypt, the Egyptians beheld the woman that she was very fair. The princes also of Pharaoh saw her, and commended her before Pharaoh: and the woman was taken into Pharaoh's house. And he entreated Abram well for her sake: and he had sheep, and oxen, and he asses, and menservants, and maidservants, and she asses, and camels."

What Abraham thought would happen did happen. Pharaoh treated Abraham wonderfully because he thought Abraham was Sarah's brother, and he wanted to have Sarah for his wife. But we see what the Lord thought of Abraham's hypocrisy, for the Scriptures say that "the Lord plagued Pharaoh and his house with great plagues because of Sarai Abram's wife" (v. 17). Others are always affected when we fall into sin and backslide. While Abraham was the guilty person, others suffered also.

### Open Rebuke

Abraham's downward steps away from God eventually led to open rebuke. The Bible says that "Pharaoh called Abram, and said, What is this that thou hast done unto me? why didst thou not tell me that she was thy wife? Why saidst thou, She is my sister? so I might have taken her to me to wife: now therefore behold thy wife, take her, and go thy way" (vv. 18,19). It is sad when a child of God has to be corrected by the world. All of this came about because of Abraham's lack of faith, which resulted in his going to Egypt—a symbol of the world of unbelief.

We, too, need to be careful about our friendship with the world. The Word of God says, "Know ye not that the friendship of the world is enmity with God? whosoever therefore will be a friend of the world is the enemy of God" (James 4:4). Check your life. Are you a friend of the world? According to this verse, if you are a friend of the world, you are an enemy of God.

The time that the Christian spends in a backslidden state is wasted time. Abraham's time in Egypt was wasted as far as his spiritual progress was concerned. While trying to be a friend of the world, the believer is only building with wood, hay and stubble—which someday will be consumed by the fire of judgment. The believer will receive no reward for this kind of work. First Corinthians 3:12-15 says, "Now if any man build upon this foundation gold, silver, precious stones, wood, hay, stubble; Every man's work shall be made manifest: for the day shall declare it, because it shall be revealed by fire; and the fire shall try every man's work of what sort it is. If any man's work abide which he hath built thereupon, he shall receive a reward. If any man's work shall be burned, he shall suffer loss: but he himself shall be saved; yet so as by fire."

## God Intervenes

God was not frustrated nor defeated by Abraham's failure. He intervened by bringing a plague on Pharaoh's household and by causing Pharaoh to rebuke Abraham and send him away. Genesis 12:20 tells us that "Pharaoh commanded his men concerning him: and they sent him away, and his wife, and all that he had."

God did not cast Abraham away; neither is the disobedient and sinning believer cast away. Psalm 37:23,24 says, "The steps of a good man are ordered by the Lord: and he delighteth in his way. Though he fall, he shall not be utterly cast down: for the Lord upholdeth him with his hand." Crucial to this statement is the fact that God cannot deny Himself. We are told in II Timothy 2:13: "If we believe not, yet he abideth faithful: he cannot deny himself." He is God, and He will not deny what He has said He is going to do. In Abraham's case, God had a purpose for him; and even though Abraham was unfaithful at this point, God remained faithful and brought Abraham back to Himself.

Verses that may take on new meaning for you as you see them in this context are verses 27 and 28 of John 10. In these verses Christ Himself said, "My sheep hear my voice, and I know them, and they follow me: And I give unto them eternal life; and they shall never perish, neither shall any man pluck them out of my hand." Notice in these parallel thoughts that Christ first referred to eternal life and then to those who follow Him. Of those He is leading in the Christian life, He says that no man is able to "pluck them out of my hand."

As this spiritual principle is applied to Abraham, we see that God eventually led him to the fullness of what He planned to do with him. This spiritual principle is also stated in Philippians 1:6: "Being confident of this very thing, that he which hath begun a good work in you will perform it until the day of Jesus Christ." Notice it says *in* you, not *through* you.

That Christ goes after His lost sheep is clear from the parable He spoke, recorded in Luke 15: "What man of you, having an hundred sheep, if he lose one of them, doth not leave the ninety and nine in the wilderness, and go after that which is lost, until he find it? And when he hath found it, he layeth it on his shoulders, rejoicing" (vv. 4,5). This is what you can also expect when you have tried your best and failed. I am not referring to presumptuous sin—a willful disobedience—but to circumstantial sin—a failure as a result of overwhelming circumstances. The record of the prodigal son, recorded in this same chapter, also shows how God does not cast us away simply because we have failed Him.

## God Knows What We Are Like

While we cannot condone nor emulate Abraham's failures, there is encouragement as we see how God is willing to use ordinary, fallible men and women to accomplish His will. It is also encouraging to realize that God knows how to bring men back to Himself. Although Abraham's life was marred by failures—sometimes repeated—and his faith was checkered by doubt, God remembered that Abraham was an earthen vessel. In II Corinthians 4:7 we are told, "But we have this treasure in earthen vessels, that the excellency of the power may be of God, and not of us." God wants to prove that He can bring about His will in our lives even though we are earthen vessels and subject to frailties.

Psalm 103 has been a tremendous encouragement to me in this regard. It says of God, "He hath not dealt with us after our sins; nor rewarded us according to our iniquities" (v. 10). The psalmist was not referring to the time of salvation but to our lives as believers. He said also, "For he knoweth our frame; he remembereth that we are dust" (v. 14). God knows what we are. He knows that in these earthen vessels there is nothing but failure. Therefore, He works through us that the excellency of the power may be of Him and not of us.

God was able to use Abraham because these failures were incidental and not fundamental to his life; that is, Abraham did not presume upon God's mercy and grace. Be very careful about the sin of presumption. Do you think that just because God is so long-suffering you can live as you please? If this is the way you think, then I seriously doubt whether you are a child of God. If you are a child of God and think this way, you will have some great tests and trials ahead of you as God endeavors to bring you back to Himself.

When we have tried our best and have failed Him—perhaps again and again—what then? Remember that God knows we are but dust. When Abraham stumbled from the path, God drew him back—and Abraham always responded. This is what is important. Obedience is the key. It is regrettable that Abraham had his lapses of faith, but it is wonderful that he kept coming back to God and was so responsive to the Lord's dealing in his life.

## God Is Long-Suffering

For the most part, Abraham's failures were in the area of his greatest strength—his faith. He failed temporarily when he was overcome by doubt. However, only once did he fall into the same trap a second time. How wonderful is the long-suffering of God and the assurance that "as the heaven is high above the earth, so great is his mercy toward them that fear him. As far as the east is from the west, so far hath he removed our transgressions from us. Like as a father pitieth his children, so the Lord pitieth them that fear him" (Ps. 103:11-13).

God's long-suffering is also seen in II Peter 3:9: "The Lord is not slack concerning his promise, as some men count slackness; but is longsuffering to us-ward, not willing that any should perish, but that all should come to repentance." Isaiah 30:18 also has a wonderful statement about the Lord's long-suffering: "Therefore will the Lord wait, that he may be gracious unto you, and therefore will he be exalted, that he may have mercy upon you: for the Lord is a God of judgment: blessed are all they that wait for him." Notice especially that we are to "wait for him," which involves trusting Him.

After Pharaoh had rebuked Abraham and sent him away, the Scriptures tell us that "Abram went up out of Egypt, he, and his wife, and all that he had, and Lot with him, into the south. And Abram was very rich in cattle, in silver, and in gold. And he went on his journeys from the south even to Beth-el, unto the place where his tent had been at the beginning, between Beth-el and Hai; Unto the place of the altar, which he had made there at the first: and there Abram called on the name of the Lord" (Gen. 13:1-4).

## Abraham's Restoration

Abraham left Egypt in humiliation—not in a blaze of glory. He had gone down into Egypt because of his lack of faith, and now he was returning to the place he had left. He had repented and had come back to the place of the altar which he had made at first. There he called on the name of the Lord. This reminds us of Christ's words to the Church of Ephesus: "Remember therefore from whence thou art fallen, and repent, and do the first works; or else I will come unto thee quickly, and will remove thy candlestick out of his place, except thou repent" (Rev. 2:5).

Abraham's sojourn in Egypt was lost time. He went back to Bethel ashamed, rebuked, beaten and repentant. He had built no altar in Egypt—the place of disobedience. There is no fellowship with God when we walk by sight and not by faith. First John 1:5,6 makes this clear when it says, "This then is the message which we have heard of him, and declare unto you, that God is light and in him is no darkness at all. If we say that we have fellowship with him, and walk in darkness, we lie, and do not the truth."

The only remedy for backsliding is to come again to the place of the altar—the place of fellowship which is made possible by the cross of Jesus Christ. Do you feel condemned? Remember Calvary. Remember that Jesus died for all of your sin and that your fellowship with God can be restored if you will come to Him and confess your sin. There can be no restoration until you confess your sin. It was the Lord who said, "Ye have forsaken me" (Judg. 10:13), but it was also the Lord who said, "Return, ye backsliding children, and I will heal your backslidings" (Jer. 3:22). How wonderful it is to know that when we fall into sin we can return to God and be restored to fellowship because of what Christ has accomplished on the cross.

## The Results of Backsliding

Even though Abraham returned to fellowship with God, irreparable damage had been done. When a believer backslides he does things he will never be able to undo. Abraham's testimony had been weakened, and damage beyond repair had been done to worldly Lot, Abraham's nephew. Lot had gone with Abraham down to Egypt. The backslider never backslides alone; he always takes others with him.

Even though Abraham had backslidden and had brought about much damage, Genesis 13:3,4 tells us that he went back "to Beth-el, unto the place where his tent had been at the beginning, between Beth-el and Hai; Unto the place of the altar, which he had made there at the first: and there Abram called on the name of the Lord."

God has made provision for every backslider. Just as Abraham returned to fellowship with the Lord, you, too, can come back into fellowship with Him if you have backslidden. First John 2:1 says, "My little children, these things write I unto you, that ye sin not. And if any man sin, we have an advocate with the Father, Jesus Christ the righteous." In the first chapter of I John, every believer is assured: "If we confess our sins, he is faithful and just to forgive us our sins, and to cleanse us from all unrighteousness" (v. 9). Do not stay in the miserable place of disobedience. Come back to God and confess your sin.

After David had come back to the Lord and fellowship was restored through confession of sin, he wrote: "Blessed is he whose transgression is forgiven, whose sin is covered. When I kept silence, my bones waxed old through my roaring all the day long. For day and night thy hand was heavy upon me: my moisture is turned into the drought of summer. Selah [think on these things]. I acknowledged my sin unto thee, and mine iniquity have I not hid. I said, I will confess my transgressions unto the Lord; and thou forgavest the iniquity of my sin. Selah" (Ps. 32:1,3-5).

In other words, David was saying that when he was out of fellowship, the Lord stayed after him and His hand was heavy upon him. God will not let His backsliding children enjoy their backsliding. Though your sin may not be as grievous as David's—as far as society is concerned—God's hand will be heavy on you until you return to Him and confess your sin. Perhaps your sin is that you have gone away from the altar and from the place of tent-living. That is, you have neglected your fellowship with God and have begun to take on an attitude of friendship with the world. If so, your need is to come back to God and confess your sin. Remember, He has promised to forgive you and to cleanse you from all unrighteousness when you confess your sin to Him (I John 1:9).

Chapter 5

# Totally Separated to God

Once Abraham was back in the land, there came an extremely important time in his life—total separation unto God. God had called Abraham to leave his country, his kindred and his father's house. Abraham had not completely obeyed the commands of God because he still had Lot with him. It was necessary for him to separate from Lot in order to be completely separated unto God.

When Abraham returned to the land from Egypt, Lot was still with him. The Word of God tells us, "And Lot also, which went with Abram, had flocks, and herds, and tents. And the land was not able to bear them, that they might dwell together: for their substance was great, so that they could not dwell together. And there was a strife between the herdmen of Abram's cattle and the herdmen of Lot's cattle: and the Canaanite and the Perizzite dwelled then in the land" (Gen. 13:5-7).

In considering the lives of Abraham and Lot, we see that Abraham's life was symbolic of the Spirit-controlled Christian, whereas Lot's life was symbolic of the carnal Christian. Unconsecrated Christians who are living according to the flesh are referred to as "carnal" in the Scriptures (I Cor. 3:1,3). Lot was a believer, but he was not living by faith—he was living by sight. By contrast, Abraham was a believer who lived by faith on the promises of God. He failed at times, as all believers do, but he was not set aside because his sins were not presumptuous; that is, they were not willful acts of disobedience. While Lot mainly sought his own pleasure and profit, Abraham sought to please God above all else.

It is never recorded that Lot built an altar. He was not known for his communion with God. As a result, he got into trouble, just as any believer gets into trouble when he does not take time for daily fellowship with God. I am not referring to a time when the entire family reads the Bible and prays together. This, too, is extremely important, but I refer in particular to your personal time alone with God. Perhaps you say you do not have enough time because you are too busy with life's activities. Anything that takes you away from this time of fellowship with God is sin. Regardless of how much work you have to do, you can find some time to spend with God alone. As a believer, this is your number one prerogative. Just as the well-watered plains had more attraction to Lot than worship did, so the busyness of life can have more attraction for us than time spent alone with God. The Devil will always see to it that we have little or no time to fellowship with God. But we can—and we must—make time for such fellowship. We must put first things first.

We are beginning to see some of the direct results of Abraham's backsliding. While God in His faithfulness restores His wandering child, the effects of backsliding cannot be set aside. The principle of sowing and reaping is a timeless principle, and it applied in Abraham's life also. Galatians 6:7,8 says, "Be not deceived; God is not mocked: for whatsoever a man soweth, that shall he also reap. For he that soweth to his flesh shall of the flesh reap corruption; but he that soweth to the Spirit shall of the Spirit reap life everlasting."

Abraham sowed to the flesh and reaped accordingly. He was forgiven when he returned to fellowship with God, but he had to reap the results of his disobedience. God had clearly commanded Abraham to leave his father's house, but Terah, his father, had journeyed with him to Haran. It is possible that Abraham would not have left Haran if it were not for the death of his father. Perhaps God had to bring death into Abraham's family in order to cause him to be obedient. It is also possible that God will have to deal with us in this same way if we refuse to obey His voice. This is why God allows certain things to be taken away from us when we become too attached to them. The things in themselves may not be wrong, but we have grown so close to them that God has second place and can no longer speak to us.

Abraham entered the land after God had taken away his father. Along with him came Lot, his nephew. Abraham had still not completely obeyed the command of God. God had not called Abraham's relatives to do a particular task; He had called Abraham. Because it was a personal call, God called Abraham to leave his relatives and to go into the land that He promised to show him.

So, too, God deals with us personally. Any call we receive from God is not general, but personal. God deals with His children as sons. He speaks to them individually. Frequently well-meaning relatives are a believer's greatest hindrance. Christ warned of this when He said, "A man's foes shall be they of his own household" (Matt. 10:36). Therefore, let us be extremely careful that our well-meaning relatives do not deter us from God's call.

## Great Hindrances

There were two things that Abraham obtained during his sojourn in Egypt, and both of them proved to be great hindrances to him. One of these was Sarah's maid, Hagar. Later, it was Hagar whom Sarah gave to Abraham so that an heir could be born. Genesis 16:3 says, "And Sarai Abram's wife took Hagar her maid the Egyptian, after Abram had dwelt ten years in the land of Canaan, and gave her to her husband Abram to be his wife." We shall examine this incident in greater detail later in our study.

While in Egypt Abraham also obtained much earthly wealth, and this, too, became a great hindrance. Both he and Lot obtained riches in Egypt. When they returned to Canaan it is recorded: "And Abram was very rich in cattle, in silver, and in gold. And Lot also, which went with Abram, had flocks, and herds, and tents" (13:2,5).

When Lot left Egypt he took something else with him which did him far more damage than his possessions—a worldly spirit. He developed a taste for the fleshpots of Egypt. When Abraham came back to the land, he returned to his fellowship with God and was not controlled by the riches he had. He continued to live in a tent. However, Lot's heart was with his riches. He moved into the city. He now had prestige. He had everything he needed. But the Scriptures state the timeless principle: "No servant can serve two masters: for either he will hate the one, and love the other; or else he will hold to the one, and despise the other. Ye cannot serve God and mammon [wealth]" (Luke 16:13). Lot was controlled by his riches.

These two men had become great in riches, and a harmonious relationship was now impossible. Conflict resulted between their herdsmen. How frequently there is strife between relatives because of earthly possessions and wealth. The Scriptures ask, "Can two walk together, except they be agreed?" (Amos 3:3). Abraham and Lot could no longer continue walking together because they disagreed over basic values.

Concerning Abraham and Lot, the Scriptures say, "And the land was not able to bear them, that they might dwell together: for their substance was great, so that they could not dwell together. And there was a strife between the herdmen of Abram's cattle and the herdmen of Lot's cattle: and the Canaanite and the Perizzite dwelled then in the land" (Gen. 13:6,7).

The conflict between Abraham and Lot illustrates the struggle that takes place between the Spirit and the flesh. This conflict was clearly set forth by Paul in the New Testament: "For I know that in me (that is, in my flesh,) dwelleth no good thing: for to will is present with me; but how to perform that which is good I find not. For the good that I would I do not: but the evil which I would not, that I do. For I delight in the law of God after the inward man: But

I see another law in my members, warring against the law of my mind, and bringing me into captivity to the law of sin which is in my members. O wretched man that I am! who shall deliver me from the body of this death?" (Rom. 7:18,19,22-24).

As we compare Abraham and Lot, we see that Abraham represents that which is of the Spirit; Lot, that which is of the flesh. Abraham walked by faith; Lot walked by sight. Abraham was generous and spiritual; Lot was greedy and worldly. Abraham looked for a city whose builder and maker was God; Lot made his home in a city which was built by man and later destroyed by God. Abraham became the father of all who believe; Lot became the father of those who perpetuated infamy–namely, the Ammonites and Moabites. Abraham was made heir of the land of Canaan; Lot lost all of his possessions when Sodom was destroyed.

Lot's history is a tragic one and is full of admonition to our generation which is so materialistically minded. The flesh and the Spirit are in conflict with each other and cannot dwell in harmony. This is evident from Galatians 5:16,17: "This I say then, Walk in the Spirit, and ye shall not fulfil the lust of the flesh. For the flesh lusteth against the Spirit, and the Spirit against the flesh: and these are contrary the one to the other: so that ye cannot do the things that ye would." Verse 24 of this same chapter tells us that "they that are Christ's have crucified the flesh with the affections and lusts."

## Abraham's Generosity

As the conflict between Abraham and Lot continued, it became evident that Abraham was a man of great generosity. It was Abraham who suggested to Lot: "Let there be no strife, I pray thee, between me and thee, and between my herdmen and thy herdmen; for we be brethren. Is not the whole land before thee? separate thyself, I pray thee, from me: if thou wilt take the left hand, then I will go to the right;

or if thou depart to the right hand, then I will go to the left" (Gen. 13:8,9).

What a generous man! Have you ever wondered why Abraham was so generous? Notice that verse 7 says, "The Canaanite and the Perizzite dwelled then in the land." This fact must have affected Abraham's decision. These ungodly people were doomed because of their sin, even though God gave them every chance. Yet, in their midst were two God-fearing men who were even finding it difficult to live together harmoniously. Abraham was obviously concerned about how his and Lot's testimony was affecting these ungodly people. No doubt this was one reason why he was so concerned about restoring harmony that he was willing to give Lot his choice of the land.

The world today is also carefully observing the Christian. What do unbelievers see when they watch you? None of us lives to himself. We are reminded of this in Romans 14:7,8: "For none of us liveth to himself, and no man dieth to himself. For whether we live, we live unto the Lord; and whether we die, we die unto the Lord: whether we live therefore, or die, we are the Lord's." Because we do not live to ourselves, it is important that we have a good testimony to those who are around us.

The main reason that Abraham was so generous was that he was a man of faith. He lived in a tent, which showed his attitude toward earthly possessions. He was willing to trust God for everything. God had promised that the land would belong to Abraham, and Abraham was willing to leave that matter in God's control. Do you have enough faith in God to leave things to Him without worrying about the outcome?

Abraham, not Lot, had been called to Canaan. Abraham could have insisted on his rights, but because he was a man of faith he left the outcome to God and was generous toward his fellow believer.

As we consider our attitude toward earthly possessions, we should ponder much the words of Christ: "If any man will come after me, let him deny himself, and take up his cross daily, and follow me. For whosoever will save his life shall lose it: but whosoever will lose his life for my sake, the same shall save it. For what is a man advantaged, if he gain the whole world, and lose himself, or be cast away?" (Luke 9:23-25). To be "cast away" is not to lose one's salvation, but to be set aside and receive no rewards because the heart has been set on the things of life. However, this was not so with Abraham. He walked by faith and was generous to those around him.

Abraham could have insisted on his rights for several reasons. He had been called to Canaan—not Lot. God had made a covenant to give Abraham the land—not Lot. Also, Abraham was the eldest of the two and the first choice should have been his. Yet Abraham gave up all of his rights. Because Abraham had a quiet, unshakable faith in God, he knew he did not need to assert himself in order to have God's best.

The Christian need not insist on his rights either, because he is an heir to all that is reserved for him in Christ. Many verses assure us of this fact. First Corinthians 3 says, "For all things are your's; . . . And ye are Christ's; and Christ is God's" (vv. 21,23). Ephesians 1:3 assures us that God the Father has "blessed us with all spiritual blessings in heavenly places in Christ." Romans 8:17 tells us, "If children, then heirs; heirs of God, and joint-heirs with Christ; if so be that we suffer with him, that we may be also glorified together." Everything that is the Lord's is ours, if we have received Him as Saviour. Nor should we forget that we are totally His and should seek to please Him in all that we do. Even concerning the Christian's physical body, the Scriptures say, "What? know ye not that your body is the temple of the Holy Ghost which is in you, which ye have of God, and ye are not your own? For ye are bought with a price: therefore glorify God in your body, and in your spirit, which are God's" (I Cor. 6:19,20).

Abraham was the friend of God, and a friend of God can easily afford to let others have the first choice. Abraham saw things from God's view instead of from man's view. He knew that brethren should have peace among themselves. In the New Testament, James wrote: "But if ye have bitter envying and strife in your hearts, glory not, and lie not against the truth. This wisdom descendeth not from above, but is earthly, sensual, devilish. For where envying and strife is, there is confusion and every evil work. But the wisdom that is from above is first pure, then peaceable, gentle, and easy to be intreated, full of mercy and good fruits, without partiality, and without hypocrisy. And the fruit of righteousness is sown in peace of them that make peace" (3:14-18). Abraham chose peace.

The Apostle Paul emphasized the same spiritual principle: "If it be possible, as much as lieth in you, live peaceably with all men" (Rom. 12:18). The Christian is not to insist on his rights, even as the Lord Jesus Christ did not insist on His. Philippians 2 tells us how Christ gave up the glory He had with the Father in order to come to earth, take upon Himself the form of man, and die on the cross. In the light of Christ's humility, the Apostle Paul said, "Let this mind be in you, which was also in Christ Jesus" (v. 5).

## Lot's Selfishness

In contrast to Abraham's attitude, notice how worldly minded Lot responded to the situation. Genesis 13 tells us that "Lot lifted up his eyes, and beheld all the plain of Jordan, that it was well watered every where, before the Lord destroyed Sodom and Gomorrah, even as the garden of the Lord, like the land of Egypt, as thou comest unto Zoar. Then Lot chose him all the plain of Jordan; and Lot journeyed east: and they separated themselves the one from the other. Abram dwelled in the land of Canaan, and Lot dwelled in the cities of the plain, and pitched his tent toward Sodom. But the men of Sodom were wicked and sinners before the Lord exceedingly" (vv. 10-13).

Lot looked for the best the world could offer and made that his choice. As other worldly believers, Lot set little value on fellowshipping with holy men of God. Lot's mind was set on earthly prosperity, not on heavenly things. He preferred to walk by sight rather than by faith. He and Abraham could not walk together because they were not agreed on spiritual values. The New Testament tells us where we should set our hearts when it says, "If [since] ye then be risen with Christ, seek those things which are above, where Christ sitteth on the right hand of God. Set your affection on things above, not on things on the earth. For ye are dead [have died], and your life is hid with Christ in God" (Col. 3:1-3).

Abraham's eyes were not set on temporal blessings but on eternal blessings. This was also true of Moses, who "forsook Egypt, not fearing the wrath of the king: for he endured, as seeing him who is invisible" (Heb. 11:27). Abraham saw beyond the things of earth because of his faith in God. God says, "Faith is . . . the evidence of things not seen," but man says, "Sight is the evidence—seeing is believing."

Lot's confidence was in what he could perceive through the eye-gate, apparently not realizing that this is the chief avenue through which temptation assails the soul. The Scriptures say, "For all that is in the world, the lust of the flesh, and the lust of the eyes, and the pride of life, is not of the Father, but is of the world" (I John 2:16).

This was the beginning of the complete decline and utmost shame for Lot. Walking by sight is the cause of most of the failures and sorrows of man. It was Eve who saw that the forbidden tree looked good; then she ate of it (Gen. 3:6). It was Achan who first saw and then took of the forbidden spoils of battle that later caused a defeat for Israel. In confessing his sin, Achan said, "I saw . . . I coveted . . . [I] took" (Josh. 7:21).

What are you looking at today? Whatever it is, it is influencing your life. I think one of the greatest curses in this respect is television. We see sin before us so much that the tendency is to lower our standards and to follow by act what we see on the screen.

When Abraham gave Lot the opportunity to choose what he wanted, Lot looked over the land and saw the well-watered area near the Jordan River. The Scriptures tell us that "Lot chose him all the plain of Jordan; and Lot journeyed east: and they separated themselves the one from the other" (Gen. 13:11).

God does not see as man sees. The worldly eye of Lot saw the well-watered plain even as the Garden of Eden, but the holy eye of God saw something else. Verse 13 tells us what the Lord saw: "But the men of Sodom were wicked and sinners before the Lord exceedingly." It always pays to seek the Lord's will and trust Him when selecting a direction for life. The psalmist said, "Delight thyself also in the Lord; and he shall give thee the desires of thine heart. Commit thy way unto the Lord; trust also in him; and he shall bring it to pass" (Ps. 37:4,5). These were the verses we claimed when we began the Back to the Bible Broadcast in 1939. We have used them for spiritual support thousands of times.

In Psalm 32:8 we are also told how God leads: "I will instruct thee and teach thee in the way which thou shalt go: I will guide thee with mine eye." If we will allow God to do the seeing for us, He will guide us. Our need is to trust Him fully.

## Lot's Sojourn in Sodom

The Scriptures clearly indicate the downward steps of Lot: he lifted up his eyes, and beheld" (Gen. 13:10); he "chose him all the plain of Jordan" (v. 11); he "separated" from Abraham—from spiritual fellowship (v. 11); he "dwelled in the cities of the plain" (v. 12); he "pitched his tent toward Sodom" (v. 12); he "dwelt in Sodom" (14:12); and finally, he "sat in the gate of Sodom [a position of great importance]" (19:1).

Lot became one of the city councilors and his daughters married Sodomites. At first he only looked, but at last he was an official in a wicked city. Sin is like cancer—it might begin with only a skin rash but it can lead to death. The Scriptures refer to Lot as "just" and as "that righteous man" (II Pet. 2:7,8), but he was dragged downward by his appetite for the things of the world.

The psalmist was well acquainted with the way sin can drag man down a step at a time. He wrote: "Blessed is the man that walketh not in the counsel of the ungodly, nor standeth in the way of sinners, nor sitteth in the seat of the scornful" (Ps. 1:1). Notice the three steps: walking, standing, and sitting. First, it is the counsel of the ungodly, then it is the way of sinners, and finally it is the seat of the scornful. This is the downward road of sin, and the psalmist said that the man who does not go this direction is blessed. The believer who avoids the downward path of sin finds that "his delight is in the law of the Lord; and in his law doth he meditate day and night. And he shall be like a tree planted by the rivers of water, that bringeth forth his fruit in his season; his leaf also shall not wither; and whatsoever he doeth shall prosper" (vv. 2,3). Whereas Psalm 1:1 shows the path that Lot took, verses 2 and 3 show the path that Abraham took. What path are you taking?

## Lot's Deliverance From Sodom

God gave Lot many opportunities to realize that things were very ungodly in Sodom. God even allowed foreign kings to come up against the cities of Sodom and Gomorrah and take Lot captive. Lot lost all of his goods and his life was in constant danger. He was so calloused, however, that he failed to learn the lesson. He finally recovered his freedom and his property—thanks to Abraham and his faith—but he again went back to Sodom. His heart was not moved by the grace of God. Many believers today also fail to see God's grace and love in dealing with them, and their lives become sad spectacles.

Because of God's long-suffering, He again moved to deliver Lot when the destruction of Sodom was imminent. In the 19th chapter of Genesis we see how God warned His child, Lot, before He destroyed the city. Two angels first came to Sodom to talk to Lot (v. 1). God was moving to save him from the destruction of the city. It was a difficult matter getting Lot out of the city because he realized its destruction would take the very things he desired so much to have.

Lot's moral values had also sunk to an all-time low. When the angels were visiting Lot in his house, the Scriptures say, "The men of Sodom, compassed the house round, both old and young, all the people from every quarter: And they called unto Lot, and said unto him, Where are the men which came in to thee this night? bring them out unto us, that we may know them" (vv. 4,5). Lot's reply revealed how low his standards had become: "I pray you, brethren, do not so wickedly. Behold now, I have two daughters which have not known man; let me, I pray you, bring them out unto you, and do ye to them as is good in your eyes: only unto these men do nothing; for therefore came they under the shadow of my roof" (vv. 7,8). The angels caused blindness to overcome those who were at the door, and they warned Lot to tell any other relatives he had that destruction was coming.

When Lot told his married daughters and their husbands of the coming judgment on the city, "he seemed as one that mocked unto his sons in law" (v. 14). Lot's married daughters and their husbands would not listen to him. Lot had no testimony among his own family. What is your testimony like among your family, friends and business associates? Do they see you as one who desires to please the Lord or only as one who is trying to get all the world has to offer?

Genesis 19:15 says that the next morning "the angels hastened Lot, saying, Arise, take thy wife, and thy two daughters, which are here; lest thou be consumed in the iniquity of the city." Notice where Lot's heart was. Lot and his family lingered because their hearts were so set on the things of Sodom. Lot could not make up his mind "and while he lingered, the men laid hold upon his hand, and upon the hand of his wife, and upon the hand of his two daughters; the Lord being merciful unto him: and they brought him forth, and set him without the city" (v. 16). All of this was done because God was merciful, but Lot could not appreciate God's mercy.

The harvest of Lot's sowing to the flesh is seen in that which happened to his married daughters and to his wife. His daughters apparently remained in the city with their husbands, and his wife "became a pillar of salt" (v. 26) when she looked back as she was fleeing the city. The angels had clearly instructed Lot and his family: "Escape for thy life; look not behind thee" (v. 17). But Lot's wife had her heart so set on the things of Sodom that she looked back to see if there was anything she could save. Because of her disobedience, she was turned into a pillar of salt.

After Lot and his two remaining daughters fled from the city, they lived in a cave because they were afraid to dwell in Zoar (v. 30). Lot had lost everything. Whereas he had had so much that he had to separate from Abraham, now he had nothing. While living in the cave with his two daughters, Lot committed a great sin and fathered two sons by means of his daughters. It is true that his daughters did the scheming, but he allowed them to do it. All of this resulted because Lot's heart was set on the things of the world.

The divine commentary on Lot is given in II Peter 2:7,8, where it is said that God "delivered just Lot, vexed with the filthy conversation of the wicked. (For that righteous man dwelling among them, in seeing and hearing, vexed his righteous soul from day to day with their unlawful deeds)." The things of Sodom vexed Lot's soul because he was a child of God, but he continued to live in Sodom.

How many of us are saying, This world is so wicked. What is happening to our young people? What is happening to our churches? These are the questions we are asking, but we also need to ask ourselves, Where are we? It is time we quit talking about others and examine our own hearts. Lot was snatched as a "brand plucked out of the fire"—saved yet so as by fire—because *God* was faithful. Let us not wait until God has to use such drastic measures in our lives. Although we live *in* the world, let us not be *of* the world. Let us be separated from sin and separated unto God that we may walk in fellowship with Him. Of Moses, Hebrews 11:26 says that "he had respect unto the recompence of the reward." Because of this he considered "the reproach of Christ greater riches than the treasures in Egypt." Moses looked to the future. Are you? What are your eyes fixed on? Where is your heart? "Where your treasure is, there will your heart be also" (Matt. 6:21).

### Abraham's Faith Rewarded

By contrast, let us see the path of Abraham after he was separated from Lot. Abraham had finally fulfilled God's requirements in not only leaving his country but also his kindred and his father's house. Lot was no longer with him, and Abraham was now alone with God. Later, God said to the nation of Israel, "Look unto Abraham your father, and unto Sarah that bare you: for I called him alone, and blessed him, and increased him" (Isa. 51:2).

After Lot and Abraham separated, the Lord said to Abraham, "Lift up now thine eyes, and look from the place where thou art northward, and southward, and eastward, and westward: For all the land which thou seest, to thee will I give it, and to thy seed for ever. And I will make thy seed as the dust of the earth: so that if a man can number the dust of the earth, then shall thy seed also be numbered. Arise, walk through the land in the length of it and in the breadth of it; for I will give it unto thee. Then Abram removed his tent, and came and dwelt in the plain of Mamre, which is in Hebron, and built there an altar unto the Lord" (Gen. 13:14-18).

What a different story we have in Abraham's life! Lot had lifted up his eyes in selfishness and had taken the best he could see, according to his values. But for Abraham, the place of separation now becomes the place of larger vision. Lot took what he saw and lost everything. Abraham lifted up his eyes at God's command and received the title deed to all the land. The Lord had told Abraham that He would give the land to his seed, but now God promises for the first time to give the land to Abraham personally as well. First, God told Abraham to go to a land that He would show him; then God promised to give the land to his seed; and finally—after complete separation—God promised to give the land to Abraham as well.

Notice further that God told Abraham, "Arise, walk through the land in the length of it and in the breadth of it; for I will give it unto thee" (v. 17). The Lord first told Abraham to look; then He told him to walk. Abraham then had God's perspective as he looked at the land. This was the first time that God had told Abraham to walk through the land.

The significance of Abraham's walking through the land was that this indicated his claiming the land. It had been promised him, but now he was appropriating it for himself. In effect, God was saying to him, "Go and take it."

Later, God spoke to Joshua and said, "Every place that the sole of your foot shall tread upon, that have I given unto you" (Josh. 1:3). This shows the principle or law of faith. Jesus Himself said, "If any man thirst, let him come unto me, and drink" (John 7:37). Notice that we are not only to come and ask, but also to drink. In this regard, drinking refers to taking. Faith demands taking, because this is appropriating what God has given us.

First Peter 1:4,5 tells of the inheritance that is reserved in heaven for those who believe; that is, for those who are willing to take it. God has made many things available to the Christian, but the Christian must appropriate them by faith.

Again we see a contrast between Lot and Abraham which reminds us of the contrast between the worldly Christian and the faithful one. One is moved by self-interest; the other is moved by the Word of God. One leans on his own understanding; the other, on the promises of God.

Proverbs 3:5-7 tells us, "Trust in the Lord with all thine heart; and lean not unto thine own understanding. In all thy ways acknowledge him, and he shall direct thy paths. Be not wise in thine own eyes: fear the Lord, and depart from evil." Every believer is also charged: "Wherefore come out from among them, and be ye separate, saith the Lord, and touch not the unclean thing; and I will receive you, And will be a Father unto you, and ye shall be my sons and daughters, saith the Lord Almighty" (II Cor. 6:17,18). The following verse says, "Having therefore these promises, dearly beloved, let us cleanse ourselves from all filthiness of the flesh and spirit, perfecting holiness in the fear of God" (7:1).

After God promised to give the land to Abraham and commanded him to walk through it, "Abram removed his tent, and came and dwelt in the plain of Mamre, which is in Hebron, and built there an altar unto the Lord" (Gen. 13:18). This was a living testimony. Lot later lost his testimony because of his choice, but Abraham's testimony became greater because he was willing to trust God. For the most part, Lot's communion with God dwindled and dropped off, but Abraham's communion kept growing. The spiritual principle is that "the just shall live by faith" (Rom. 1:17). God calls Himself the God of Abraham, but not the God of Lot.

God wants to be our God, too, and He will be in the truest sense if we will "cleanse ourselves from all filthiness of the flesh and spirit" (II Cor. 7:1). In this verse, the filthiness of the spirit refers to the sins of the mind; that is, our thinking and attitudes. We must be careful to confess the sins of the spirit as well as the sins of the flesh if we are going to be what God really wants us to be.

After God commanded Abraham to walk through the land, Abraham "removed his tent, and came and dwelt in the plain of Mamre, which is in Hebron, and built there an altar unto the Lord" (Gen. 13:18). It was not until there was complete separation on Abraham's part that he was fully in the will of God. His fellowship with God was evidenced by the fact that he built an altar.

Chapter 6

# The Discipline of Faith

After Abraham experienced the awakening of his faith, he had even richer experiences as he was tested through the disciplining of his faith.

Genesis 14 gives us the account of the first war mentioned in the Scriptures. In this great war, four kings opposed five others. Lot and everything he had was taken captive. (This war occurred before God destroyed Sodom and Gomorrah.) The Bible says, "The vale of Siddim was full of slimepits; and the kings of Sodom and Gomorrah fled, and fell there; and they that remained fled to the mountain. And they took all the goods of Sodom and Gomorrah, and all their victuals, and went their way. And they took Lot, Abram's brother's son, who dwelt in Sodom, and his goods, and departed" (vv. 10-12).

The conflict between the kings devastated Sodom and Gomorrah, and Lot was taken captive. Since Abraham lived in the same general area, you may ask, How did Abraham escape? He was not involved in the conflict because he lived in a tent. The kings would not have been interested in such a nomad. If they would have captured him and taken over his possessions, they would have gained much wealth. But from his outward appearance it was not evident that Abraham was rich.

In addition, he had an altar. This marked him as one whose pursuits were of quite another character than that of Lot, who was involved in Sodom and Gomorrah's activities. Abraham was a man who was obviously concerned about heavenly things, so the kings could see no value in taking him captive. How wonderful it is when the believing pilgrim can look from his high elevation with God down on the battlefield of the evil world. Abraham could literally look down from the hilltops toward the valley. This was the same view Lot had had earlier when it had seemed so luxurious and inviting to him. There the rich people lived, and Lot wanted to be one of them. Abraham could now look down on this battle and see the results of seeking the world's riches. Although Abraham was a man of great wealth, it would not have been tragic even if he had lost all of his riches. His trust was in the Lord, not in his possessions.

What would it mean to you if you were to lose your earthly possessions today? Do you have your heart set on the riches of this world or on the riches of heaven?

As we hear about the present conditions of the world, we can be very upset. Although I refuse to be upset by the things of the world, I am very upset by our anti-God attitude. What happens to the material things of this world is not of the greatest significance. Our personal relationship with God is what really matters. In the midst of a world of confusion, I realize that my task is to finish the course that God has laid out for me and to leave the outcome with God.

Although Abraham was not concerned about his own possessions, notice that he was a person of great sympathy. The Scriptures tell us that "there came one that had escaped, and told Abram the Hebrew; for he dwelt in the plain of Mamre. . . . And when Abram heard that his brother was taken captive, he armed his trained servants, born in his own house, three hundred and eighteen, and pursued them unto Dan" (vv. 13,14). Abraham was not indifferent to Lot's needs, nor was he bitter toward him. Abraham could have been calloused and unmoved by Lot's situation because of the selfish attitude Lot had displayed earlier. Abraham did not say, "This is none of my business. Lot is reaping what he sowed." When a person is in fellowship with God, he will not be indifferent to his brother who is in need.

What should be our attitude when a brother is taken captive by the things of this world? Some have a distorted concept of separation. When they see a brother fall into sin they shout it from the housetops and publish it in their magazines. This is not what Christ instructed. He said that when one sheep is lost we are to leave the other sheep in good keeping and go out after the lost one.

Galatians 6 tells us what our attitude should be toward a fallen Christian brother. The Apostle Paul exhorted: "Brethren, if any person is overtaken in misconduct or sin of any sort, you who are spiritual—who are responsive to and controlled by the Spirit—should set him right and restore and reinstate him, without any sense of superiority and with all gentleness, keeping an attentive eye on yourself, lest you should be tempted also. Bear (endure, carry) one another's burdens and troublesome moral faults, and in this way fulfill and observe perfectly the law of Christ, the Messiah, and complete what is lacking [in your obedience to it]" (vv. 1,2, *Amp.*).

This is the attitude we should take toward a fallen brother, but this is so different from what is usually done today. So often a self-righteous attitude is taken toward the fallen brother and he is only further harmed and hurt.

When Abraham realized what had happened to Lot, he became very bold. "When Abram heard that his brother was taken captive, he armed his trained servants, born in his own house, three hundred and eighteen, and pursued them unto Dan. And he divided himself against them, he and his servants, by night, and smote them, and pursued them unto Hobah, which is on the left hand of Damascus" (Gen. 14:14,15). God rewarded his courage because Abraham "brought back all the goods, and also brought again his brother Lot, and his goods, and the women also, and the people" (v. 16).

## A Holy Boldness

Abraham had a holy boldness. When a man walks with God as Abraham did, he can be bold against sin and the

Enemy. Proverbs 28:1 says, "The wicked flee when no man pursueth: but the righteous are bold as a lion." Although these were mighty kings, one of them as noted as Napoleon, Abraham went against them with only 318 men—and God. These were only a handful in comparison to the other armies, but the man of faith attempts great things. He knows his God. This was a righteous cause and Abraham knew what God could do. He knew that God could use what the world considered foolish in order to confound what the world considered wise.

When Paul wrote to the Christians at Corinth, he said, "For ye see your calling, brethren, how that not many wise men after the flesh, not many mighty, not many noble, are called: But God hath chosen the foolish things of the world to confound the wise; and God hath chosen the weak things of the world to confound the things which are mighty; And base things of the world, and things which are despised, hath God chosen, yea, and things which are not, to bring to nought things that are: That no flesh should glory in his presence" (I Cor. 1:26-29).

These verses have been of tremendous encouragement to me. Many times they have prevented me from becoming very discouraged. God has given me a great responsibility in the Back to the Bible Broadcast. Yet I am keenly aware of my limitations. I am not a great preacher. I am not an orator. I do not have command of a large vocabulary. But one thing I know is that God chose me for this ministry and my responsibility is to follow Him. I leave the results to God, and I bless and thank Him for what He is doing. It is impossible for me to personally boast about what the Broadcast ministry is accomplishing, because only God could be producing such results.

I am reminded of D. L. Moody, who was approached by a person who said, "Mr. Moody, you made 18 grammatical mistakes in your sermon today." Mr. Moody was quick to answer, "Young man, I use all the grammar I have for the Lord. What are you doing with yours?" The responsibility that each of us has is to dedicate all that he is to Jesus Christ.

The weapons that we have in Christ Jesus are tremendous. We are told in II Corinthians 10:3-5 that "though we walk in the flesh, we do not war after the flesh: (For the weapons of our warfare are not carnal, but mighty through God to the pulling down of strong holds;) Casting down imaginations, and every high thing that exalteth itself against the knowledge of God, and bringing into captivity every thought to the obedience of Christ." The spiritual weapons we have are able to bring even our thoughts into captivity. What are these spiritual weapons? The greatest of these is given in Ephesians 6:18: "Praying always with all prayer and supplication in the Spirit." Prayer is the greatest weapon we have. Along with faith, prayer can overcome anything and everything. Nothing is impossible with God.

We must always remember that God can use only the separated man—the person who will dare to stand alone if necessary. That is why Paul could say, "I can do all things through Christ which strengtheneth me" (Phil. 4:13). Paul was a man who was separated unto God. Have you ever tried earnest praying? Real praying? Have you tried earnestly praying for a separated brother rather than merely exposing or murdering his character? God's approach is for the Christian in fellowship to earnestly pray for the restoration of the fallen brother. It does not take a bold man to murder a person's character; any coward can do it. Such a person is a coward before God and usually a coward before his fallen brother. If we are not seeking to restore the fallen brother to fellowship, this indicates that we are not being led by the Spirit. When the Holy Spirit controls our lives there is always gentleness, love and compassion for others.

## A Man of Power

Abraham went up against the kings with great power. He had power, not because of his physical resources, but because he went in the name of the Lord. His power was evidenced by the fact that he "brought back all" (Gen. 14:16). There is nothing impossible to the man who is totally separated unto God.

God's power was later seen when He led the children of Israel out of Egypt. Yet God told Moses concerning the Israelites: "I am come down to deliver them out of the hand of the Egyptians, and to bring them up out of that land unto a good land and a large, unto a land flowing with milk and honey; unto the place of the Canaanites, and the Hittites, and the Amorites, and the Perizzites, and the Hivites, and the Jebusites" (Ex. 3:8). When God appeared to Moses at this time, He identified Himself as "the God of Abraham, the God of Isaac, and the God of Jacob" (v. 6). God chose to use Moses to display His power, so He said to him, "Come now therefore, and I will send thee unto Pharaoh, that thou mayest bring forth my people the children of Israel out of Egypt" (v. 10). This is the kind of God we have. He does impossible deeds, using those who are totally separated unto Him. God works through man.

Abraham had tremendous power from God, but Lot could not do anything. He could not even save himself because, even though he was a child of God, he was not separated unto God. Jesus said to the believers of His day—and to us also: "Abide in me, and I in you. As the branch cannot bear fruit of itself, except it abide in the vine; no more can ye, except ye abide in me. I am the vine, ye are the branches: He that abideth in me, and I in him, the same bringeth forth much fruit: for without me ye can do nothing. If ye abide in me, and my words abide in you, ye shall ask what ye will, and it shall be done unto you" (John 15:4,5,7). Abraham did not know these verses, but he knew the principle of them. He knew he had power only as he lived in fellowship with God. Because of Lot's lack of fellowship, he had no such power.

### The Test of Worldly Ambition

It is wonderful to read how Abraham had enough confidence in God to go after Lot and bring back everything.

But it is important to see that Abraham faced a great test after this significant victory. After Abraham brought back all the people and their possessions, out of gratefulness the king of Sodom said to him, "Give me the persons, and take the goods to thyself" (Gen. 14:21). Since God had promised Abraham all the land, Abraham might have thought, Well, this may be it. This is perhaps the way God is going to give the land to me. This must be God's method.

God had promised to make of Abraham a great nation. Now that Abraham had conquered some great kings, it would be only logical for him to think that this was the time that God was going to do it. This teaches us that we must be on guard concerning the world's attractions. Too many Christians allow circumstances to dictate God's will to them. In this way many become ensnared by Satan. How wonderful it is to see, however, that Abraham refused to let circumstances dictate God's will for his life. He continued to walk by faith and not by sight.

In Genesis 14:18-20 we are told that "Melchizedek king of Salem brought forth bread and wine: and he was the priest of the most high God. And he blessed him, and said, Blessed be Abram of the most high God, possessor of heaven and earth: And blessed be the most high God, which hath delivered thine enemies into thy hand. And he gave him tithes of all."

Suddenly there came on the scene this person by the name of Melchizedek. He was a remarkable character—a stranger commissioned by God to fortify Abraham's faith. It was at this time that the Enemy was ready to attack Abraham by having the king of Sodom offer him the earthly goods. Abraham did not have the Word of God as we have; therefore, he was not able to go to the Word and fortify himself. Instead, God sent Melchizedek to strengthen his faith.

God is always on time. When a person is characterized by a tent-life on earth and lives by his altar of communion, God is always there to help and strengthen in time of need. Perhaps you have discovered that when temptation arises, you yield to it easily. If this is the case, how much time are you spending in the Word of God to fortify yourself against these temptations? If you do not have a good devotional life, during which time you read and meditate on God's Word and spend time in prayer, you cannot expect to be able to withstand temptation. If we would spend more time in the Word and prayer, fortifying ourselves against temptations to come, we would spend less time in a backslidden condition wondering how we can get back in fellowship with God. Of course, believers are assured that "if we confess our sins, he is faithful and just to forgive us our sins, and to cleanse us from all unrighteousness" (I John 1:9). But the struggle of the soul who finally comes to his spiritual senses and confesses his sins to God could largely be avoided if the life was fortified ahead of time against the temptations.

Melchizedek was the king of Salem. The word "Salem" means "peace." Melchizedek brought forth bread and wine. Bread is used in the Scriptures to refer to the Word of God because it gives sustenance. Wine is symbolic of the Holy Spirit. Melchizedek blessed Abraham and reminded him that the most High God is "possessor of heaven and earth" (Gen. 14:19). Abraham was reminded that all things belong to God—even the deliverance from the enemy, which might attack him in retaliation for his recent victory over them.

When the king of Sodom tempted Abraham by urging him to take the earthly goods, Abraham's attitude was the same as the Apostle Paul's. In II Corinthians 4:18 Paul said, "We look not at the things which are seen, but at the things which are not seen: for the things which are seen are temporal; but the things which are not seen are eternal."

Because Abraham had been spiritually fortified beforehand, he was ready when the king of Sodom offered him earthly riches. There was no problem because he had already made his choice between that which is temporal and that which is eternal. Joshua told the people of his day, "Choose you this day whom ye will serve" (Josh. 24:15). The greatest need among present-day believers is to realize there is a choice that has to be made.

### Abraham's Choice

When the choice was presented to Abraham, he gave a very pointed answer to the king of Sodom: "I have lift up mine hand unto the Lord, the most high God, the possessor of heaven and earth, That I will not take from a thread even to a shoelatchet, and that I will not take any thing that is thine, lest thou shouldest say, I have made Abram rich" (Gen. 14:22,23).

Abraham was ready and his answer was quick, concise and final. Abraham declared God to be his God and that he was confident and determined that God alone would provide his portion. Abraham declared unashamedly that he would trust God for his every need. He did not want to give either Satan or man the opportunity to say that he had made him rich.

The man who has made God his God can afford to say this. Paul said, "Not that I speak in respect of want: for I have learned, in whatsoever state I am, therewith to be content. I know both how to be abased, and I know how to abound: every where and in all things I am instructed both to be full and to be hungry; both to abound and to suffer need" (Phil. 4:11,12). Paul was saying, "I can take it any way it comes, but I will take it only from God." He refused to rely on the manipulations of man.

In Hebrews 13:5 we are told: "Be content with such things as ye have: for he hath said, I will never leave thee, nor forsake thee." Because of this promise, we can say with the writer of Hebrews, "Let us go forth therefore unto him without the camp, bearing his reproach. For here we have no continuing city, but we seek one to come" (vv. 13,14).

All things are ours in Christ Jesus. May God open our inner eyes to see the riches we have in Him. Paul wrote in Ephesians 1:18: "The eyes of your understanding being enlightened; that ye may know what is the hope of his calling, and what the riches of the glory of his inheritance in the saints." Ask God to open your eyes so you can see all that He has for you in Christ.

Abraham chose that which was eternal instead of that which was temporal. Lot's choice was just the opposite. Abraham's refusal of the goods which the king of Sodom offered included Lot's goods. His refusal enabled Lot to take back all of his earthly riches. Lot did so. A spiritual principle is stated in Proverbs 13:7 that is significant in Lot's case: "There is that maketh himself rich, yet hath nothing: there is that maketh himself poor, yet hath great riches."

Even though Abraham refused anything for himself, notice how considerate he was of the others who labored with him. He said he would not take anything "save only that which the young men have eaten, and the portion of the men which went with me" (Gen. 14:24). Abraham told the king of Sodom that he could give the 318 men who went with him what they had eaten and what was needed to take care of their expenses. Abraham did not force others to walk according to his elevated standards. Our walk should always be as Paul described it in Romans 12:3: "According as God hath dealt to every man the measure of faith." We need to be considerate of our fellow believers and not force them to take the same definite stand for God as we have chosen. By our example, however, we should lead them on to deeper things.

## 'Fear Not'

Abraham had been successful with his 318 men, but this was not the end of his problems. Obviously, the four kings might return at any time against this small band of men. But after Abraham had been blessed by Melchizedek and had taken his stand regarding the offer of the king of Sodom, the Scriptures tell us that "after these things the word of the Lord came unto Abram in a vision, saying, Fear not, Abram: I am thy shield, and thy exceeding great reward" (Gen. 15:1). The phrase "after these things" is very important in connecting chapter 15 with chapter 14. Abraham had just had a mountaintop experience with God. However, after such experiences we often go into the valley of despair. Although

Abraham had reason to fear that the kings might retaliate, God said, "Fear not."

The command, "Fear not," appears over 300 times in the Bible. In Isaiah 41:10 God says, "Fear thou not; for I am with thee: be not dismayed; for I am thy God: I will strengthen thee; yea, I will help thee; yea, I will uphold thee with the right hand of my righteousness." In Isaiah 43:1,2 God assures us, "Fear not: for I have redeemed thee, I have called thee by thy name; thou art mine. When thou passest through the waters [of sorrow], I will be with thee; and through the rivers [of danger], they shall not overflow thee: when thou walkest through the fire [of testing], thou shalt not be burned; neither shall the flame kindle upon thee."

Even as God said to Abraham, so he says to present-day believers that He will be our Shield. Nothing evil can befall those who walk as pilgrims and strangers—those who have a tent-life and who live by the altar of communion with God. Although some circumstances may seem evil to us while we are passing through them, we need to remember Romans 8:28, which assures us that "all things work together for good to them that love God, to them who are the called according to his purpose."

### The Believer's Reward

God also assured Abraham that He was Abraham's "exceeding great reward." The king of Sodom had offered Abraham all the riches that Abraham and his servants had brought back, but he turned them down. Notice that the tense is not past or future, but present. Not "I was" or "I will be," but "I am"—"I am thy shield, and thy exceeding great reward" (Gen. 15:1). God assured Abraham that He was his reward at the present time and also forever. The reward which the king of Sodom offered was valueless as far as eternity is concerned, but it would have been very attractive as far as the world is concerned.

We see from God's promise to be Abraham's reward that God never permits His children to lose for honoring Him and seeking His glory. God never leaves His child without spiritual blessings after His child has taken a stand for the glory of God.

After God promised to be Abraham's exceeding great reward, Abraham said, "Lord God, what wilt thou give me, seeing I go childless, and the steward of my house is this Eliezer of Damascus? And Abram said, Behold, to me thou hast given no seed: and, lo, one born in my house is mine heir" (vv. 2,3). Notice God's glorious response to Abraham, who was concerned about future descendants: "This shall not be thine heir; but he that shall come forth out of thine own bowels shall be thine heir. And he brought him forth abroad, and said, Look now toward heaven, and tell the stars, if thou be able to number them: and he said unto him, So shall thy seed be" (vv. 4,5).

Although Abraham had no children at this time, his faith in the Lord is recorded in verse 6: "He believed in the Lord; and he counted it to him for righteousness." Because of Abraham's faith in God, he was able to look into the future and trust God for everything. At a later time, Moses also set his eyes on the future and believed God for the reward. It is said of Moses in Hebrews 11:24,25 that he "refused to be called the son of Pharaoh's daughter; Choosing rather to suffer affliction with the people of God, than to enjoy the pleasures of sin for a season." Because Abraham and Moses had their hearts fixed on eternal treasures, they were able to overlook any difficulties of the present. They put their confidence in the promises of God for the future.

Ephesians 1:3 tells us that present-day believers have been blessed with "all spiritual blessings in heavenly places in Christ. But we, too, must set our eyes on the future. We must be those who look to their reward for glorifying God, rather than looking at the temporal satisfactions of the present.

Chapter 7

# Abraham's Test of Patience

In the New Testament, James told us, "My brethren, count it all joy when ye fall into divers temptations [testings]; Knowing this, that the trying of your faith worketh patience. But let patience have her perfect work, that ye may be perfect and entire, wanting nothing" (1:2-4). Testings are God's means of helping the believer to become mature.

In Romans 5:3, the Apostle Paul wrote: "And not only so, but we glory in tribulations also: knowing that tribulation worketh patience." God sends tribulation (testing) into the life of a believer to produce patience. Have you prayed for patience and found that things became worse? They became worse because God was answering your prayer by sending tribulation to produce patience. This is the way God works.

Abraham's patience was greatly tested because he found it extremely difficult to wait for God's time regarding an heir. It apparently seemed to Abraham that he had been waiting endlessly and God's time had not arrived. Abraham had no children of his own, yet God had promised to make of him a great nation. Abraham was seriously wondering how God was going to fulfill His promises since he had no children and was now getting too old to have them.

When Abraham talked to God about this matter, he alluded to the promises God had made. God had told Abraham, "Unto thy seed will I give this land" (Gen. 12:7). Later, God had also assured him: "For all the land which thou seest, to thee will I give it, and to thy seed for ever. And

I will make thy seed as the dust of the earth: so that if a man can number the dust of the earth, then shall thy seed also be numbered" (13:15,16).

Seven years had gone by and still there was no child. There are great dangers involved when we look at the promises of God rather than at the God of the promises. We should not look from the promises to God: instead we should look from God to the promises. Abraham was looking at God from the vantage point of promises. Thus, he was accusing God because seven years had gone by and nothing had been done.

We are this way too, and it shows that our need is to keep our eyes fixed on God. When we realize what a wonderful God we have—that He cannot lie, that time is no factor with Him—we will not have a problem with His promises.

## Israel at Kadesh-barnea

What can happen when we get our eyes on the promises instead of on God is illustrated by the Israelites at Kadesh-barnea. It was from this place that Israel sent 12 spies to see what the land of Canaan and its inhabitants were like. God had assured them that He was going to give them the land. Twelve spies were sent to observe the land for 40 days and bring back a report. When they returned, 10 of them had looked at the promises only. Two of them looked at God first.

When the 10 spies compared the promises with the circumstances, they said it was impossible to enter the land. The 10 spies said, "The people be strong that dwell in the land, and the cities are walled, and very great: and moreover we saw the children of Anak there" (Num. 13:28). Their conclusion was: "We be not able to go up against the people; for they are stronger than we" (v. 31). But there were two men among the spies—Joshua and Caleb—whose eyes were fixed on God. When they looked from God to the circumstances, the circumstances amounted to nothing. Caleb spoke for both himself and Joshua and said, "Let us go up at once, and possess it; for we are well able to overcome it" (v. 30). Joshua and Caleb had confidence that what God had promised He was able to bring to pass. The Word of God assures us that "God is not a man, that he should lie; neither the son of man, that he should repent: hath he said, and shall he not do it? or hath he spoken, and shall he not make it good?" (23:19). How great is your God? Always keep your eyes on the God of the promises rather than on the promises of God.

## Why God Delays

Viewing the promises first allows self to creep in. Abraham and Sarah were not getting any younger, and the impossibility of the fulfillment of the promise seemed more acute. Abraham was about 80 years old at this time and Sarah was about 70, so it is understandable that they began to question how God was going to fulfill His promise. But they were looking at themselves first, rather than at God. Remember that circumstances always look different when we look to God first.

God's delay in fulfilling His promise was for a special purpose—that Abraham might learn to know Him better. God's promises are as sure as He is, but our faith needs to be tested so that we learn to glory in God instead of in His promises or in ourselves. If faith is not tested, the danger is that man will take some of the glory himself.

God knows how frail we are. "He knoweth our frame; he remembereth that we are dust" (Ps. 103:14). Thus, He knows that we need much encouragement. He reminded Abraham that the time element was no issue; neither was the deadness of Sarah's womb or Abraham's natural inability. Hebrews 11:12 describes Abraham as one who was "as good as dead"—an obvious reference to his procreative powers. But when God wills to do something there is nothing that can stop Him.

Because God knows how impatient man is, and that he can even become sinful in impatience, in His mercy He appeared to Abraham and gave him an even greater promise. Abraham was wondering whether Eliezer, the steward of his house, was to be his heir. God told Abraham, "This shall not be thine heir; but he that shall come forth out of thine own bowels shall be thine heir. And he brought him forth abroad, and said, Look now toward heaven, and tell the stars, if thou be able to number them: and he said unto him, So shall thy seed be" (Gen. 15:4,5).

Previously God had promised Abraham that his seed would be as "the dust of the earth" (13:16). This emphasized Abraham's earthly posterity. In Genesis 15, however, God gives Abraham an even greater promise—that his seed would be as the stars of heaven (v. 5). This emphasized Abraham's spiritual posterity. Abraham was to become "the father of all them that believe" (Rom. 4:11), and God likened the number of this posterity to the number of stars in heaven.

## Faith Unto Righteousness

God's word was sufficient for Abraham. Genesis 15:6 tells us that "he believed in the Lord; and he counted it to him for righteousness." God had spoken and that was enough for Abraham. He took God at His word. God then reminded Abraham, "I am the Lord that brought thee out of Ur of the Chaldees" (v. 7). God was saying in effect, "I am the One who began this, and I am the One who is going to finish it." The same principle is stated in Philippians 1:6: "Being confident of this very thing, that he which hath begun a good work in you will perform it until the day of Jesus Christ." God never begins anything that He does not finish.

In Ephesians 1:3 we have the beautiful statement: "Blessed be the God and Father of our Lord Jesus Christ, who hath blessed us with all spiritual blessings in heavenly places in Christ." Here the blessing is put in the past tense—"hath blessed us." Although much of the blessing is yet future, it is so certain in Christ that it is put in the past tense. To this promise God adds a seal. In verses 13 and 14 of this same chapter we are told, "In whom [Christ] ye also trusted, after that ye heard the word of truth, the gospel of your salvation: in whom also after that ye believed, ye were sealed with that holy Spirit of promise, Which is the earnest of our inheritance until the redemption of the purchased possession, unto the praise of his glory." God's seal assures us that He will keep us until the day of redemption.

God had to assure Abraham that what He had begun He was able to perform. He reminded Abraham that He had not only brought him up out of Ur of the Chaldees and into the land of promise, but that He also would finish that which He had begun. However, Abraham asked for a sign, and God, in His long-suffering and mercy, granted one. Abraham asked the Lord, "Whereby shall I know that I shall inherit it?" (Gen. 15:8). Verses 9-18 of this chapter tell us of the sign God gave Abraham. At this time God told Abraham, "Know of a surety that thy seed shall be a stranger in a land that is not theirs, and shall serve them; and they shall afflict them four hundred years; and also that nation, whom they shall serve, will I judge: and afterward shall they come out with great substance. And thou shalt go to thy fathers in peace; thou shalt be buried in a good old age. But in the fourth generation they shall come hither again: for the iniquity of the Amorites is not yet full" (vv. 13-16).

This was a detailed prophecy concerning Abraham and his descendants. It was predicted that Abraham's descendants would be strangers in a land that was not theirs (Egypt), and that they would be afflicted for 400 years. The deliverance from this land would take place in the fourth generation. (In Abraham's time a generation was considered to be 100 years.) The Israelites were delivered from Egypt under the leadership of Moses after 400 years in that land. It is important to see, however, that their servitude and deliverance were predicted in Genesis 15.

Genesis 15:18 gives the dimensions of the land promised to Abraham. God told Abraham, "Unto thy seed have I given this land, from the river of Egypt unto the great river, the river Euphrates."

### Sarah's Suggestion

Three years passed after God had told Abraham to look at the stars and had said, "So shall thy seed be" (v. 5). All of Abraham's hopes centered on the promised heir, but no heir had yet been given. Abraham was having a great test of patience. Because they could have no children, Sarah said to Abraham, "I pray thee, go in unto my maid; it may be that I may obtain children by her. And Abram hearkened to the voice of Sarai" (16:2).

Ten years had passed since God had first promised Abraham descendants, and now three years had gone by since God had reassured Abraham of this same thing. Whereas in chapter 15 Abraham is seen as a man of faith, in chapter 16 we see him as a man of unbelief. He could wait no longer for God to fulfill His promise. A lack of patience tends to foster unbelief. In chapter 15 Abraham believed the Lord; in chapter 16 he hearkened unto the voice of his wife. In chapter 15 Abraham walked after the Spirit; in chapter 16 he walked after the energy of the flesh. What a sad inconsistency in the life of this man of God. Only Jesus Christ could say, "I do always those things that please him" (John 8:29).

It is apparent from Genesis 16 that a wife can either be a curse or a blessing to her husband. She can be overambitious for him and can encourage him in selfish pursuits that would be a tremendous hindrance to him. On the other hand, a wife can be a great asset to her husband. Proverbs 31 tells of the virtuous woman and says that "her price is far above rubies. The heart of her husband doth safely trust in her" (vv. 10,11). Of such a woman it is said that "her children arise up, and call her blessed; her husband also, and he praiseth her" (v. 28). The Bible not only tells us what a great asset a virtuous woman is to her husband, but it also describes what can take place when the opposite is true. In I Kings 16 we are told that "Ahab the son of Omri did evil in the sight of the Lord above all that were before him. And it came to pass, as if it had been a light thing for him to walk in the sins of Jereboam the son of Nebat, that he took to wife Jezebel the daughter of Ethbaal king of the Zidonians, and went and served Baal, and worshipped him" (vv. 30,31). The divine commentary on Ahab's life is: "But there was none like unto Ahab, which did sell himself to work wickedness in the sight of the Lord, whom Jezebel his wife stirred up" (21:25). What a difference a good or bad wife can make to her husband!

Sarah was not necessarily a bad wife, but she lacked faith. Up to this time it is not recorded that Sarah had been promised a child. The promises had been made to Abraham, though obviously he shared them with Sarah. But Sarah's suggestion for Abraham to take her handmaid, Hagar, brought new testing for Abraham.

Up to this time Abraham had victoriously passed five special testings. First, he was tested to see if he would leave his country, his kindred and his father's house. This was a testing of the fervor of his faith. It was to prove whether he loved God more than he loved his home and kindred.

Second, after Abraham arrived in Canaan his faith was tested by trying circumstances—there was a famine in the land. This was a test of the sufficiency of Abraham's faith. It was to determine whether or not Abraham believed God was sufficient for his every need.

Third, there was a test regarding his nephew, Lot. There was strife between their herdsmen and it became necessary for them to separate. This was a test of the humility of Abraham's faith. Would he assert his rights and claim the land, or would he yield to Lot and let him have his choice? For Abraham to yield to Lot meant that he was willing to let God fulfill His promise to give him the land in His own time.

Fourth, Abraham faced a test when Lot was captured. This was a test of the courage of Abraham's faith. Would he dare go up against the four great kings and their armies in order to rescue Lot?

Fifth, Abraham was tested when the king of Sodom offered to let him keep the possessions he had confiscated. This was testing the dignity or honorableness of Abraham's faith. Would he accept gifts and honor from the godless king of Sodom?

Abraham was victorious in all of these tests. But now he is tested by the suggestion of a well-meaning wife. Would he take matters out of the hand of God and act in the energy of the flesh? This sixth test was the trying of the patience of his faith. Would he wait on God to fulfill His word in His own time and way, or would Abraham's patience give out and the flesh take over? These six tests involved different aspects of Abraham's faith. God wanted him to have a mature faith.

## Testing Follows Triumph

It seems to be a principle that after every great triumph there comes a test. This was certainly true in Abraham's life. Imagine the triumph of his faith when God assured him that his seed, or descendants, would be as the stars of heaven (Gen. 15:5). But now there comes this severe test of the patience of Abraham's faith. God first blesses and enriches His people and then tests them to see if they will continue to believe and trust Him.

Even the Lord Jesus Christ experienced testing after triumph. When He was baptized, the heavens were opened and the Spirit descended upon Him like a dove. He heard a voice from heaven saying, "Thou art my beloved Son, in whom I am well pleased" (Mark 1:11). What a moment of triumph!

But the very next verses say, "And immediately the spirit driveth him into the wilderness. And he was there in the wilderness forty days, tempted of Satan; and was with the wild beasts; and the angels ministered unto him" (vv. 12,13). Jesus was victorious in all of his testings, but even in His life we see that triumph was followed by testing.

Sarah's suggestion tested the patience of Abraham's faith. Waiting is what the natural heart does not like to do. Rather than wait on God, man prefers to work out his own plans.

A wonderful verse for those who are having the patience of their faith tested is Psalm 37:5: "Commit thy way unto the Lord; trust also in him; and he shall bring it to pass." This verse has meant a great deal to me through the years as I have faced the test of waiting on the Lord.

Had Abraham not gone into Egypt during one of his previous tests, it is possible he would never have faced the test concerning Hagar. When he came out of Egypt he had great riches and many servants, including Hagar who became Sarah's handmaid. She was in his household as a result of his earlier backsliding.

Why didn't Abraham shrink from Sarah's suggestion involving Hagar as much as he did from the thought that his steward might be his heir? Abraham could not bear to think of Eliezer's being the heir, yet Sarah's suggestion that he take Hagar to produce seed was not as repugnant to him.

It is always dangerous to take things into our own hands—to adopt carnal means to achieve spiritual ends. God will not be hurried. But God is never late. He jealously keeps the time factor in His own hands as He deals with men. Abraham had to learn the difficult lesson of waiting on God. He learned it the hard way.

We often have to learn things the hard way too. Those who are older in the Lord have sometimes related their sad experiences to us in hopes that we will avoid the same pitfalls. However, we often go through the same experiences and learn things the hard way. Those of us who want to guide our children in the right paths face the same problem. We want them to avoid many of the things we experienced, but often they learn only by going through the very same experiences.

The Scriptures say that "Sarai Abram's wife took Hagar her maid the Egyptian, after Abram had dwelt ten years in the land of Canaan, and gave her to her husband Abram to be his wife. And he went in unto Hagar, and she conceived: and when she saw that she had conceived, her mistress was despised in her eyes" (16:3,4). Abraham's patience had run out—he could no longer wait on God. What Sarah had suggested was a logical way to solve their dilemma. But the flesh only produces flesh. The timeless principle of sowing and reaping is given in Galatians 6:7,8: "Be not deceived;

God is not mocked: for whatsoever a man soweth, that shall he also reap. For he that soweth to his flesh shall of the flesh reap corruption; but he that soweth to the Spirit shall of the Spirit reap life everlasting."

Abraham and Sarah were to reap what they had sown. The child that was born to Abraham and Hagar brought family trouble, international trouble and spiritual trouble.

## Family Trouble

Genesis 16:4 says that "when she [Hagar] saw that she had conceived, her mistress [Sarah] was despised in her eyes." Not only was there trouble between Hagar and Sarah, but also between Sarah and Abraham. Sarah said to Abraham, "My wrong be upon thee: I have given my maid into thy bosom; and when she saw that she had conceived, I was despised in her eyes: the Lord judge between thee and me" (v. 5). Everyone wants to blame someone else for his trouble. Adam blamed Eve, and Eve blamed the serpent. Sarah blamed Abraham even though she had made the suggestion and was really the one who had led him astray. She blamed Abraham for the family trouble which resulted from her suggestion.

Abraham told Sarah, "Behold, thy maid is in thy hand; do to her as it pleaseth thee" (v. 6). The last part of this verse is a sad commentary on Sarah, for it says, "And when Sarai dealt hardly with her, she fled from her face." Abraham not only succumbed to Sarah's suggestion but he also gave up his place as head of the house. Instead of directing Sarah in this bad situation in the home, he let Sarah make the decision about what should be done. But the family trouble didn't stop there. When Isaac was born 14 years later, he was mocked by Ishmael (21:9).

## International Trouble

After Hagar fled from Sarah's presence, before Ishmael was born, the angel of the Lord said to her, "Behold, thou art with child, and shalt bear a son, and shalt call his name Ishmael; because the Lord hath heard thy affliction. And he will be a wild man; his hand will be against every man, and every man's hand against him; and he shall dwell in the presence of all his brethren" (16:11,12). The Arabs are the descendants of Ishmael, and this prophecy of international trouble is being fulfilled today. The centuries-old conflict between the Arabs and the Jews had its beginning when Abraham tried to use the means of the flesh to produce a spiritual result. We are now, 4000 years later, seeing the international conflict that resulted from Abraham's lapse of faith.

The results of our lack of faith may not be as long-lasting or globe-encircling, but we are not called for the same task that Abraham was. He was to be the father of many nations and the father of them that believe. Because of his unique position in relation to God's chosen nation, great responsibility rested on him and made the results of his sin far-reaching.

## Spiritual Trouble

Not only did Abraham's sin produce family and international trouble, but it also produced spiritual trouble. In the New Testament the Apostle Paul wrote: "For it is written, that Abraham had two sons, the one by a bondmaid, the other by a freewoman. But he who was of the bondwoman was born after the flesh; but he of the freewoman was by promise. Which things are an allegory: for these are the two covenants; the one from the mount Sinai, which gendereth to bondage, which is Agar. For this Agar is mount Sinai in Arabia, and answereth to Jerusalem which now is, and is in bondage with her children. But Jerusalem which is above is free, which is the mother of us all" (Gal. 4:22-26).

Paul was referring to Ishmael, who was born of a bondmaid, and to Isaac, who was born of a freewoman. He stressed that the birth by the bondwoman brought nothing but bondage. So, too, when churches or believers leave the simplicity and liberty which is in Christ and return to the works of the flesh, there is nothing but bondage. When religious ceremonies or other activities are substituted for the work of the Holy Spirit, bondage results. From this incident in Genesis we see the sad results of relying on the flesh to bring about spiritual results.

Chapter 8

# God Revealed as Almighty

In Genesis 17:1 we are told, "And when Abram was ninety years old and nine, the Lord appeared to Abram, and said unto him, I am the Almighty God; walk before me, and be thou perfect." Thirteen years had gone by since Abraham had hearkened unto Sarah, and during this time there was no mention of God appearing to Abraham. In the Scriptures these 13 years are passed over as a period of spiritual barrenness. For Abraham it was what is known spiritually as a time of wood, hay and stubble.

But why all of this waiting? God had promised Abraham a son, and by this time only Ishmael had been born into his home—by a means that was not pleasing to the Lord. The reason for God's delay was so God could bring Abraham to the end of himself. Later it was said of Abraham: "And being not weak in faith, he considered not his own body now dead, when he was about an hundred years old, neither yet the deadness of Sarah's womb" (Rom. 4:19). Before divine power is put forth, man must learn his own impotency. Not until Abraham's body was as good as dead would God fulfill His word. Man's extremity is God's opportunity. Though to Abraham this seemed like a long delay, God was right on time.

At the time when Sarah suggested to Abraham that he go into her handmaid, Abraham's body still had its full procreative powers. But 13 years later Abraham's body was past this stage, and he was cast totally on the Lord.

God has a perfect time for everything. Even of the birth of Jesus Christ we read: "When the fulness of the time was come, God sent forth his Son" (Gal. 4:4). The same will be true concerning the Second Coming of Christ. Second Peter 3:9 assures us that "the Lord is not slack concerning his promise, as some men count slackness; but is longsuffering to us-ward, not willing that any should perish, but that all should come to repentance." Christ's delay in returning for His own is due to His long-suffering in waiting for others to turn to Him and receive Him as Saviour.

By the time of the 17th chapter of Genesis, it had been 24 years since God's first promise to Abraham that he would have a seed and that the land would be given to his seed. When God now appears to Abraham, He appears to him as "the Almighty God" (v. 1). The Hebrew name for God here is actually *El Shaddai. El* means "God" or "the Strong One." *Shaddai* means "nourisher" or "strength-giver." As *El Shaddai*, God is "the all-sufficient One." In his note on this verse, C. I. Scofield commented: "Almighty God (*El Shaddai*) not only enriches, but makes *fruitful*. This is nowhere better illustrated than in the first occurrence of the name (Gen. 17:1-8). To a man ninety-nine years of age, and 'as good as dead' (Heb. 11:12), He said: 'I am the Almighty God [*El Shaddai*] . . . I will . . . multiply thee exceedingly' " (*Scofield Reference Bible*, p. 26).

Thus, when Abraham was 99 years old God appeared to him and gave him a promise that was greater than ever: "I am the Almighty God . . . [I] will multiply thee exceedingly" (Gen. 17:1,2). Whereas Abraham longed for physical seed so that God's promises could be fulfilled, do we long for spiritual seed—for others to come to know Christ under our ministry? Christ has told all believers, "Ye have not chosen me, but I have chosen you, and ordained you, that ye should go and bring forth fruit, and that your fruit should remain" (John 15:16). Perhaps in your life you have found times when spiritual fruit does not come. This frequently happens to pastors and evangelists. The tendency then is to resort to unworthy methods to produce results, maintaining that the end justifies the means. How patiently God bore with Abraham! After the first promise 24 years earlier, God now reveals Himself to Abraham as "the Almighty God." No one but the all-powerful, all-sufficient God could meet Abraham's need at this time. Abraham was now 99 years old and Sarah was 89. But with God all things are possible. Why? Because He is *El Shaddai*–the all-sufficient One.

At this time God even changed Abraham's name. God told Abraham, "As for me, behold, my covenant is with thee, and thou shalt be a father of many nations. Neither shall thy name any more be called Abram, but thy name shall be Abraham; for a father of many nations have I made thee" (Gen. 17:4,5). "Abram" means "high father," whereas "Abraham" means "father of many nations."

## A Spiritual Walk

God instructed Abraham, "Walk before me, and be thou perfect" (v. 1). There are four passages in the Scriptures that refer particularly to the walk of believers. To Abraham He said, "Walk before me." This has to do with walking ahead of God. This is what Abraham did. Unlike Jacob who was always running away from God, Abraham was pushed out by God. Though God pushed him on to new horizons, all the time Abraham seemed to feel insecure. At that time it was as if God was saying, "Walk before Me in perfect security for I am the Almighty; I am just behind you; I will take care of all this and will give you seed." This speaks of spiritual maturity.

In another passage God spoke to Israel through Moses and said, "Ye shall walk after the Lord your God" (Deut. 13:4). This is as a servant following his master. The nation of Israel was like a child, immature and needing a leader. Many Christians are like this because they are not spiritually mature.

Concerning Enoch and Noah, it is said that they "walked with God" (Gen. 5:24; 6:9). This indicates friendship, fellowship and full harmony as the believer walks side by side with God.

For present-day believers there is an even more precious truth. We do not walk *before* or walk *after*, or even walk *with*, but rather we walk *in* Christ (Col. 2:6). This denotes union—we are united with Christ because we are in Christ and He is in us. This is full possession of Him.

Because we are in Christ we form the true Church, which is His Body. In Ephesians 1:23 we learn that "the Church is his body, and in that body lives fully the one who fills the whole wide universe" (*Phillips*). The Apostle Paul was actually addressing his question to all believers when he asked, "What? know ye not that your body is the temple of the Holy Ghost which is in you, which ye have of God, and ye are not your own? For ye are bought with a price: therefore glorify God in your body, and in your spirit, which are God's" (I Cor. 6:19,20). This glorious truth of being in Christ and of Him being in the Christian is also seen in Colossians 1:27: "Christ in you, the hope of glory."

We walk before God as children, after God as servants, with God as friends, and in Christ as members of His Body.

God instructed Abraham to be "perfect," which means "upright" or "sincere." The Hebrew word translated "perfect" in Genesis 17:1 is translated "without blemish" 44 times in the Old Testament. It does not mean perfect in the sense of sinless perfection. The Apostle Paul wanted to attain this spiritual maturity and he said, "Not as though I had already attained, either were already perfect: but I follow after, if that I may apprehend that for which also I am apprehended of Christ Jesus" (Phil. 3:12). The following two verses show us how Paul pressed on to spiritual maturity: "Brethren, I count not myself to have apprehended: but this one thing I do, forgetting those things which are behind, and reaching forth unto those things which are before, I press toward the mark for the prize of the high calling of God in Christ Jesus" (vv. 13,14).

Perhaps you ask, Is it possible to live on such a high plane? It is when you realize that we have an all-mighty God to enable us. The Almighty God is the all-sufficient God who told the Apostle Paul, "My grace is sufficient for thee: for my strength is made perfect in weakness" (II Cor. 12:9). Ours is a God who is able to make alive the dead and to cause the stones to cry out if need be. Because He is the Almighty God—able to do everything—no flesh is to glory in His presence. Thus we see that when He instructed Abraham to be "perfect," He meant for him to be upright, sincere, without blemish—always walking before Him.

Abraham was so overwhelmed with the grace of God that he "fell on his face" (Gen. 17:3). He fell on his face and worshiped as he saw the grace of God in spite of his previous unbelief.

## God's 'I Wills'

It is at this time that God changes Abram's name to Abraham and confirms His covenant with him. There are seven significant times in Genesis 17 that God says to Abraham, "I will. . . ." God told Abraham, "I will make thee exceeding fruitful" (v. 6); "I will make nations of thee" (v. 6); "I will establish my covenant between me and thee and thy seed after thee" (v. 7); "I will give unto thee, and to thy seed after thee, the land wherein thou art a stranger" (v. 8); "I will be their God" (v. 8); "I will establish my covenant with him [Isaac] for an everlasting covenant" (v. 19); and "my covenant will I establish with Isaac" (v. 21).

These promises were given to Abraham when God revealed Himself as "the Almighty God." Because all power is at His disposal, He will be able to fulfill the promises.

Later, God spoke to Moses when the Israelites were in Egypt, and again the expression "I will" appears frequently. In Exodus 6 God said, "I will bring you out from under the burdens of the Egyptians . . . I will rid you out of their bondage . . . I will redeem you with a stretched out arm, and with great judgments" (v. 6); "I will take you to me for a people . . . I will be to you a God" (v. 7); "I will bring you in unto the land . . . I will give it you for an heritage" (v. 8). Such promises could only be made because God is the Almighty God.

In Genesis 17, when God changed Abram's name to Abraham, the reason is given: "For a father of many nations have I made thee" (v. 5). Notice the expression "have I made thee." At this time no child has been born to Abraham and Sarah, yet God says He has made Abraham "a father of many nations." What God has promised, He is able to perform. What He has begun, He is able to finish. When God says it, it is as good as done.

This same principle is seen in Romans 8:30: "Moreover whom he did predestinate, them he also called: and whom he called, them he also justified: and whom he justified, them he also glorified." We have not yet been glorified, but God speaks of it as a finished work. Why? Because what He begins, He finishes. When it is His undertaking, He sees it through. The time element is in His hands.

We need to realize that Abraham's God is our God. The promises made to Abraham were promises which almighty grace alone could utter and which almighty power alone could fulfill. When the almighty, all-sufficient God displays Himself, man's self must be excluded. Abraham is set aside in the account at this point. He only listens. Sarah is not mentioned. The bondwoman and her son are, for the moment, not in view. Nothing is seen but the Almighty God in the fullness of His grace and sovereign power. Thus, in faith, Abraham lies prostrate in the dust in silent adoration to behold the display of God's divine glory.

Present-day believers ought also to present themselves to God. Paul exhorted, "I beseech you therefore, brethren, by the mercies of God, that ye present your bodies a living sacrifice, holy, acceptable unto God, which is your reasonable service" (Rom. 12:1). Because of what God has done for us, we ought to gladly present our bodies as a "living sacrifice" to Him.

How vastly different is Genesis 17 from Genesis 16! In chapter 16 Ishmael was born as a result of the flesh running ahead of God. There Abraham hearkened to Sarah's suggestion; in chapter 17 he hearkened to the voice of God Almighty. It is this God who was about to make alive the dead womb of Sarah and to make alive Abraham's body which was impotent. By waiting until this time God had made sure that no flesh would glory in His presence. In chapter 16 Abraham and Sarah excluded God; in chapter 17 God is seen as so powerful that He could work even without Abraham and Sarah. In chapter 16 it was the flesh; in chapter 17 it was the Spirit. Chapter 16 portrays a walking by sight; chapter 17 portrays a walking by faith.

## Abraham Continues to Doubt

All of this was too much for Abraham. He could not comprehend it. He was now almost 100 years old and Sarah was nearly 90. He could not understand how they could have a child so that God's promises could be fulfilled. In his wondering, Abraham said to God, "O that Ishmael might live before thee!" (17:18). Abraham was asking, "What about this young man, Ishmael?" Weighing the impossibility of having children, it seems that Abraham was asking if Ishmael could not be representative of his seed. Certainly Ishmael was Abraham's son, even though not by Sarah. It is sad to see that Abraham was still experiencing doubts.

It was at this time that the name of Abraham's wife was changed to Sarah. God told Abraham, "As for Sarai thy wife, thou shalt not call her name Sarai, but Sarah shall her name be. And I will bless her, and give thee a son also of her: yea, I will bless her, and she shall be a mother of nations; kings of people shall be of her" (vv. 15,16). It was after this incredible promise concerning Sarah that the Bible says, "Then Abraham fell upon his face, and laughed, and said in his heart, Shall a child be born unto him that is an hundred years old? and shall Sarah, that is ninety years old, bear?" (v. 17). Because of his doubts, it was then that Abraham said to God, "O that Ishmael might live before thee!" (v. 18).

Before Genesis 17 there is no record that Sarah was to be included in God's promise to raise up seed for Abraham. Though there had been several repetitions of the promise,

Sarah had not once been mentioned as the mother of this seed until chapter 17.

All of this was too much for Abraham to comprehend. We must remember that Abraham did not have the Bible as we have. All he had to go on was God's limited communication with him. He was not able to read about the great number of miracles which we are able to read about. It is understandable, therefore, that Abraham had a difficult time comprehending the promises of God.

After Abraham had suggested Ishmael, God said to him even more plainly, "Sarah thy wife shall bear thee a son indeed; and thou shalt call his name Isaac: and I will establish my covenant with him for an everlasting covenant, and with his seed after him" (v. 19).

God did not exclude Ishmael entirely, for He told Abraham, "And as for Ishmael, I have heard thee: Behold, I have blessed him, and will make him fruitful, and will multiply him exceedingly; twelve princes shall he beget, and I will make him a great nation" (v. 20). However, in contrast to Ishmael, God said, "But my covenant will I establish with Isaac, which Sarah shall bear unto thee at this set time in the next year" (v. 21).

## Flesh and Spirit in Conflict

God did not refuse to bless Ishmael, but He caused Abraham to clearly understand that the covenant would be established with Isaac, who was not yet born. Ishmael was not to be an heir with Isaac. The Scriptures build on this principle in showing that the flesh (Ishmael) cannot be heir with the Spirit (Isaac).

In the New Testament, the Apostle Paul referred to Ishmael and Isaac and drew a parallel to Christians. Paul was emphasizing that the Christian is made mature through the freedom of the Spirit and not through the bondage of the law. He wrote: "Nevertheless what saith the scripture? Cast out the bondwoman and her son: for the son of the bondwoman shall not be heir with the son of the freewoman.

So then, brethren, we are not children of the bondwoman, but of the free" (Gal. 4:30,31).

Paul continued the parallel in Galatians 5 when he said, "This I say then, Walk in the Spirit, and ye shall not fulfil the lust of the flesh. For the flesh lusteth against the Spirit, and the Spirit against the flesh: and these are contrary the one to the other: so that ye cannot do the things that ye would" (vv. 16,17). In this same chapter, Paul also wrote: "They that are Christ's have crucified the flesh with the affections and lusts. If we live in the Spirit, let us also walk in the Spirit" (vv. 24,25).

Regarding the flesh and the Spirit, Paul went on to say, "He that soweth to his flesh shall of the flesh reap corruption; but he that soweth to the Spirit shall of the Spirit reap life everlasting" (6:8). The birth of Ishmael resulted from the efforts of the flesh to work out a plan as a substitute for God's plan. However, God absolutely refused to accept Ishmael as a substitute.

Because God would accept no substitute, it eventually became necessary for Abraham to have a complete separation from Ishmael. This took place after the birth of Isaac when "Sarah saw the son of Hagar the Egyptian, which she had born unto Abraham, mocking. Wherefore she said unto Abraham, Cast out this bondwoman and her son: for the son of this bondwoman shall not be heir with my son, even with Isaac. And the thing was very grievous in Abraham's sight because of his son" (Gen. 21:9-11). Even though Ishmael was a product of Abraham's works of the flesh, it was not easy for Abraham to part with him. So it is in the spiritual realm. The flesh loves itself. The flesh (the old man) that you and I possess loves itself. But there must be a complete separation from it if we are to live lives pleasing to God. Romans 6:11 exhorts all Christians: "Likewise reckon ye also yourselves to be dead indeed unto sin, but alive unto God through Jesus Christ our Lord." Because we have died to sin, we do not need to let it have dominion over us any longer.

There was a glad note in Abraham's life at this time because through faith he was to become a blessing to all nations. This blessing, in particular, was that of his lineage Jesus Christ was born, who provided salvation for all the world. But there was also a sad note in Abraham's life at this time. Through unbelief he had become the father of Ishmael, who in turn became the progenitor of a people who have been at enmity with the chosen nation of God through the centuries. Because Abraham was destined to be such a great leader, his lapses of faith had far-reaching effects. His final year of waiting, before the birth of Isaac, is especially abundant in spiritual lessons.

Chapter 9

# The Final Year of Waiting

Abraham's final year of waiting for the birth of Isaac was a year of rich experiences. They were experiences that caused Abraham to be called "the Friend of God" (James 2:23). This touching description can also be applied to present-day believers. Christ Himself said, "Ye are my friends, if ye do whatsoever I command you. Henceforth I call you not servants; for the servant knoweth not what his lord doeth: but I have called you friends; for all things that I have heard of my Father I have made known unto you" (John 15:14,15).

Our friendship with Christ is based on our union with Him. Christ commanded: "Abide in me, and I in you" (v. 4). In verse 10 of this same chapter Jesus explained what He meant by abiding: "If ye keep my commandments, ye shall abide in my love; even as I have kept my Father's commandments, and abide in his love." We are friends of Christ because of our union with Him. Because we are His friends, He has made known to us the heartthrob of the Father.

In Genesis 18 we see Abraham entering into a new and intimate relationship with God. Verse 1 reveals that "the Lord appeared unto him in the plains of Mamre: and he sat in the tent door in the heat of the day." This was the sixth time the Lord had appeared to Abraham. Notice where He found him—in the plains of Mamre. After Abraham had separated from Lot, God had instructed him to walk throughout all the land because He would give it to him. We are told that "then

Abram removed his tent, and came and dwelt in the plain of Mamre, which is in Hebron, and built there an altar unto the Lord" (13:18).

When the Lord appeared to Abraham the sixth time, as recorded in Genesis 18, Abraham was still in the place of his tent and altar. It is significant that in spite of all that had taken place, Abraham was still characterized as a man of the tent and a man of the altar.

The Scriptures attribute much importance to Abraham's tent-life and altar life. In the great faith chapter of the Bible it says that "by faith he sojourned in the land of promise, as in a strange country, dwelling in tabernacles [tents] with Isaac and Jacob, the heirs with him of the same promise: For he looked for a city which hath foundations, whose builder and maker is God" (Heb. 11:9,10).

Abraham was rich and had no special earthly needs because God had revealed Himself as "the Almighty God" (Gen. 17:1). Even though Abraham served the all-sufficient God, he remembered that he was but a pilgrim in this world and continued to live in a tent. God's new revelation of Himself to Abraham had not altered Abraham's attitude toward worldly possessions.

Genesis 18 records how God greatly honored Abraham: "He lift up his eyes and looked, and, lo, three men stood by him: and when he saw them, he ran to meet them from the tent door, and bowed himself toward the ground, And said, My Lord, if now I have found favour in thy sight, pass not away, I pray thee, from thy servant" (vv. 2,3). The Lord Himself, together with two angels, appeared to Abraham. Think of it! The Lord did not honor the sumptous halls and princely palaces of Egypt with His presence, but He accepted hospitality in the tent of a pilgrim and stranger. Nor did God go to Lot, who was a believer with many worldly possessions, although later He sent two angels to him. Think of the high privilege of Abraham, the stranger and pilgrim, to host the Lord and two angels!

We, too, are privileged because of our union with Christ. After Christ's resurrection, before He ascended to heaven, He told the believers, "I will not leave you comfortless: I will come to you. Yet a little while, and the world seeth me no more; but ye see me: because I live, ye shall live also. At that day ye shall know that I am in my Father, and ye in me, and I in you" (John 14:18-20). The believer has God Himself dwelling in him! No higher privilege can be known by those in this life.

## God's Final Announcement

As the Lord and the two angels appeared to Abraham in the form of men, they asked him, "Where is Sarah thy wife?" (Gen. 18:9). Abraham responded that she was in the tent, and the Lord said, "I will certainly return unto thee according to the time of life, and, lo, Sarah thy wife shall have a son" (v. 10). This was the first time Sarah heard she was to be the mother of this son. Perhaps she had hoped to be, but now she was too old to hope any longer.

The Scriptures make it clear that there was no natural possibility for Abraham and Sarah to have a son. Verse 11 says, "Now Abraham and Sarah were old and well stricken in age; and it ceased to be with Sarah after the manner of women." Sarah had overheard the Lord saying she would have a son; "therefore Sarah laughed within herself, saying, After I am waxed old shall I have pleasure, my lord being old also? (v. 12). Then the Lord asked Abraham, "Wherefore did Sarah laugh, saying, Shall I of a surety bear a child, which am old? Is any thing too hard for the Lord? At the time appointed I will return unto thee, according to the time of life, and Sarah shall have a son" (vv. 13,14).

Sarah was surprised the Lord had detected her laugh and she "denied, saying, I laughed not; for she was afraid. And he said, Nay; but thou didst laugh" (v. 15).

Even though Sarah found it difficult to believe, God had given His final announcement that she and Abraham would have a son. They had waited nearly 25 years, but now was God's time. Abraham was as good as dead and Sarah was past the age of childbearing, but what God had promised, He was able to perform.

Even though God was going to work the impossible, He was going to use human means. God also wants to work the impossible through us if we will allow Him to do so. Christ said, "If ye abide in me, and my words abide in you, ye shall ask what ye will, and it shall be done unto you" (John 15:7). God wants to perform the impossible by using believers as His human instruments. Realizing this, the Apostle Paul was able to say, "I can do all things through Christ which strengtheneth me" (Phil. 4:13).

God asked Abraham and Sarah, "Is any thing too hard for the Lord?" (Gen. 18:14). We, too, must respond to this question. As we face seeming impossibilities, do we think God is unable to perform what He has promised?

### Abraham's Response

The fourth chapter of Romans reveals Abraham's response: "And being not weak in faith, he considered not his own body now dead, when he was about an hundred years old, neither yet the deadness of Sarah's womb: He staggered not at the promise of God through unbelief; but was strong in faith, giving glory to God; And being fully persuaded that, what he had promised, he was able also to perform. And therefore it was imputed to him for righteousness" (vv. 19-22).

It was not until this time that Abraham believed God so completely that there was no question whatsoever in his mind. This was a test concerning the impossible for Abraham. But even though it seemed impossible, he had confidence in God. He drew strength from his faith while giving glory to God.

Faith does not stop with saying, "God is able." It goes beyond that and says, "God will." This is seen in Mark 11:22-24: "And Jesus answering saith unto them, Have faith in God. For verily I say unto you, That whosoever shall say unto this mountain, Be thou removed, and be thou cast into the sea; and shall not doubt in his heart, but shall believe that those things which he saith shall come to pass; he shall have whatsoever he saith. Therefore I say unto you, What things soever ye desire, when ye pray, believe that ye receive them, and ye shall have them." Faith is more than believing that God is able to do it.

Abraham's faith grew and developed through the spiritual exercise of testing. This is also why God permits our faith to be tested. First Peter 1:7 says the purpose of testing is so "the trial of your faith, being much more precious than of gold that perisheth, though it be tried with fire, might be found unto praise and honour and glory at the appearing of Jesus Christ."

In Genesis 18 there are some very significant statements about Abraham. The Lord said, "Shall I hide from Abraham that thing which I do; Seeing that Abraham shall surely become a great and mighty nation, and all the nations of the earth shall be blessed in him?" (vv. 17,18). The Lord was going to destroy the cities of Sodom and Gomorrah, but He told Abraham first. Truly, Abraham was the friend of God.

God said of Abraham, "For I know him, that he will command his children and his household after him, and they shall keep the way of the Lord, to do justice and judgment; that the Lord may bring upon Abraham that which he hath spoken of him" (v. 19). What a tremendous statement—and to think it was spoken by God Himself! God knew Abraham intimately, and He knows every detail about us. Are we determined to do His will at any cost? Does He have first place in our lives and thinking? Do we command our children and our household after Him?

The Lord said, "Because the cry of Sodom and Gomorrah is great, and because their sin is very grievous; I will go down now, and see whether they have done altogether according to the cry of it, which is come unto me; and if not, I will know" (vv. 20,21). Then the two angels, appearing in the form of men, "turned their faces from thence, and went toward Sodom" (v. 22). Notice especially the last phrase of this verse: "But Abraham stood yet before the Lord."

Another great man of the Old Testament was also described as standing before the Lord. When Elijah appeared to Ahab, he said to the king, "As the Lord God of Israel liveth, before whom I stand, there shall not be dew nor rain these years, but according to my word" (I Kings 17:1). Elijah could speak in boldness because he stood before the Lord.

We, too, can come before the Lord with boldness and confidence. Hebrews 4:14-16 tells us, "Seeing then that we have a great high priest, that is passed into the heavens, Jesus the Son of God, let us hold fast our profession. For we have not an high priest which cannot be touched with the feeling of our infirmities; but was in all points tempted like as we are, yet without sin. Let us therefore come boldly unto the throne of grace, that we may obtain mercy, and find grace to help in time of need." Or, as we read in Hebrews 10: "Having therefore, brethren, boldness to enter into the holiest by the blood of Jesus, . . . Let us draw near with a true heart in full assurance of faith, having our hearts sprinkled from an evil conscience, and our bodies washed with pure water. Let us hold fast the profession of our faith without wavering; (for he is faithful that promised)" (vv. 19,22,23).

## Abraham's Intercessory Prayer

Genesis 18:23-33 records Abraham's intercessory prayer for Sodom, the city where Lot lived. Abraham asked the Lord, "Wilt thou also destroy the righteous with the wicked?" (v. 23). Abraham asked the Lord if the city could be spared if 50 righteous people could be found (v. 24). The Lord answered, "If I find in Sodom fifty righteous within the city, then I will spare all the place for their sakes" (v. 26).

Abraham apparently realized how difficult it would be to find 50 righteous people in Sodom, so he asked the Lord if He would spare the city if he could find 40 righteous people. The Lord agreed to spare the city if 40 righteous people could be found. Then Abraham lowered the figure to 30 and then to 20. Finally, Abraham said, "Oh let not the Lord be angry, and I will speak yet but this once: Peradventure ten shall be found there. And he said, I will not destroy it for ten's sake" (v. 32).

Abraham knew the responsibility of intercessory prayer. Are you aware of this responsibility? Ours is the responsibility of authoritative prayer in the name of Jesus Christ. It is a spiritual warfare against principalities and powers in high places (Eph. 6:12). This principle is nowhere better seen than in Matthew 12:29,30 where Jesus Himself said, "How can one enter into a strong man's house, and spoil his goods, except he first bind the strong man? and then he will spoil his house. He that is not with me is against me; and he that gathereth not with me scattereth abroad." Jesus has given us the ministry of praying authoritatively and binding the Strong Man. It is in this way that those who are spiritually bound can be released. Such intercessory prayer is our responsibility.

After the Lord assured Abraham that He would spare the city if ten righteous people could be found, we are told that "the Lord went his way, as soon as he had left communing with Abraham: and Abraham returned unto his place" (Gen. 18:33). What blessed communion Abraham had with God! This is our wonderful privilege also. Although we cannot see the Lord as Abraham did, we can enter His very presence, as made possible by the Lord Jesus Christ.

Abraham was unable to find ten righteous persons in Sodom and Gomorrah, as evidenced by God's destruction of the city. In Genesis 19, just before judgment was rained out of heaven on Sodom and Gomorrah, it is said that "Abraham gat up early in the morning to the place where he stood before the Lord" (v. 27). From this vantage point he saw the destruction of Sodom and Gomorrah, for "he looked toward Sodom and Gomorrah, and toward all the land of the plain, and beheld, and, lo, the smoke of the country went up as the smoke of a furnace" (v. 28). What a terrible destruction. However, God's grace was seen at the same time for He "remembered Abraham, and sent Lot out of the midst of the overthrow, when he overthrew the cities in which Lot dwelt" (v. 29).

Even as Abraham stood and watched the overthrow of Sodom and Gomorrah, I think the Lord is going to allow Christians to observe the Great White Throne Judgment before which all unbelievers will appear. How sad it will be in that day to see unbelievers cast into the lake of fire and to realize that we did not intercede for them as we should have. Today we have the privilege of intercession and of telling others about Jesus Christ. Soon He will appear for us and then we who are believers will stand before Him to give an account of what we have said and done—and what we have not done. We are God's appointed ambassadors to represent Him before the world. What will your reaction be on that day when you witness the judgment of the unbelievers to whom you failed to witness and for whom you failed to intercede?

## Abraham's Lapse at Gerar

Have you found that after having a mountaintop experience you were suddenly tempted or tested and perhaps fell lower than you thought you possibly could fall? This can happen to anyone. Certainly it has happened to many Christians. It even happened to Abraham—that great pioneer of faith.

Without question, Abraham must have been having a mountaintop experience. He had met and talked with the Lord, who announced to him that within a year he would have the son for whom he had been waiting 24 years. Everything was glorious and wonderful in Abraham's life—then suddenly there came a great fall. It is a sad story that is recorded in Genesis 20. As we examine what happened, we want to ask ourselves the question, Why did Abraham have this lapse at Gerar?

The Scriptures tell us that "Abraham journeyed from thence toward the south country, and dwelled between Kadesh and Shur, and sojourned in Gerar. And Abraham said of Sarah his wife, She is my sister: and Abimelech king of Gerar sent, and took Sarah" (vv. 1,2).

This is the same thing that had happened to Abraham before when he was in Egypt. At that time Pharaoh took Sarah, and now Abraham allows Abimelech to take her. At 89 years of age she was still so beautiful that she was desired by Abimelech. He took her into his home and, as a result, God sent him much trouble. God did not allow Abimelech to touch Sarah, but appeared to him in a dream and warned Abimelech that he and all those with him would die if he did not restore Sarah to Abraham.

Abimelech was not aware that Sarah was Abraham's wife until after God revealed this to him. Abimelech then called Abraham and asked, "What hast thou done unto us? and what have I offended thee, that thou hast brought on me and on my kingdom a great sin? thou hast done deeds unto me that ought not to be done" (v. 9). Abraham answered: "Because I thought, Surely the fear of God is not in this place; and they will slay me for my wife's sake. And yet indeed she is my sister; she is the daughter of my father, but not the daughter of my mother; and she became my wife" (vv. 11,12).

The key to Abraham's backsliding appears in verse 1 of Genesis 20: "Abraham journeyed from thence toward the south country, and dwelled between Kadesh and Shur, and sojourned in Gerar." He journeyed from Hebron, the place of fellowship, and from Mamre, the place of fatness. Why would he leave these places after such wonderful fellowship with the Lord, during which he received the promise of a son to be born the following year? Why would Abraham leave these places and journey to the south country, toward Egypt—a symbol of the world?

It is not difficult to understand why. Even the best of men still have the old nature remaining in them. There is no eradication of this old nature when we are born again. Instead, the Scriptures make it very clear that we have to constantly cope with the old nature. Galatians 5:16 says, "Walk in the Spirit, and ye shall not fulfil the lust of the flesh."

Abraham went away from his altar into the south country. Perhaps he reasoned that he could surely raise up another altar there even though it was a place of wickedness. It is sad indeed that a man of such caliber should fall. This was not the fall of a young, inexperienced believer. It was the lapse of a mature, well-experienced disciple of God. This is something for us to seriously ponder.

Abraham was willing to sacrifice the honor of his wife. He was willing to give up the one who was to be the mother of the promised seed. What kind of man was he? What hope was there for such a man? There was no hope for him except in God.

Have you ever wondered why God recorded the failure of Abraham? He could have easily omitted it from His inspired revelation to us. However, it seems that God gave us this account so we might be well-grounded and see the sad and terrible failures that can occur even in the lives of the honored servants of God. In giving us this account of Abraham's failure, God underscored the weakness of the flesh and the necessity for us to trust Him moment by moment.

In the New Testament the Apostle Paul said, "I know that in me (that is, in my flesh,) dwelleth no good thing: for to will is present with me; but how to perform that which is good I find not" (Rom. 7:18). Paul also wrote that he and other Christians who were rejoicing in Christ Jesus had "no confidence in the flesh" (Phil. 3:3). In Romans 13:14, all Christians are charged to "put ye on the Lord Jesus Christ, and make not provision for the flesh, to fulfil the lusts thereof."

Abraham had made provision for the flesh. He went down to the south country again—to the place of the world—and this made provision for the flesh. What Abraham did was not a sudden thing, but a reoccurrence of an old sin. He had really not made things right with God after his first lapse in Egypt when he had done exactly the same thing.

## Premeditated Sin

We see how far back Abraham's sin went when we read his reply to Abimelech in Genesis 20:13: "It came to pass, when God caused me to wander from my father's house, that I said unto her [Sarah], This is thy kindness which thou shalt shew unto me; at every place whither we shall come, say of me, He is my brother." Abraham's sin could be traced back before the time he left Ur of the Chaldees. It was a premeditated sin which he had never dealt with properly and now he had fallen into it again. It was a sin of his younger days which had not been confessed and forsaken. As a result, when the circumstances were ripe, Abraham again committed the sin. His weak point was manifested again.

Through Jeremiah, the Lord said, "The heart is deceitful above all things, and desperately wicked: who can know it?" (Jer. 17:9). You cannot trust your heart. Your inner feelings will deceive you. God allowed these circumstances to test Abraham in order to expose him to his own unclean heart. The Lord has said, "I the Lord search the heart, I try the reins, even to give every man according to his ways, and according to the fruit of his doings" (v. 10).

God tests and tries men to bring out the best in them and to expose any sin that needs confessing. For a challenge to your own life in this regard, read Psalm 139. It will frighten you if you have been living in sin, for this psalm emphasizes that the Lord knows everything. After the psalmist declared the greatness of God, he said, "Search me, O God, and know my heart: try me, and know my thoughts: And see if there be any wicked way in me, and lead me in the way everlasting" (vv. 23,24). The psalmist asked God to search his heart and point out anything that was not right. Then he asked to be led in the way that he should go. We need to ask the Lord to do this for us also.

When the Lord brings something to our attention that is wrong, we need to apply I John 1:9: "If we confess our sins, he is faithful and just to forgive us our sins, and to cleanse us from all unrighteousness." If we do not apply this verse, there is danger that our sin will recur. Two things are emphasized in I John 1:9—the Lord forgives us, and He cleanses us when we confess.

We must deal with the old self according to Romans 6. In this chapter the Apostle Paul was writing to Christians when he said, "Knowing this, that our old man is crucified with him, that the body of sin might be destroyed, that henceforth we should not serve sin" (v. 6). Paul also exhorted: "Likewise reckon ye also yourselves to be dead indeed unto sin, but alive unto God through Jesus Christ our Lord" (v. 11). Paul went on to explain that Christians ought not to yield themselves to sin but to God, "for sin shall not have dominion over you: for ye are not under the law, but under grace" (v. 14).

The key to victory for the Christian is also found in Galatians 2:20: "I am crucified with Christ: nevertheless I live; yet not I, but Christ liveth in me: and the life which I now live in the flesh I live by the faith of the Son of God, who loved me, and gave himself for me." It is only through the indwelling, enabling Christ that the believer is able to live as he should.

From the lesson of Abraham, and from other statements of Scripture, there should be no doubt about the vileness of the flesh. The old nature (old man) is utterly corrupt and is incapable of doing anything which deserves merit before God.

Romans 8:13 tells us, "For if ye live after the flesh, ye shall die: but if ye through the Spirit do mortify the deeds of the body, ye shall live." The word "mortify" means "put to death." We need to put to death the deeds of the body and commit ourselves to the Lord for His keeping. Having done this, the Apostle Paul was able to say, "I know whom I have believed, and am persuaded that he is able to keep that which I have committed unto him against that day" (II Tim. 1:12).

In the record of Scripture, Abraham's sin involving Sarah was the only sin he committed twice. He confessed his other sins to the Lord and forsook them, but not so with this one regarding Sarah. Notice how God dealt with him after this sin was repeated. God did not lose patience with him and cast him off for being so inconsistent. Satan would have us to think that God is just looking for people he can cast away because of disobedience and inconsistency. But this is not so. God is seeking to save, and Hebrews 7:25 emphasizes that "he [Christ] is able also to save them to the uttermost that come unto God by him, seeing he ever liveth to make intercession for them." He not only wants to save us from the guilt of sin but also from the power of sin.

### The Grace of God

God's abundant grace is seen in Abraham's life. God did not forsake Abraham, nor did He abandon him to his foe, Abimelech. Why was God so merciful? Because His gifts and callings are without repentance. He had bestowed them on Abraham by sovereign choice. Abraham did not receive them because he had merited them. Since it was all of grace, it wasn't that Abraham had lost something he had earned. He had never merited God's gifts and calling in the first place.

The same is true with us. Salvation is of grace, as is made clear in Ephesians 2:8,9: "By grace are ye saved through faith; and that not of yourselves: it is the gift of God: Not of works, lest any man should boast." The following verse records God's call to service, which is also by His sovereign will: "For we are his workmanship, created in Christ Jesus unto good works, which God hath before ordained that we should walk in them" (v. 10).

The fact that God has done it all is not a license for us to sin. Paul dealt with this very matter in Romans 6 where he asked, "What shall we say then? Shall we continue in sin, that grace may abound? God forbid. How shall we that are dead to sin, live any longer therein?" (vv. 1,2). Because the grace of God was seen more clearly when contrasted to sin, the question arose as to whether we should sin so that the grace of God might be more prominent. Paul's answer was, "God forbid."

Our need is to appropriate the grace of God and to live moment by moment in dependence on Him. Our finite minds are not able to understand all the details of God's grace, but if we submit ourselves to Him, He will work out His grace through us. As the Apostle Paul told the Corinthian believers, "God is able to make all grace abound toward you; that ye, always having all sufficiency in all things, may abound to every good work" (II Cor. 9:8).

In order for God to work out His grace through us, we must come to Him and appropriate what He has made available. Concerning this very thing Christ said, "If any man thirst, let him come unto me, and drink. He that believeth on me, as the scripture hath said, out of his belly shall flow rivers of living water" (John 7:37,38).

When Abraham was guilty of the same sin regarding Sarah, he was rebuked by an unbeliever, Abimelech (Gen. 20:9,10). It is tragic when a believer who is out of fellowship has to be rebuked by an unbeliever. Certainly this is to the believer's shame. However, this brought Abraham to the root of the problem and he confessed the sin which he had conceived when he left Ur of the Chaldees (v. 13). God knew that Abraham would confess his sin, as is evident from what God told Abimelech in the dream: "Now therefore restore the man his wife; for he is a prophet, and he shall pray for thee, and thou shalt live" (v. 7). God vindicated Abraham, His friend. God not only forgave Abraham but He also made Abimelech a debtor to Abraham's prayers, for "Abraham prayed unto God: and God healed Abimelech, and his wife, and his maidservants; and they bare children. For the Lord had fast closed up all the wombs of the house of Abimelech, because of Sarah Abraham's wife" (vv. 17,18).

God enabled Abraham to overcome. The God of Abraham, Isaac and Jacob is also the God of the overcomer. Revelation 21:7 records the promise, "He that overcometh shall inherit all things; and I will be his God, and he shall be my son." What God was to Abraham, Isaac and Jacob, He will be to you too, because He is the God of the overcomer.

## 'The Father of Us All'

Romans 4:16 refers to Abraham as "the father of us all." It is logical to ask, How can this be? Inasmuch as Abraham separated himself unto God, he is the father of all those who are separated. Abraham was a forerunner of believers in showing how to live a separated life. In this respect, he is the father of all those who live a separated life unto God.

There are two aspects of separation indicated by the words "from" and "unto." The believer is to be separated *from* the world *unto* God. The command for present-day believers to have such separation is recorded in II Corinthians 6:14: "Be ye not unequally yoked together with unbelievers: for what fellowship hath righteousness with unrighteousness? and what communion hath light with darkness?" The two aspects of separation are seen in verse 17 of this passage: "Wherefore come out from among them, and be ye separate, saith the Lord, and touch not the unclean thing; and I will receive you." What a wonderful promise!

The Book of Genesis is a living book–it is charged with vitality. It is a book which speaks to our day because what it says is pertinent and applicable to our times. Since Jesus Christ is "the same yesterday, and to day, and for ever" (Heb. 13:8), it logically follows that His ways of working with men are basically the same in every age. Throughout all of time He deals with mankind–especially with His own people–on the same spiritual principle. Often we have heard the statement: "History repeats itself." Certainly it is true as far as God's working with mankind–He works on the same spiritual principle with us today as He did with Abraham. Therefore, God's dealings with Abraham foreshadow His dealings with us who are believers. When the incidental details are omitted from Abraham's life, his experiences illustrate our experiences.

Because Abraham was such a spiritual giant in the walk of faith, he is also called "the father of all them that believe" (Rom. 4:11). We are not his physical descendants, but we are his spiritual descendants. We are the children of Abraham in the sense that we walk by faith even as he walked. Galatians 3:29 says, "And if ye be Christ's then are ye Abraham's seed, and heirs according to the promise." We are the children of Abraham in the sense that we live by faith in the promises of God even as Abraham lived.

## A Sample Believer

Abraham was the father of us all inasmuch as he was a sample of believers. As we have followed his history, we have seen that he was separated from God as a lost sinner before God called him. This is also true of us. Writing to the Ephesian Christians, the Apostle Paul said, "That at that time ye were without Christ, being aliens from the commonwealth of Israel, and strangers from the covenants of promise, having no hope, and without God in the world" (Eph. 2:12).

Even as God called Abraham into relationship with Himself, He has also called us. Paul wrote: "But now in Christ Jesus ye who sometimes were far off are made nigh by the blood of Christ" (v. 13). We who know Jesus Christ as Saviour have been brought into a right relationship with Him through receiving Him as Saviour. We responded to God's call to salvation.

God's call to Abraham also meant separation. It was to be a separation from the world and unto God. At first, Abraham only partially obeyed his call to separation. We, too, have been called to be separated unto God from the world. How far have we gone? Has ours also been only a partial obedience?

When there was a famine in Canaan, Abraham went his own way instead of seeking God's way out. He went down to Egypt. In times of great need in our lives, have we turned to God to have these needs met or have we turned to the world?

Abraham remained childless even after repeated promises from God that he would have descendants. Finally, Abraham could wait no longer and he relied on fleshly means to solve his problem. Abraham used Hagar to assist God in fulfilling His promises. God did not need such help, nor did He desire it. The result was the birth of Ishmael, whose descendants have long been in conflict with the descendants of Isaac.

Even though Abraham wavered in his faith, God did not give him up. In His grace, God is faithful and long-suffering. If it were not for this, none of us would have a chance. What if God lost patience with us? Where would you and I be today?

Remember how God suffered along with the people of Israel. They wandered in the desert for 40 years because of their unbelief, but God never lost patience. Because He knew the end as well as the beginning, He was long-suffering toward Israel. In patience God waited on Abraham; in patience He waited on Israel; and in patience He has been waiting on you and me.

Abraham came out of his many trials triumphantly. So also Jesus tells us, as He told His disciples, "In the world ye shall have tribulation: but be of good cheer; I have overcome the world" (John 16:33). God patiently waits on us to bring us through triumphantly.

Later, when we study the life of Isaac, we will see the wonderful results of God's having patience with Abraham. While Isaac was still quite a young man, God called upon Abraham to sacrifice him as an offering. It is then that we see the great triumph of Abraham. As God used severe testings to mold Abraham into what He wanted him to be, He also brings circumstances to bear in our lives to prepare us for what is to come.

Romans 8:28 assures us that "all things work together for good to them that love God, to them who are the called according to his purpose." The question might well be, How do we know this? The following verses give us the answer: "For whom he did foreknow, he also did predestinate to be conformed to the image of his Son, that he might be the firstborn among many brethren. Moreover whom he did predestinate, them he also called: and whom he called, them he also justified: and whom he justified, them he also glorified" (vv. 29,30). The point of these verses is that what

God has begun, He is going to finish; therefore, "all things work together for good to them that love God."

In contrast to Abraham, there were men like Terah, his father, and Lot, his nephew. These men were not willing to pay the price that Abraham was willing to pay. Their relationship with God was not so vital that they would have been willing to give up a son if God had asked them to do so. Because they had never come to this place in their relationships with God, they never reached this place of maturity and triumph as Abraham did.

It took much patience on God's part to wait for Abraham to come to this point. But what God had begun in Abraham's life, He was continuing to perfect until the very end. So, too, present-day believers are promised: "He which hath begun a good work in you will perform it until the day of Jesus Christ" (Phil. 1:6). Or as Ephesians 5 tells us, "Christ . . . loved the church, and gave himself for it; That he might sanctify and cleanse it with the washing of water by the word, That he might present it to himself a glorious church, not having spot, or wrinkle, or any such thing; but that it should be holy and without blemish" (vv. 25-27). This presentation will be in the future, but Christ is preparing the Church with patience today so that it might be ready for that time.

## The Man of Faith

Abraham's life was not only a sample of the believer's life, but it was also a sample of the life of the man of faith. Three times in Hebrews 11 the words "by faith" are used in describing Abraham. We are told that "by faith Abraham, when he was called to go out into a place which he should after receive for an inheritance, obeyed; and he went out, not knowing whither he went. By faith he sojourned in the land of promise, as in a strange country, dwelling in tabernacles [tents] with Isaac and Jacob, the heirs with him of the same promise. By faith Abraham, when he was tried, offered up

Isaac: and he that had received the promises offered up his only begotten son" (vv. 8,9,17).

It was the quality of Abraham's faith that resulted in his being called "the father of all them that believe" (Rom. 4:11). It is not exaggerating to say that Abraham's faith was tried more severely, more repeatedly, and more strenuously than any other person's.

Abraham was called to leave his country, his kindred, and his house, and to go to a land that God would show him. At this time, God did not even promise to give the land to Abraham. On the basis of God's promise, Abraham started out although he did not know where he was going. Finally, after arriving in the land, he did not occupy it as an owner but lived in it as a pilgrim and stranger—living in tents for nearly a century.

It was necessary for Abraham to wait 25 years for the seed God had promised him. Can we not learn from this too? Time belongs to God. We must learn to wait on Him.

Also, in Abraham's experience of having to offer up Isaac, his faith was tested far more severely than it had ever been tested before, but he believed God.

Although Abraham's faith wavered in the beginning stages of his walk with God, he continued to grow spiritually strong by learning to keep his eyes on God. Because he had learned to know God so intimately, Abraham was able to fully trust Him during the hour of crisis when he offered Isaac.

## A Life of Contrasts

There are also many contrasts in the life of Abraham. By faith he obeyed God, but in unbelief he disobeyed. By faith he left his country; in unbelief he stopped short at Haran. By faith he entered the land; in unbelief he forsook it for Egypt. By faith he returned to the land to sojourn; in unbelief he took Hagar to bear a child rather than waiting on God. By faith he rescued Lot; in unbelief he lied to Abimelech.

In Abraham we see the conflict of the two natures. The sin nature was constantly in conflict with the nature he had received from God. This conflict of present-day believers is described in Galatians 5:16,17: "This I say then, Walk in the Spirit, and ye shall not fulfil the lust of the flesh. For the flesh lusteth against the Spirit, and the Spirit against the flesh: and these are contrary the one to the other: so that ye cannot do the things that ye would." Verses 24 and 25 of this same chapter tell us, "And they that are Christ's have crucified the flesh with the affections and lusts. If we live in the Spirit, let us also walk in the Spirit."

Like Abraham, we are frequently inconsistent. But God is calling so He might lead us through to triumph. The Lord referred to Himself as the God of Abraham, not because Abraham was always consistent, but because he allowed God to bring him through to victory. God did not abandon His man, and in His mercy He will not abandon us. Grace is always at hand.

Hebrews 13:5,6 exhorts believers: "Let your conversation [manner of life] be without covetousness; and be content with such things as ye have: for he hath said, I will never leave thee, nor forsake thee. So that we may boldly say, The Lord is my helper, and I will not fear what man shall do unto me." As a result, the writer of Hebrews could say, "Now the God of peace, that brought again from the dead our Lord Jesus, that great shepherd of the sheep, through the blood of the everlasting covenant, Make you perfect in every good work to do his will, working in you that which is wellpleasing in his sight, through Jesus Christ; to whom be glory for ever and ever. Amen" (vv. 20,21).

Abraham's call is also an example of how the Lord has called us. In both cases, God's call was not based on the merit of the persons involved. The calling (election) has been all of grace. Ephesians 1:4 tells believers that they have been "chosen . . . in him before the foundation of the world." Referring to believing Jews living during the Church Age, the Apostle Paul said, "Even so then at this present time also there is a remnant according to the election of grace" (Rom.

11:5). Thus we see that God's calling is based on His infinite grace.

In Abraham we also see a person who was the object of God's love. Although at times Abraham was a lonely person in his walk of faith, God never forsook him. God's love always remained fixed on Abraham. So, too, we can say with the Apostle Paul: "Who shall separate us from the love of Christ? shall tribulation, or distress, or persecution, or famine, or nakedness, or peril, or sword? As it is written, For thy sake we are killed all the day long; we are accounted as sheep for the slaughter. Nay, in all these things we are more than conquerors through him that loved us. For I am persuaded, that neither death, nor life, nor angels, nor principalities, nor powers, nor things present, nor things to come, Nor height, nor depth, nor any other creature, shall be able to separate us from the love of God, which is in Christ Jesus our Lord" (8:35-39). We must never forget that the God of Abraham is our God, and He loves us.

Chapter 10

# The Spiritual Value of an Ordinary Life

Abraham's ordinary daily living made a deep impression on the outside world of his day. The uneventful days are usually better tests of one's true character than an emergency or crisis. When we face times of crises, we seek God for special help and spend extra time in the study of the Word and in prayer. However, we often fail in the simple routine of daily living. We need to remember that people are watching us. They are watching us in our homes, in our churches and in our businesses. As they watch us in these different phases of life, what are they seeing?

In a sense, it was Abraham's consciousness of the world watching him that made him the great man that he was. After the birth of Isaac, Abimelech came to Abraham with this testimony: "God is with thee in all that thou doest" (21:22). This was several years after Isaac was born. This simple testimony revealed that Abraham lived a genuine life of witness for God in the presence of Abimelech. This was not the same Abimelech to which Abraham had lied earlier about Sarah. The name "Abimelech" is a ruler's title, not a man's name. Although Abraham had sinned before a previous Abimelech, he was now walking victoriously with the Lord and was a great witness to this and other kings.

We are also to be good witnesses for the Lord Jesus Christ. In Acts 1:8 Christ promised: "Ye shall receive power, after that the Holy Ghost is come upon you: and ye shall be witnesses unto me both in Jerusalem, and in all Judaea, and in Samaria, and unto the uttermost part of the earth."

What does it mean to be a witness? Being a witness includes a verbal expression of what we believe. We witness to that which we have seen, heard and experienced. But witnessing includes more than just speaking; it also involves witnessing with our lives. What do people see in your everyday life? Do they see only a front you are putting up before others, or do they see the reality of Jesus Christ in you? It is in the routine of daily living that you are seen most clearly. If you wait for crises to come before you demonstrate your faith, you will fail to do God's will. Christians should make every occasion great by faithful loyalty to God's grace. We will then have a good witness before those who are observing us.

The Bible has much to say about how believers should live before those who do not know Jesus Christ as Saviour. Colossians 4:5 exhorts us to "walk in wisdom toward them that are without." First Thessalonians 4:12 commands us to "walk honestly toward them that are without." In I Timothy 3:7 the qualification given for a leader of the church is that he "must have a good report of them which are without; lest he fall into reproach and the snare of the devil."

In our walk before others we are to "walk circumspectly, not as fools, but as wise, Redeeming the time, because the days are evil" (Eph. 5:15,16). Romans 12:17 tells every believer, "Recompense to no man evil for evil. Provide things honest in the sight of all men." Thus we see that the Bible has much to say about how we should live before others. The believer has Christ within his life, and if he yields to Christ's control he will not find it difficult to live a good testimony before others.

When Abimelech came to Abraham and said, "God is with thee in all that thou doest," Abraham spoke to him about a particular matter. Abraham had waited until the proper time, and even then we can be sure he spoke with much compassion as he reproved Abimelech. Abimelech's servants had violently taken away a well which belonged to Abraham. Whoever dug a well had rights to the area of the well. It was a hard job to dig a well, and once it was dug the owner wanted to retain it because of its importance to the well-being of his livestock.

Abraham apparently thought this was the right time to mention this matter to Abimelech. Abimelech was shocked by this news and told Abraham he had not heard about it before (Gen. 21:26). Abraham and Abimelech then made a covenant. Abraham gave Abimelech seven ewe lambs as a witness that the well belonged to Abraham. It was obviously of the Lord that Abraham brought this matter before Abimelech at this time. Because Abraham dealt with the problem in the right way, it resulted to his advantage. Abraham was a good witness to those without.

We never know who is watching us. Nearly 30 years ago my wife and I rented a home and lived on the first floor. The owner of the home, a widow, lived in the basement. This widow was not a Christian; in fact, she was practically an atheist. She once said, "If my husband is in hell, that's where I want to go." There seemed to be nothing we could do to testify to this woman about Jesus Christ. After living in the home for about two years, this lady came to us one day and said, "I have been watching your family, and I want what you have." It was our joy to lead her to a personal relationship with Jesus Christ. Although we moved from the home not too long after that, we visited her several times before she went to be with the Lord. We had the joy of seeing how God had been working in her heart. This also shows us the importance of living a life that is pleasing to Christ even in the routine of daily living. We never know who is watching us.

## Sarah's Burying Place

Abraham had daily contact with his unbelieving neighbors, but he was always careful that they knew where he stood with God. Especially was this true at the time of Sarah's death. Sarah lived 37 years after Isaac was born and died at the age of 127. Abraham mourned for her and sought for a place to bury her. He said to the sons of Heth, "I am a stranger and a sojourner with you: give me a possession of a buryingplace with you, that I may bury my dead out of my sight" (23:4). Abraham referred to himself as a "stranger" and a "sojourner" even though he was a man of much wealth. He owned several wells and that alone made him wealthy. In addition, he had many cattle. But even with all of this, Abraham had not allowed himself to become attached to worldly possessions. He unashamedly confessed by his words and actions where he stood with God.

The sons of Heth recognized Abraham's stature and said to him, "Hear us, my lord: thou art a mighty prince among us: in the choice of our sepulchres bury thy dead; none of us shall withhold from thee his sepulchre, but that thou mayest bury thy dead" (v. 6). They were willing to let Abraham take any piece of ground he wanted for a burying place. However, Abraham refused to accept the land as a gift.

Abraham especially wanted the cave of Machpelah and offered to pay for it (vv. 8,9). Although the owner of the cave wanted to give it to him, Abraham paid him what it was worth.

These people recognized Abraham's greatness because of the way he lived before them. Although they were not concerned about Abraham's God, he had made such an impact on them by the way he lived that they were willing to give him any land he wanted for a burying place for Sarah. Abraham refused to be chargeable to his ungodly neighbors. He let it be known that he was a separated man and was going to stay in this separated position.

Faith makes men independent of the men of the world, yet it results in the believer's walking honestly toward all men. Romans 13:8 says, "Owe no man any thing, but to love one another: for he that loveth another hath fulfilled the law." Christians need to be very careful about obligating themselves to others. In business matters, they should have a special concern for doing things honestly before their fellowmen. Abraham was one who took favors only from God and not from man. He paid the sons of Heth for the burying place, and he looked to God to give him all of Canaan.

The fact that Abraham purchased this burying place for Sarah indicated he planned to stay in the land of Canaan rather than returning to Mesopotamia. Although he could have buried Sarah in his old country, he buried her in the land to which God had called him. Thus, even in purchasing Sarah's burying place, Abraham declared his faith in God.

## Choosing Isaac's Bride

Later, Abraham also declared his faith when he sent for a bride for Isaac. This account is given in Genesis 24. The way the servant did Abraham's bidding is a beautiful picture of the way the Holy Spirit serves God the Father. It is also a great example of the importance of faithfulness in our lives. By sending his servant to Mesopotamia to procure a bride for Isaac, Abraham once again declared his intention to stay in the land to which God had called him. Abraham said to his servant, "I will make thee swear by the Lord, the God of heaven, and the God of the earth, that thou shalt not take a wife unto my son of the daughters of the Canaanites, among whom I dwell: But thou shalt go unto my country, and to my kindred, and take a wife unto my son Isaac" (vv. 3,4).

Abraham's servant had a good question: "Peradventure the woman will not be willing to follow me unto this land: must I needs bring thy son again unto the land from whence thou camest?" (v. 5). Abraham answered his servant with a serious charge: "Beware thou that thou bring not my son thither again" (v. 6).

Abraham told his servant of God's promises and said, "He shall send his angel before thee, and thou shalt take a wife unto my son from thence. And if the woman will not be willing to follow thee, then thou shalt be clear from this my oath: only bring not my son thither again" (vv. 7,8).

We see how important it was to Abraham that a wife for Isaac not be taken from the unbelieving people of Canaan. Although Abraham wanted Isaac's wife to come from

Mesopotamia, he did not want Isaac himself to go there. Isaac showed weaknesses in some areas of his life, and apparently Abraham feared that Isaac would not return if he went to Mesopotamia. Thus, God—working through Abraham—would not give Isaac a chance to have his weakness challenged. God does not test a man beyond what he is able to bear but always provides a way of escape (I Cor. 10:13). Abraham's act revealed the strong determination of faith. Faith determines to do God's will and God's will only.

### Abraham's Last Days

Genesis 25 records the closing events in Abraham's life. In his last days, he made provision that Isaac would receive all of his inheritance. "Abraham gave all that he had unto Isaac. But unto the sons of the concubines, which Abraham had, Abraham gave gifts, and sent them away from Isaac his son, while he yet lived, eastward, unto the east country" (vv. 5,6). In addition to Isaac, Abraham had a son by Hagar and six others by Keturah. Abraham had married Keturah after Sarah's death. Abraham wanted to make it clear to his other sons that Isaac was the chosen son of promise. By giving gifts to the other sons and sending them away, Abraham took the necessary steps to make Isaac's position free from as many difficulties as possible.

After Abraham had given all that he had unto Isaac, we are told, "Then Abraham gave up the ghost, and died in a good old age, an old man, and full of years; and was gathered to his people. And his sons Isaac and Ishmael buried him in the cave of Machpelah" (vv. 8,9). This was the cave that Abraham had purchased to bury Sarah in. God's ways of working are seen in the last statement concerning Abraham: "And it came to pass after the death of Abraham, that God blessed his son Isaac" (v. 11).

### Summary

In Abraham's life we have seen the relationship that God wants to have with man. First, there was *God's purpose*. The fact that God was fulfilling His program through Abraham is the most important thing we can learn from Abraham's life. Through Abraham, God purposed to accomplish His sovereign will. In the New Testament, believers are told, "For it is God which worketh in you both to will and to do of his good pleasure" (Phil. 2:13). Thus, God works within the believer to create the desire to do His will. Doing God's will is utterly important. Ask anyone whom God has used to accomplish something spiritually significant, and he will tell you he has no special secret with God but that he has simply done what God told him to do. D. L. Moody was one who determined to do God's will at any cost, and this has been the determination of the Back to the Bible Broadcast also.

From Abraham's life in the Old Testament, and from verses recorded in the New Testament, we see that God's purpose in placing man on earth is so that man might do His will. Our highest goal is to glorify God by doing His will. Notice the words in the prayer the Lord taught the disciples to pray: "Thy will be done in earth, as it is in heaven" (Matt. 6:10). Jesus Himself said, "Lo, I come to do thy will, O God" (Heb. 10:9).

Second, in Abraham's life we have seen *God's power.* God never commands without enabling, and there is no limit to His power. God revealed Himself to Abraham as "the Almighty God" (Gen. 17:1). God provided Abraham with all the strength he needed to fulfill His will. God will also supply all that is needed for you and me to do His will.

God's grace is all-sufficient, but it must be accepted on our part. When the Apostle Paul was experiencing severe trials, God said to him, "My grace is sufficient for thee: for my strength is made perfect in weakness" (II Cor. 12:9). What Paul wrote to the Corinthian believers is also true for us: "God is able to make all grace abound toward you; that ye, always having all sufficiency in all things, may abound to every good work" (II Cor. 9:8).

God never leaves us without strength to do His will. He has assured us that "as thy days, so shall thy strength be" (Deut. 33:25). Whatever the calling, whatever the task, whatever God's purpose and will is for you, He will give you the strength you need for the day. But you must appropriate it; you must accept it for yourself. You do this by taking God at His word that He will give you strength for each day. As you go forward to do His will, you will discover that His strength is there as you need it.

Third, in Abraham's life we have seen *God's plan*. A very practical question is, By what means can the divine purpose be accomplished and the divine power be utilized by man? Abraham's life gave us not only the answer but also the demonstration of the answer. We accomplish the divine purpose and utilize the divine power by faith. We accomplish His will by faith, and we appropriate His power to do His will by faith. God promises power and, in response to our faith, He makes it available to each one of us. Jesus said, "If any man thirst, let him come unto me, and drink" (John 7:37). So also we utilize God's power by coming to Him and taking what He has promised to give.

God emphasized the same truth to Joshua when He said, "This book of the law shall not depart out of thy mouth; but thou shalt meditate therein day and night, that thou mayest observe to do according to all that is written therein: for then thou shalt make thy way prosperous, and then thou shalt have good success. Have not I commanded thee? Be strong and of a good courage; be not afraid, neither be thou dismayed: for the Lord thy God is with thee whithersoever thou goest" (Josh. 1:8,9). What a wonderful promise from God! All things are possible to he who believes. When we are willing to take God at His word, we can say with the Apostle Paul, "I can do all things through Christ which strengtheneth me" (Phil. 4:13).

## Conclusion

From Abraham's life we see the *believer's greatest privilege*—to be associated with God. Perhaps you say, "I do not think I can have such a close relationship." But you can. God has made the same provision for you as He made for

Abraham; actually, you have even more because you have the indwelling Christ. Abraham would have been nothing without God, but with God he was an overcomer. In Revelation 21:7 God promises, "He that overcometh shall inherit all things; and I will be his God, and he shall be my son." Will you accept this great privilege to be what God wants you to be? Will you appropriate the enabling power of God to glorify Him by doing His will?

In Abraham's life we also see the *believer's greatest glory*—unrelenting faithfulness to God. There is nothing greater than to live a humble, consistent, determined life to the glory of God. In I Corinthians 10:31 every believer is exhorted: "Whether therefore ye eat, or drink, or whatsoever ye do, do all to the glory of God." In John 17, Jesus prayed to the Father and said, "I have glorified thee . . . : I have finished the work which thou gavest me to do. . . . I have manifested thy name unto the men which thou gavest me out of the world. . . . I have given unto them the words which thou gavest me" (vv. 4,6,8). The Lord Jesus gave absolute obedience to His Father. Our greatest glory is to be unrelenting in our faithfulness to God.

In Abraham's life we also see the *believer's simplest secret*—believing God. This is the key to spiritual success. God was able to do all that He did through Abraham because Abraham believed Him. God cannot lie; therefore, let us take Him at His word and act accordingly. Abraham learned, not to trust himself, but to trust God.

Ultimately, faith rests on God, receives from God, responds to God, relies on God, realizes God, rejoices in God, and reproduces God's life and character.

Two blind men once followed Jesus because they wanted to be healed by Him. He asked them, "Believe ye that I am able to do this?" (Matt. 9:28). They responded, "Yea, Lord." The Scriptures record, "Then touched he their eyes, saying, According to your faith be it unto you" (v. 29). Here we see that faith determines what we receive from God. It is faith that proportions everything else.

Faith in God is the key to spiritual success. This is so simple, yet it embraces the whole secret of daily living for God. Faith has always been the principle by which God has worked with man. Romans 10:17 tells us where we obtain faith: "Faith cometh by hearing, and hearing by the word of God." Hebrews 11:6 tells us that "without faith it is impossible to please him." Each Christian is to live by the faithfulness of the Son of God, just as the Apostle Paul said, "I am crucified with Christ: nevertheless I live; yet not I, but Christ liveth in me: and the life which I now live in the flesh I live by the faith [faithfulness] of the Son of God, who loved me, and gave himself for me" (Gal. 2:20).

Chapter 11

# The God of Isaac

The birth of Isaac was the second great step toward the fulfillment of God's purpose. The first was the selection of Abraham to be the father of the chosen nation. In our study we have already looked at what was involved in Abraham's call. Isaac's birth marked a crisis in connection with the history of the chosen line of Christ.

Genesis 21:1-8 tells us, "And the Lord visited Sarah as he had said, and the Lord did unto Sarah as he had spoken. For Sarah conceived, and bare Abraham a son in his old age, at the set time of which God had spoken to him. And Abraham called the name of his son that was born unto him, whom Sarah bare to him, Isaac. And Abraham circumcised his son Isaac being eight days old, as God had commanded him. And Abraham was an hundred years old, when his son Isaac was born unto him. And Sarah said, God hath made me to laugh, so that all that hear will laugh with me. And she said, Who would have said unto Abraham, that Sarah should have given children suck? for I have born him a son in his old age. And the child grew, and was weaned: and Abraham made a great feast the same day that Isaac was weaned."

Even though Ishmael had been born 13 years earlier, God made it clear to Abraham that "in Isaac shall thy seed be called" (v. 12). This was the crisis concerning the line of Christ. God had promised Abraham a son but none had been given. Abraham had gone into Hagar, Sarah's handmaid, and a son had resulted from their union—but not the son of God's choice. But at this time in Genesis, God provided the son He had promised. Isaac's birth was also the beginning of the second great period in Abraham's life.

It is significant that God calls Himself the God of Isaac as well as the God of Abraham and Jacob. Although Isaac lived the longest of the three of them (180 years), the least is recorded about him. In fact, there is only one chapter, Genesis 26, which is devoted exclusively to his life. Most of the account of his life is interwoven with that of his father, Abraham, and with that of his sons, Jacob and Esau.

Isaac led a quiet, peaceful life. He was the ordinary son of a great father, and he was the ordinary father of a great son. Isaac's life was commonplace. Yet the ordinary life is the ordered life. Better yet, it is the ordained life. Thus, God calls Himself the God of Isaac. The God of Isaac is the God of the ordinary people—those involved in the routine of daily living.

Isaac's life was not filled with glory and spectacular events. Yet he had a very meaningful life. He filled his place in life with complete contentment, not looking for the spectacular, but seeking to please God in the ordinary things of life. Therefore, a study of Isaac's life will greatly benefit us because most of us are ordinary people desiring to please God in the routine of daily living.

Even though little happened to Isaac that was irregular, in his relationship with God he was no less honored than his great father and his great son. He was included in the inner family, for God called Himself the God of Abraham, the God of Isaac and the God of Jacob.

Because the record of Isaac's life is interwoven with that of his father, as we study Isaac we will gain further insights into the life of Abraham.

There were only two divine communications with Isaac. When God spoke to him on those two occasions, nothing new was added to what God had given Abraham. There was no special call for action or for Isaac to venture out in a new step of faith. God did not ask Isaac to forsake his country and kindred in order to serve Him as He had Abraham. God spoke to Isaac simply to ratify what He had already promised Abraham.

Both of God's communications with Isaac are recorded in Genesis 26. The first is recorded in verses 2-5: "And the Lord appeared unto him, and said, Go not down into Egypt; dwell in the land which I shall tell thee of: Sojourn in this land, and I will be with thee, and will bless thee; for unto thee, and unto thy seed, I will give all these countries, and I will perform the oath which I sware unto Abraham thy father; And I will make thy seed to multiply as the stars of heaven, and will give unto thy seed all these countries; and in thy seed shall all the nations of the earth be blessed; Because that Abraham obeyed my voice, and kept my charge, my commandments, my statutes, and my laws."

According to verse 5, God was going to do these things for Isaac because Isaac's father had obeyed His voice. Some do not like to be identified as sons of great fathers. They want to stand on their own feet and make their own reputations. Isaac stood on his own feet in many ways, yet he was given the promise on the basis of Abraham's response to the call of God.

God's second communication with Isaac is recorded in verse 24: "And the Lord appeared unto him the same night, and said, I am the God of Abraham thy father: fear not, for I am with thee, and will bless thee, and multiply thy seed for my servant Abraham's sake." These are the only two communications that are recorded as taking place between God and Isaac.

As we glance at the overall picture of Isaac's life, we see there must have been some weaknesses in his life—especially regarding his stability. This is indicated by the fact that God would not permit him to go down to Egypt (v. 2), nor would He permit him to return to his father's home country to obtain a wife. Chapter 24 of Genesis tells us how Abraham sent his servant to Mesopotamia to obtain a wife for Isaac. Although Isaac was only a common person and not subjected to some of the temptations of life as others would have been, it is important to realize that he had some weaknesses. From this we also see that God knows a man's weak points as well as his strong points.

Abraham was not stopped as he entered Egypt, for God knew that He could teach him a lesson there. It was a very important lesson that Abraham needed to learn. God knew Isaac also, and apparently knew that if he went down to Egypt he would be weak and would not return at the call of God.

Another comparison is that Jacob—as we shall see later—was not prevented from going to Mesopotamia to find a wife, for God knew He could depend on Jacob's returning after he had learned important lessons. But not so with Isaac. It seems that Isaac was too weak in this area of his life. Thus God did not permit him to be subjected to such temptation. This reminds us of the spiritual principle stated in I Corinthians 10:13: "There hath no temptation taken you but such as is common to man: but God is faithful, who will not suffer you to be tempted above that ye are able; but will with the temptation also make a way to escape, that ye may be able to bear it." God knew Isaac thoroughly, and He knew how much testing Isaac was able to bear.

Whereas Abraham had an obedient faith and Jacob had a restless faith, Isaac had a passive faith. Isaac suffered and accepted without resisting. Rather than acting, he was acted upon. Isaac did no great adventuring by faith, but he was submissive to God as he was submissive to his father, Abraham. He was not a spiritual dwarf, but was more of a spiritual giant than most of us possibly ever will be. However, Isaac's life was not characterized by doing great, exciting things for God.

In studying Isaac's life we will examine some of the practical events connected with his birth. We will also closely examine the major event of his youth—when he was offered as a sacrifice. We will also consider the record of Isaac's manhood, which is the third major contribution that Isaac makes for our encouragement. We will also see that Isaac's carelessness and weaknesses became more prominent in his declining years.

As we study the Scriptures concerning Isaac's life, we should constantly remember that the God of Isaac is our

God. God loves ordinary people, and they can have as vital a relationship with God as did the pioneers of faith.

Chapter 12

# Isaac's Birth

From the time Abraham left Haran until the time Isaac was born was a period of 25 years. During that time Abraham had received various promises from the Lord that he would be made a great nation. God's promises had been given only to Abraham and not to Sarah. Sarah is not mentioned in relation to the promises for descendants until a year before Isaac was born. By this time Sarah was 89 years old. No doubt Abraham had told Sarah about God's promises to him, but God had not communicated directly with Sarah about the promised seed until this time. The first reference to Sarah's being the mother of the promised seed is in Genesis 17: "And God said unto Abraham, As for Sarai thy wife, thou shalt not call her name Sarai, but Sarah shall her name be. And I will bless her, and give thee a son also of her: yea, I will bless her, and she shall be a mother of nations; kings of people shall be of her" (vv. 15,16).

Abraham's reaction to God's announcement was that he "fell upon his face, and laughed, and said in his heart, Shall a child be born unto him that is an hundred years old? and shall Sarah, that is ninety years old, bear? And Abraham said unto God, O that Ishmael might live before thee! And God said, Sarah thy wife shall bear thee a son indeed; and thou shalt call his name Isaac: and I will establish my covenant with him for an everlasting covenant, and with his seed after him" (vv. 17-19).

This passage tells us that Abraham "laughed." A laugh can be the result of either scorn (unbelief) or joy. The context indicates that Abraham's laugh was a laugh of unbelief. He was 99 years old and Sarah was 89. Because it was incredible that a child would be born to them, Abraham asked God why Ishmael could not be the promised seed. At this time Ishmael was 13 years old. However, God made clear to Abraham that He would establish His covenant with Isaac, not Ishmael. Notice, however, that even at this time God did not directly communicate with Sarah. God's direct communication with Sarah about the birth of a son is recorded in Genesis 18. Verse 1 tells us, "The Lord appeared unto him [Abraham] in the plains of Mamre: and he sat in the tent door in the heat of the day." Three men appeared to Abraham at this time, but it is clearly spoken of as an appearance of the Lord. In the Old Testament, the angel of the Lord appeared frequently in this manner. The angel of the Lord is considered to be an appearance of the Lord Jesus Christ Himself. Here He appeared to Abraham with two other messengers of God, all in human form.

Abraham was asked by these men, "Where is Sarah thy wife? And he said, Behold, in the tent. And he [the angel of the Lord] said, I will certainly return unto thee according to the time of life, and, lo, Sarah thy wife shall have a son. And Sarah heard it in the tent door, which was behind him. Now Abraham and Sarah were old and well stricken in age; and it ceased to be with Sarah after the manner of women. Therefore Sarah laughed within herself, saying, After I am waxed old shall I have pleasure, my lord being old also? And the Lord said unto Abraham, Wherefore did Sarah laugh, saying, Shall I of a surety bear a child, which am old?" (vv. 9-13).

Sarah's laugh at this time was a laugh of unbelief as Abraham's laugh had been earlier.

## The Lord's Response

Notice, however, how the Lord responded to Sarah's laugh of unbelief. He asked, "Is any thing too hard for the Lord?" (v. 14). Then God promised, "At the time appointed

I will return unto thee, according to the time of life, and Sarah shall have a son" (v. 14). God not only promised a son, but He also promised to use Abraham and Sarah—in spite of their ages—in producing the son. Although God could have performed another kind of miracle, He chose to use human instruments to accomplish His will.

When God makes a promise, He will fulfill it. Numbers 23:19 tells us, "God is not a man, that he should lie; neither the son of man, that he should repent: hath he said, and shall he not do it? or hath he spoken, and shall he not make it good?"

Abraham and Sarah faced the test of the impossible. Although Abraham had faced many tests before, this was the greatest test he had faced up to this point in his life. He had laughed in unbelief earlier, but now his faith became steadfast in the Lord.

In commenting on this experience of Abraham, the Apostle Paul described Abraham as a person "who against hope believed in hope, that he might become the father of many nations; according to that which was spoken, So shall thy seed be. And being not weak in faith, he considered not his own body now dead, when he was about an hundred years old, neither yet the deadness of Sarah's womb: He staggered not at the promise of God through unbelief; but was strong in faith, giving glory to God; And being fully persuaded that, what he had promised, he was able also to perform. And therefore it was imputed to him for righteousness" (Rom. 4:18-22).

Abraham's faith had grown and developed through much exercise over the years. He was now able to fully believe God's promise that a son was to be born to him and Sarah, although he was nearly 100 years old and she was nearly 90. Such a thing had no precedent in history. All the evidence was against him. Human reasoning would only have led him to more unbelief.

God was testing Abraham's faith to prove its genuineness and to bring out the best in it. So also, the Word of God tells present-day believers, "That the trial of your faith, being much more precious than of gold that perisheth, though it be tried with fire, might be found unto praise and honour and glory at the appearing of Jesus Christ" (I Pet. 1:7).

In referring to the birth of Isaac in Genesis 21, these significant statements are made: "And the Lord visited Sarah as he had said, and the Lord did unto Sarah as he had spoken. For Sarah conceived, and bear Abraham a son in his old age, at the set time of which God had spoken to him" (vv. 1,2). Notice in particular the phrases, "as he had said," "as he had spoken" and "which God had spoken to him."

## Profitable Lessons

From the account of Isaac's birth there are many important lessons we should learn. Five are extremely significant.

First, God is in no hurry to work out His plans. He is never too late; He is always on time. Man frets and worries and is always in a hurry to work out his plans. But God has all eternity at His disposal, so with great deliberation and leisure He accomplishes His purposes. He always knows the right time to perform a certain work. Because we serve such a God as this, we should not be in a hurry or anxious for plans to develop. The Lord has said, "He that believeth shall not make haste" (Isa. 28:16). Take time. Believe God.

Second, God is almighty. Nothing can hinder or thwart the outworking of God's purpose. Abraham was old and Sarah was barren, but these obstacles presented no difficulty to God. He who has infinite power—who created the earth and man—was fully capable of fulfilling His promise to Abraham and Sarah. No matter how serious we consider our problems to be, they are no barrier to God when He wills to do something. Let us place our full confidence in God, therefore, and be willing to trust Him for everything regardless of how difficult the circumstances may seem. The Apostle Paul's desire was to please the Lord Jesus Christ in all that he did. When he came to the end of his life, Paul was able to say, "I have fought a good fight, I have finished my course, I have kept the faith" (II Tim. 4:7). Let this be true of us also.

Third, God is faithful. He promised Sarah a son. From the standpoint of human reasoning it seemed like a foolish promise. However, the promise of God was sure because He is always faithful in keeping His promises. Because God's word is absolutely sure, in times of doubt and discouragement we need to come to the Word of God to check our spiritual lives and to remind ourselves of His faithfulness. Although we may not be able to understand how God can fulfill His promises to us, our attitude should be: If God says it, that settles it.

Fourth, faith is tested so it might be proven to be genuine. A faith that cannot endure trial is really no faith at all. Although Abraham's faith was severely tested concerning the birth of Isaac, this test proved that his faith was genuine. Faith does not fail even under severe testing. However, feelings or experiences will fail.

Fifth, God has a set time for everything. It is important that we learn this lesson well. God has an appointed time for accomplishing His will. Nothing is left to chance. Nothing is contingent on the creature. Everything is fixed before time by God Himself. God gave Abraham and Sarah a son at the time He had set. Abraham was impatient for God to fulfill His promises, but God did not act until His appointed hour. Abraham wanted God to use Ishmael in His program, but God said, "My covenant will I establish with Isaac, which Sarah shall bear unto thee at this set time in the next year" (Gen. 17:21). When God promised that Sarah would bear a son, He said, "At the time appointed I will return unto thee, according to the time of life, and Sarah shall have a son" (18:14).

The Scriptures abound with other examples which show God has an appointed time for everything. The Lord told Habakkuk, "The vision is yet for an appointed time, but at the end it shall speak, and not lie: though it tarry, wait for it; because it will surely come, it will not tarry, . . . but the just shall live by his faith" (Hab. 2:3,4).

The New Testament emphasizes how God acts at His appointed time when it says, "When the fulness of the time was come, God sent forth his Son, made of a woman, made under the law, To redeem them that were under the law, that we might receive the adoption of sons" (Gal. 4:4,5). There was an appointed time for the Lord Jesus to be born.

In God's program we also find that there was an appointed time for the Holy Spirit to come. This set time was on the Day of Pentecost, and Acts 2:1 emphasizes this when it says, "And when the day of Pentecost was fully come, they were all with one accord in one place." The praying of the saints did not bring the coming of the Spirit even one day earlier. Their prayers prepared them for His coming, but the Holy Spirit came at God's appointed time.

Isaac's birth was at the time God had set. He was not born too early nor too late, as far as God's program was concerned. Isaac was born 25 years after God first promised Abraham that he would have seed. This seemed like a long time to Abraham, but it was the appointed time of God.

## A Child of Promise and Miracle

The birth of Isaac was a great climax in the life of Abraham. The Scriptures tell us that "Abraham called the name of his son that was born unto him, whom Sarah bare to him, Isaac" (Gen. 21:3). This was in accordance with what God had told Abraham earlier: "Sarah thy wife shall bear thee a son indeed; and thou shalt call his name Isaac" (17:19).

Isaac was the child of promise. There were progressive promises made to Abraham, and at first there was some doubting on his part. But in the New Testament, when God recounted Abraham's life, He completely passed over the fact that Abraham doubted at first. In Hebrews 11:11 we are told, "Through faith also Sara herself received strength to conceive seed, and was delivered of a child when she was past age, because she judged him faithful who had promised." How beautiful! Because of God's mercy and forgiving grace, the doubt of the parents is not mentioned in the New Testament. So also, our sins are blotted out once they have come under the blood of Jesus Christ.

Isaac was a child of miracle because Sarah's womb was "dead." In describing Abraham, the Apostle Paul said, "Being not weak in faith, he considered not his own body now dead, when he was about an hundred years old, neither the deadness of Sarah's womb" (Rom. 4:19). At first Sarah did not think there was any possibility she could bear a child, but God asked, "Is any thing too hard for the Lord?" (Gen. 18:14).

This reminds us of the virgin birth of Christ. When the angel Gabriel appeared to Mary and told her she would have a son and that she should call His name Jesus, Mary asked, "How shall this be, seeing I know not a man?" (Luke 1:34). Gabriel assured Mary, "With God nothing shall be impossible" (v. 37). Then Mary responded, "Behold the handmaid of the Lord; be it unto me according to thy word" (v. 38).

## Regeneration and Sanctification

In Isaac's birth we also see truths that remind us of regeneration and sanctification. Sarah's womb was dead and had to be made alive before she could bear a child. It is the same principle with our salvation. Ephesians 2:4,5 tells us, "But God, who is rich in mercy, for his great love wherewith he loved us, Even when we were dead in sins, hath quickened us [made us alive] together with Christ, (by grace ye are saved)." The state of the natural (unregenerated) man is that of spiritual death. As such, he is alienated from the life of God and destitute of the Holy Spirit. Because man is spiritually dead—totally depraved—it is essential that he have a new birth if he is to have eternal life. Christ's words to Nicodemus are true for all mankind: "Except a man be born again, he cannot see the kingdom of God" (John 3:3). How wonderful it is that the words of John 1:12 also apply to all:

"As many as received him, to them gave he power to become the sons of God, even to them that believe on his name."

Sanctification has to do with being set apart. As it relates to the Christian, it has to do with his being set apart for God. Such a person no longer lives by natural values but by supernatural values. Regarding the birth of Isaac, something had to be done that was not natural to man. God works on a far higher principle and frequently does things that are opposed to the thinking of mankind. Such a principle was stated by Christ Himself when He said, "Except a corn of wheat fall into the ground and die, it abideth alone: but if it die, it bringeth forth much fruit. He that loveth his life shall lose it; and he that hateth his life in this world shall keep it unto life eternal" (John 12:24,25).

In order to be separated unto God, there must be death to the old life. For the present-day believer, death to the old life was taken care of judicially by the death of Jesus Christ. This is emphasized in the sixth chapter of Romans. Although it has taken place judicially, we must appropriate the benefits to our lives if we are going to live for the Lord as He intends. We have to apply the fact that we have died with Christ and have been made alive unto a glorious life. Thus, Romans 6:11 tells us, "Likewise reckon ye also yourselves to be dead indeed unto sin, but alive unto God through Jesus Christ our Lord."

Matthew 10:38,39 emphasizes similar truths when it says, "He that taketh not his cross, and followeth after me, is not worthy of me. He that findeth his life shall lose it: and he that loseth his life for my sake shall find it." You "take your cross" when you take your place as having died with Christ. In saying that "he that loseth his life for my sake shall find it," Christ was not talking about physical life but about spiritually applying what God has done for us.

All that we have is due to our miracle-working God. Salvation and sanctification are due to His miracles, and even spiritual maturity is based on a miracle. We become spiritually mature by appropriating the position we have in Christ—a position which God has miraculously put us into. In

Ephesians 2 we are told that God "hath raised us up together, and made us sit together in heavenly places in Christ Jesus" (v. 6). This means that, in Christ, we have been given power and control over all that is evil so that we will not be overcome by it. The Apostle Paul referred to this position in Christ when he said, "That I may know him, and the power of his resurrection, and the fellowship of his sufferings, being made conformable unto his death" (Phil. 3:10).

### Isaac Grew and Was Weaned

The Scriptures say that after Isaac was born he "grew, and was weaned: and Abraham made a great feast the same day that Isaac was weaned" (Gen. 21:8). Isaac grew and was weaned—these two go together. During Old Testament times, weaning referred to the time in a child's life when he was old enough to be entrusted to strangers. This took place between three and five years of age—and sometimes older. Samuel is a biblical example. The Scriptures say that when Hannah "had weaned him, she took him up with her, with three bullocks, and one ephah of flour, and a bottle of wine, and brought him unto the house of the Lord in Shiloh: and the child was young" (I Sam. 1:24). Samuel was still a child but he was old enough to live with a stranger. He was able to get along without his mother's care.

Growth is also important to the Christian. The Bible instructs believers: "As newborn babes, desire the sincere milk of the word, that ye may grow thereby" (I Pet. 2:2). While the milk of the Word is needed for young Christians, older Christians should be feeding on the meat of the Word. Paul told the Corinthian believers, "And I, brethren, could not speak unto you as unto spiritual, but as unto carnal, even as unto babes in Christ. I have fed you with milk, and not with meat: for hitherto ye were not able to bear it, neither yet now are ye able" (I Cor. 3:1,2). The Corinthian believers were older in the Lord, but they were still babes in Christ as far as their spiritual diet was concerned.

The same truth is found in Hebrews 5:12-14: "For when for the time ye ought to be teachers, ye have need that one teach you again which be the first principles of the oracles of God; and are become such as have need of milk, and not of strong meat. For every one that useth milk is unskilful in the word of righteousness: for he is a babe. But strong meat belongeth to them that are of full age, even those who by reason of use have their senses exercised to discern both good and evil." The writer of Hebrews continued by saying, "Therefore leaving the principles of the doctrine of Christ, let us go on unto perfection [maturity]" (6:1).

When Isaac had matured enough to be weaned, Abraham made a great feast "the same day that Isaac was weaned" (Gen. 21:8). This significant time in a child's life was celebrated with a feast. So also, it is a time of much rejoicing when a believer passes from the milk stage into the meat stage in his walk with the Lord. It is at this time that the believer leaves his dependence on others and depends on the leadership of the Holy Spirit.

## Family Conflict

After the feast celebrating Isaac's weaning, we are told that "Sarah saw the son of Hagar the Egyptian, which she had born unto Abraham, mocking. Wherefore she said unto Abraham, Cast out this bondwoman and her son: for the son of this bondwoman shall not be heir with my son, even with Isaac" (vv. 9,10). Thus we see that the birth of Isaac and the feast celebrating his weaning created a conflict in the family. There should not be such conflict in a well-ordered household, but there was more involved in Abraham's family than was apparent on the surface. Ishmael, who was born to Abraham and Hagar, was the son of bondage; whereas Isaac, the son of Abraham and Sarah, was the son of freedom. One was born of a bondwoman and the other was born of a freewoman (Gal. 4:22-31). When there is only the old nature, there is no conflict. It is when the new nature is received that there becomes great opposition between the two natures in the believer. This conflict takes place in the life of every believer and is pictured in the conflict between Ishmael and Isaac.

After the birth of Isaac, the true nature of Ishmael was revealed. Nothing of his life is known before Isaac's birth. Even this points out a significant truth for the believer. It is not until a person receives the new nature, through receiving Christ as Saviour, that he discovers the real character of his old nature. The discovery is a painful one and even causes some to doubt their salvation as they see the struggle taking place in their lives. However, the very fact that there is conflict is proof of salvation. There is no conflict when there is only the old nature. But when the new nature comes in to control the life, the old nature sets up an intense conflict. Paul referred to this conflict when he said, "For the flesh lusteth against the Spirit, and the Spirit against the flesh: and these are contrary the one to the other: so that ye cannot do the things that ye would" (Gal. 5:17). This is the condition which results when a person receives Christ as Saviour. He receives a new nature, which is in opposition to the old nature. There is conflict between the spirit of liberty and the spirit of bondage. Even as in the case of Ishmael and Isaac, where one had to be expulsed, the believer cannot yield to both natures but must choose the one he will obey.

Until the time of Isaac's birth, Ishmael had occupied the prominent place in Abraham's life. Ishmael, who was 14 years old when Isaac was born, could not accept the fact that Isaac would now have first place in his father's eyes.

Ishmael was at least 17 when he made fun of Isaac, for Isaac was old enough to be weaned, according to the custom. In addition to making fun of Isaac, Ishmael no doubt ridiculed the idea that God would do such a great work through Isaac. Thinking as natural man, it seemed foolish to Ishmael to think that an insignificant person like Isaac would be greatly used of God.

In the New Testament, Paul referred to Ishmael's mocking Isaac as "persecution." In making the analogy for present-day believers, the Apostle Paul said, "But as then he that was born after the flesh persecuted him that was born after the Spirit, even so it is now" (Gal. 4:29).

The fourth chapter of Galatians also sets forth dispensational distinctions. Paul said that the births of Ishmael and Isaac were analogous to "the two covenants; the one from the mount Sinai, which gendereth to bondage, which is Agar [Hagar]. For this Agar is mount Sinai in Arabia, and answereth to Jerusalem which now is, and is in bondage with her children. But Jerusalem which is above is free, which is the mother of us all" (vv. 24-26). Thus, Ishmael exemplifies the one born after the flesh, whereas Isaac exemplifies the one born after the Spirit. Just as there were two sons in Abraham's household—one produced by the flesh and the other by the power of God—every believer has two natures—one of the flesh and the other from God. These natures are totally different and are unable to cooperate with each other in any way. The flesh lusts against the Spirit, but Paul said, "Walk in the Spirit, and ye shall not fulfil the lust of the flesh" (5:16).

## Separation Is Essential

The conflict between Ishmael and Isaac demanded that they be separated. When Sarah saw Ishmael mocking Isaac she demanded: "Cast out this bondwoman and her son: for the son of this bondwoman shall not be heir with my son, even with Isaac" (Gen. 21:10). At first this seems selfish of Sarah—and it would have been selfish if all that was involved was the two boys' living together. However, God revealed—even in the case of Ishmael and Isaac—what must be done with the believer's conflicting natures. When a person receives Christ as Saviour, his old nature is not eradicated. If this were so, there would not be a conflict between the two natures. Since the old nature is not eradicated, the believer must know what to do about the conflict that goes on within his life.

The old nature is not eradicated at the time of salvation; neither is it improved by salvation. The flesh can never be improved, and this is why there must be a new birth. The Lord Jesus reminded Nicodemus: "That which is born of the flesh is flesh; and that which is born of the Spirit is spirit. Marvel not that I said unto thee, Ye must be born again" (John 3:6,7). The flesh nature does not improve when a person is born again. Instead, it becomes antagonistic to the new nature. The flesh nature is always at enmity with God.

Because the old nature cannot be improved or brought into subjection to the law of God, there is only one remedy. This remedy is seen in Ishmael's case—it must be put out. The Apostle Paul reminded the Colossian believers that they had to "put off the old man with his deeds" (Col. 3:9). Believers must reject the desires of the old nature and yield to the desires of the new nature.

If Ishmael had been retained, Abraham would have been tempted to glory in the flesh. God wanted to make sure that Abraham understood that any right standing with Him was on the basis of faith—not works. The New Testament assures us that Abraham was not justified by works but by faith. Paul wrote: "For if Abraham were justified by works, he hath whereof to glory; but not before God. For what saith the scripture? Abraham believed God, and it was counted unto him for righteousness" (Rom. 4:2,3). In I Corinthians 1 Paul told how God works to bring about situations so "that no flesh should glory in his presence" (v. 29). In contrast to glorying in His presence, Paul reminded believers that "of him are ye in Christ Jesus, who of God is made unto us wisdom, and righteousness, and sanctification, and redemption: That, according as it is written, He that glorieth, let him glory in the Lord" (vv. 30,31).

What we are in Christ Jesus is what God has done for us in answer to our faith, even as Isaac's birth was in response to the faith of Abraham and Sarah. There is no legitimate reason to glory in the flesh, because the flesh is not capable of doing good. Paul said, "For I know that in me (that is, in my flesh,) dwelleth no good thing: for to will is present with me; but how to perform that which is good I find not" (Rom. 7:18).

### A Grievous Thing

The Scriptures say that when Sarah demanded that Ishmael be expelled from the household, "the thing was very grievous in Abraham's sight because of his son" (Gen. 21:11). The word "grievous" means "bad" or "evil." Abraham viewed the conflict between his two sons as something evil. No doubt he was also grieved over the necessity of having to send Ishmael away. Perhaps Abraham thought that Ishmael and Isaac would someday be able to live together in harmony. This is the way many believers view the conflict between their old and new natures. They mistakenly think that the old nature will improve with time and they will have less conflict.

There are also those who think that believers and unbelievers can dwell in harmony and even cooperate in promoting the same organization. This is what the proponents of the ecumenical movement are trying to tell us today. They stress organizational unity and peace, but they do not emphasize salvation by faith in Christ, which is the only thing that can bring about spiritual unity and lasting peace.

Although the situation was grievous to Abraham, God said to him, "Let it not be grievous in thy sight because of the lad, and because of thy bondwoman; in all that Sarah hath said unto thee, hearken unto her voice; for in Isaac shall thy seed be called" (v. 12). Abraham was to depend on what God had done for him and had given him in the person of Isaac. This had to do primarily with Isaac's being the covenant heir and being in the lineage of Christ. Abraham was grieved about having to part with Ishmael, so God emphasized to him again that "in Isaac shall thy seed be called."

Present-day believers also find it exceedingly difficult to part with the desires of the flesh. The struggle is intense, but to cling to the flesh only results in bondage. God has provided a way for the believer to be free from bondage to the flesh. Paul explained it when he said, "Knowing this, that our old man is [was] crucified with him, that the body of sin might be destroyed, that henceforth we should not serve sin" (Rom. 6:6). Verse 11 of this same chapter says, "Likewise reckon ye also yourselves to be dead indeed unto sin, but alive unto God through Jesus Christ our Lord." We need to recognize what has been done for us, count it as a fact, appropriate its benefits, and continually live for God.

Abraham did what the Lord told him to do. Genesis 21:14 says that "Abraham rose up early in the morning, and took bread, and a bottle of water, and gave it unto Hagar, putting it on her shoulder, and the child, and sent her away: and she departed, and wandered in the wilderness of Beer-sheba." Abraham's obedience in this matter was another step in his spiritual progress. This act made it possible for God to bless Abraham and Isaac in greater steps of faith.

The Christian must exercise spiritual discipline so he is not entangled again with the yoke of bondage. The Bible says, "Stand fast therefore in the liberty wherewith Christ hath made us free, and be not entangled again with the yoke of bondage" (Gal. 5:1). In order to do this, we must separate ourselves from the things of the world and be a living sacrifice for the Lord. The Apostle Paul wrote: "I beseech you therefore, brethren, by the mercies of God, that ye present your bodies a living sacrifice, holy, acceptable unto God, which is your reasonable service. And be not conformed to this world: but be ye transformed by the renewing of your mind, that ye may prove what is that good, and acceptable, and perfect, will of God" (Rom. 12:1,2).

Chapter 13

# The Offering of Isaac

While the offering of Isaac was Abraham's greatest test, it was also Isaac's greatest test. It was the last major test for Abraham and the first major test for Isaac.

The offering of Isaac is recorded in Genesis 22. This chapter sees father and son together in this great test. That they were "together" is one of the keys to this chapter. Verse 6 says, "And they went both of them together." Verse 8 also emphasizes: "So they went both of them together." It is significant that the first record of Isaac's active participation in life had to do with his being willing to offer his life. In this chapter we see that his response was a wonderful and complete surrender of faith. He willingly surrendered to the will of his father and to the will of Almighty God.

As the chapter opens we are told, "And it came to pass after these things, that God did tempt Abraham, and said unto him, Abraham: and he said, Behold, here I am. And he [God] said, Take now thy son, thine only son Isaac, whom thou lovest, and get thee into the land of Moriah; and offer him there for a burnt-offering upon one of the mountains which I will tell thee of" (vv. 1,2).

Notice the time element in these verses: "After these things." In particular, this was after Abraham's victory concerning Ishmael. Abraham and Sarah rejoiced over the birth of Isaac, and Abraham's hopes were raised to the highest point. Then followed the severest test of Abraham's life.

Severe tests frequently follow times of special blessing. This occurred even in the life of Christ on earth. After the time of His baptism when "the Holy Ghost descended in a bodily shape like a dove upon him, and a voice came from heaven, which said, Thou art my beloved Son; in thee I am well pleased" (Luke 3:21,22), Jesus endured one of His severest tests. After His baptism, "Jesus being full of the Holy Ghost returned from Jordan, and was led by the Spirit into the wilderness, Being forty days tempted of the devil" (4:1,2).

The Lord Jesus Christ's three closest disciples—Peter, James and John—also experienced that testing follows blessing. On the Mount of Transfiguration they had been richly blessed by what they had seen and heard, but there followed a time of severe testing for them (Matt. 17:1-21).

The principle that testing follows blessing is also seen in the history of God's chosen nation, Israel. Under the leadership of Moses, the nation experienced a miracle of God when He parted the waters of the Red Sea so the people could walk across on dry land (Ex. 14:26-31). However, not long after this they experienced the testing of thirst because they could not find water to drink (15:23-26). Later, they experienced a great victory at Jericho (Josh. 6:1-27), but they suffered defeat at Ai (7:1-5).

Testing and discipline are necessary for the believer because they prove whether his spiritual experiences have really become a part of his life and character. The tests that Abraham had successfully passed prepared him for the greatest test of his life—the offering of Isaac. The Bible says, "God did tempt Abraham" (Gen. 22:1). The word "tempt" can be used in two ways. It can mean a testing or trying to prove that which is good, or it can mean a testing which is a solicitation to do evil. The first meaning is what is intended in this passage. Abraham was tested in order to prove that which was good in his faith. The testing itself purified his faith. When Satan tempts us it is always with the purpose of trying to get us to do evil. God never tempts us to do evil. The Bible says, "Let no man say when he is tempted, I am tempted of God: for God cannot be tempted with evil, neither tempteth he any man" (James 1:13). Although God does not tempt us to do evil, He does test us to purify our faith so that it "might be found unto praise and honour and glory at the appearing of Jesus Christ" (I Pet. 1:7).

God's testing of an individual is evidence that He has confidence in that individual. God never tests a person who hasn't the capacity to pass the test. God never tested Lot to the degree He tested Abraham, because Lot never reached a spiritual plane that was high enough to warrant God's testing in his life. Sodom tempted Lot, but it was no temptation to Abraham. By his life Abraham proved he loved God more than the things of Sodom.

### The Purpose of the Test

God wanted Abraham to prove that he loved Him more than the things of this life and more than any other person. For this test God chose the person who was the dearest object of Abraham's life—Isaac. God may sometimes test you this way also. If you have attained spiritual heights with God and have shown great progress in your spiritual life, God may test you to see whether your growth is genuine. Although the test may be severe and may involve the dearest person or thing in your life, you will be a better person for God as a result of the test.

The offering of human sacrifices was a common practice of the heathen in Abraham's time. However, there is no other incident where God tested a believer in this particular way. Human sacrifices were strongly condemned by God in the Old Testament. His people, Israel, were to totally abstain from this heathen practice. But with Abraham, God chose this test to prove whom Abraham loved most. God knew what he would do.

Abraham faced the grave danger of loving Isaac more than God. It took a test like this to bring Abraham to the point of choosing so he would know what his own heart was like. Abraham had to decide whether God or Isaac came first in his life. When God promised him a son, Abraham believed God and it was counted to him for righteousness. But, having received the promised son, there was the danger that Abraham would give more of his attention to the gift than to the Giver. He knew that out of Isaac would come the descendants God had promised. Abraham was in danger of concentrating on the fulfillment of God's promise to the exclusion of God Himself, who had made the promise.

It is easy to fix our eyes on the miracle rather than on the Miracle Worker. This principle is also seen in the New Testament. It is recorded that Jesus, "seeing a fig tree afar off having leaves, he came, if haply he might find any thing thereon: and when he came to it, he found nothing but leaves; for the time of figs was not yet. And Jesus answered and said unto it, No man eat fruit of thee hereafter for ever. And his disciples heard it" (Mark 11:13,14). The passage goes on to say that "in the morning, as they passed by, they saw the fig tree dried up from the roots. And Peter calling to remembrance saith unto him, Master, behold, the fig tree which thou cursedst is withered away" (vv. 20,21).

Jesus had performed a miracle and Peter seemed to be more taken up with the miracle than with the One who had performed it. Peter drew attention to the fact that the fig tree had withered away, but Jesus did not even comment on Peter's observation. Instead, Jesus completely changed the subject so He might show Peter and the others that the important thing was not the miracle itself but the Person who performed the miracle. Jesus said to them, "Have faith in God" (v. 22). Jesus wanted Peter and the others to know that if they had faith in God, they would be able to do great things. He went on to say, "For verily I say unto you, That whosoever shall say unto this mountain, Be thou removed, and be thou cast into the sea; and shall not doubt in his heart, but shall believe that those things which he saith shall come to pass; he shall have whatsoever he saith" (v. 23). Peter and the others had seen a tree dry up at the word of Jesus, but He assured them that they would do even greater things if they would keep their eyes on God and not just on the miracle. The Lord Jesus had caused a tree to wither, but He promised they would be able to move mountains if they had faith in God. I have experienced the moving of mountains in my own life—not physical mountains, but problems that posed as great a problem as physical mountains.

Isaac was the child of a miracle; therefore, God had to teach Abraham that he was to keep his attention on the One who performed the miracle instead of on the miracle. In the test of the offering of Isaac, God really wanted Abraham—not Isaac. God did not desire the death of Isaac, but He wanted the death of Abraham—death to his self-life. God wanted Abraham to die to everything that would cause him to give Isaac preeminence over God.

The command to offer Isaac as a sacrifice was intended to show Abraham where his heart's desires were—in God or in Isaac. God has tested others to prove whether their trust was in Him or in the arm of the flesh. When Jehoshaphat was faced with invading armies, he was quick to admit to the Lord: "O our God, wilt thou not judge them? for we have no might against this great company that cometh against us; neither know we what to do: but our eyes are upon thee" (II Chron. 20:12).

Job also came to this place. Earlier in his life he had his eyes focused on the things he had done as well as on the miracles and wonderful works of God. However, after God was through dealing with him, Job said, "I have heard of thee by the hearing of the ear: but now mine eye seeth thee. Wherefore I abhor myself, and repent in dust and ashes" (Job 42:5,6).

The Apostle Paul was also tested so that he would be more concerned about the Giver than the gifts. Because of his testing he was able to write: "That I may know him, and the power of his resurrection, and the fellowship of his sufferings, being made conformable unto his death" (Phil. 3:10).

When Abraham was called upon to give up Ishmael, he was given a reason for doing so and that made it much easier.

God told Abraham that Ishmael was not the one He had chosen to be the heir. However, when God commanded Abraham to offer Isaac, He gave no reason for the test. Imagine how difficult it was for Abraham to face this test. Isaac was the promised son and if his life were offered up, how would God fulfill His promises? All God's promises were wrapped up in Isaac. No solution was given to Abraham. No reason was given for such a severe test. Everything in Abraham's life had pointed forward to the birth of his son because he knew it was God's will for descendants to come through Isaac. Then God said, in effect, "Give Me your son." For Abraham to offer up Isaac was to sacrifice the very object of his faith. Everything God had led him to believe and sacrifice for was in his son.

This brought Abraham to the place of seeing whether he was really convinced that God was able to make alive those who are dead. Abraham had to examine his heart to see if he really believed God was able to raise up children from the ashes of a sacrificed son, even as he did from the deadness of Sarah's womb.

Not only did God withhold reasons from Abraham as to why he should offer his son, but God also withheld specific instructions about where this offering should be made. God only told Abraham: "Get thee into the land of Moriah; and offer him there for a burnt-offering upon one of the mountains which I will tell thee of" (Gen. 22:2). This reveals the way God worked with Abraham. When God called Abraham to leave his country, He did not give him precise instructions where he was to go but only instructed Abraham to go "unto a land that I will shew thee" (12:1). When Abraham was called upon to offer his son, he even had to exercise faith that God would show him the place where it was to be done.

### Abraham's Prompt Response

Even though Abraham could not understand why God would command him to offer his son, he was not slow in responding. Genesis 22:3 says, "And Abraham rose up early in the morning, and saddled his ass, and took two of his young men with him, and Isaac his son, and clave the wood for the burnt-offering, and rose up, and went unto the place of which God had told him." In Abraham's response there was no reluctance, no hesitation, no doubt, no staggering, no unbelief. Abraham did not delay. He did not endeavor to reason things out or spend time consulting with other people about the matter.

So also, when the Apostle Paul was called to preach the gospel, he said, "Immediately I conferred not with flesh and blood" (Gal. 1:16). This is important. There are occasions when no time should be taken to counsel with men. In the cases of Abraham's being commanded to offer Isaac and Paul's being called into the ministry, human counsel would have added nothing. When God so deals with the inner man there is no need to discuss it with others, because they will not understand. Even other believers sometimes discourage God's child from stepping out in faith. Faith never stops to look at the circumstances or to ponder the results. It looks only at God. The moment we confer with flesh and blood, our testimony and services for the Lord are marred. We must never make our action dependent on human reasoning, but on our faith in God. When God finds ready faith, He gives both the direction and the power to perform.

God found ready faith in Abraham. Faith triumphed over natural affections, over reason, over self-will. God's grace found a ready outlet through which it could manifest itself.

Might our faith be as Abraham's faith. As we yield our lives to the Lord, He will work in us "both to will and to do of his good pleasure" (Phil. 2:13). Then we will be able to say with the Apostle Paul, "I can do all things through Christ which strengtheneth me" (Phil. 4:13).

In Abraham, the grace of God found a ready outlet. Abraham immediately obeyed God's will even though he did not understand why he should do so. Only his faith enabled Abraham to have such an immediate response. Faith can subdue every passion of the human heart and every imagination of the carnal mind by bringing everything into an obedient subjection to God.

Faith is the answer. The Apostle Paul wrote: "For though we walk [live] in the flesh, we are not carrying on our warfare according to the flesh and using mere human weapons. For the weapons of our warfare are not physical (weapons of flesh and blood), but they are mighty before God for the overthrow and destruction of strongholds, [Inasmuch as we] refute arguments and theories and reasonings and every proud and lofty thing that sets itself up against the (true) knowledge of God; and we lead every thought and purpose away captive into the obedience of Christ, the Messiah, the Anointed One" (II Cor. 10:3-5, *Amp.*). This is what Jesus Christ enables us to do as we yield to Him.

Abraham was willing to do whatever God wanted him to do—even regarding his son. God enabled Abraham to give up anything and everything as long as Abraham kept his eyes fixed on the Almighty God alone.

This is also the lesson we need to learn. If our eyes are only on the promises, we will not be able to understand when God fails to fulfill the promises in our time. But if our eyes are fixed on God, we will not be so concerned about the promises that are not fulfilled when *we* think they ought to be.

## The 12 Spies

When the Israelites had been delivered from Egypt by the power of God and were approaching the land of Canaan from Kadesh-barnea, they sent 12 men to spy out the land (Num. 13). Ten of the men had their eyes only on the promises concerning the land. When they saw the obstacles, they were sure the Israelites could never conquer the land. But two of the men had their eyes fixed on Almighty God—the God of the promises, the Creator and Sustainer of all things. Because of their confidence in God, these two men said, "Let us go up at once, and possess it; for we are well able to overcome it" (v. 30). In the reports of the ten spies and the two spies, we see the difference between looking to the promises and looking to the God of the promises.

Abraham had to decide who was his first love—Isaac or God. We also have to decide this and when we do, it answers a question that is frequently asked: How can I enjoy heaven if I know my loved ones are in hell? It is understandable that believers would ask a question like this, but I believe the question can be answered by asking another question: Who is first in your love—the Lord Jesus Christ or your family? Because we are so attached to the members of our families, it would greatly affect us if we knew for sure that one of them was in hell. Even God has said, "I have no pleasure in the death of the wicked" (Ezek. 33:11).

God does not rejoice over a person who rejects Jesus Christ as Saviour and who is therefore eternally punished. However, if we love Jesus Christ more than we love our families, we will see things differently. We will then realize that Christ died for every member of our families and, in so doing, He paid the supreme price to win them so they might receive Him as Saviour and escape eternal condemnation. He made it possible for them to stay out of hell, but they rejected Him. When we love Christ more than our families, we will feel very sorry for any member who rejects Christ and goes to hell, but we will be more concerned that Christ's great love for them was cast aside—that Christ was spurned. We will be able to rejoice in heaven because Christ will be there, and our attitudes then will be different than they are now—we will see as He sees. Each person must decide whether his affections are going to be centered on God or on his family. Centering our affections on God does not mean we exclude our families; it is only then that we can love our families as God intends.

### Abraham's Faith Demonstrated

Genesis 22:4,5 says, "Then on the third day Abraham lifted up his eyes, and saw the place afar off. And Abraham said unto his young men, Abide ye here with the ass; and I and the lad will go yonder and worship, and come again to you." In these verses there are three things in particular which reveal the tremendous faith of Abraham. First, he told the young men who were with him, "Abide ye here." Once Abraham saw the mountain that God was going to send him to, he wanted to be sure that nothing or no one would hinder what he had undertaken. Perhaps he realized that if the young men knew he was going to offer Isaac, they might prevent him from doing so. Abraham was not going to allow any provisions whatever for the flesh, so he insisted the young men wait where they were.

Second, Abraham told the young men, "I and the lad will go yonder and worship." Thus Abraham gave up all of his desires and ascribed everything to God. It was a true act of worship when Abraham was willing to give up everything for God. He was about to lay on the altar of sacrifice the one in whom all God's promises centered. He was about to prove, in the sight of heaven, earth and hell, that no other object had control of his soul more than Almighty God. His eye was upon God and God alone.

Third, Abraham told the young men, "I and the lad will . . . come again to you." Abraham not only said he would return to the young men but also that "the lad" would return. Why did Abraham indicate that both he and Isaac would return to the young men? Because his faith was in the God of the resurrection. He believed that God would bring his son back to life. It is one thing to rest in God's blessings, but it is quite another to rest in God Himself apart from the blessings. It was one thing for Abraham to trust God when he had before his eyes the channel through which the blessing was to flow; it was quite another thing for Abraham to trust God when the channel was to be sacrificed.

Can we trust God when we are totally unable to see how He is going to work out His will? Abraham demonstrated that he could. He showed he could trust God, not merely for innumerable seed while Isaac stood before him healthy, vigorous and strong; but he could trust God just as fully if

Isaac were a smoking victim on the altar. Abraham rested in God Himself. He counted on the fact that God was able even to bring Isaac back from the dead. Hebrews 11:17-19 says, "By faith Abraham, when he was tried, offered up Isaac: and he that had received the promises offered up his only begotten son. Of whom it was said, That in Isaac shall thy seed be called: Accounting that God was able to raise him up, even from the dead; from whence also he received him in a figure."

Isaac had been born to Abraham and Sarah when they were incapable of having children. Out of this state of deadness God had given them Isaac. Because God had brought life out of death once, Abraham was convinced He was able to do it again. Abraham never considered that Isaac was able, but that God was able. Isaac without God was nothing. But God without Isaac was absolutely everything.

After Abraham commanded the young men to wait for him and Isaac, the Scriptures say that "Abraham took the wood of the burnt-offering, and laid it upon Isaac his son; and he took the fire in his hand, and a knife; and they went both of them together" (Gen. 22:6). Notice the beautiful togetherness of the father of faith and the son of faith. How the angelic hosts must have watched the two of them from stage to stage in their wondrous but agonizing journey, until at last Abraham stretched forth his hand with the knife to slay his own son.

## Satan's Defeat

What an opportunity for Satan to thrust his fiery darts. He might have come to Abraham at this time and said, "What will become of all the promises? Are you sure God has said you should do this? Don't you know, and doesn't God know, that the day you sacrifice this son, all of your hopes will be obliterated?" Or Satan might have said, "Think of Sarah. What will she do if she loses Isaac? How will you ever face her without bringing Isaac back?" These are some of the many questions that Satan might have thrown at Abraham, but to all of them Abraham would have had a complete answer. His answer would have been that he accounted that God was able to raise up Isaac again, even from the dead.

Death and resurrection are what ruined Satan. Hebrews 2:14,15 says, "Forasmuch then as the children are partakers of flesh and blood, he [Christ] also himself likewise took part of the same; that through death he might destroy him that had the power of death, that is, the devil; And deliver them who through fear of death were all their lifetime subject to bondage." Ephesians 1:19-21 says, "And what is the exceeding greatness of his power to us-ward who believe, according to the working of his mighty power, Which he wrought in Christ, when he raised him from the dead, and set him at his own right hand in the heavenly places, Far above all principality, and power, and might, and dominion, and every name that is named, not only in this world, but also in that which is to come." By Christ's death and resurrection, God overcame Satan and gave Christ absolute preeminence.

Abraham accounted that God was able. God was such a reality to Abraham, and His promises were so certain, that Abraham drew the inevitable conclusion that God's power could and would effect this resurrection. Abraham's secret of faith is found in the statement "Here am I," which is recorded in Genesis 22:11. The same thought is also found in verse 1. Abraham lived in such close fellowship with God that he was always ready for and responsive to any new revelation from God.

### The Inevitable Question

As Abraham and Isaac journeyed together, finally the inevitable question came: "Isaac spake unto Abraham his father, and said, My father: and he said, Here am I, my son. And he said, Behold the fire and the wood: but where is the lamb for a burnt-offering? And Abraham said, My son, God will provide himself a lamb for a burnt-offering: so they went both of them together" (vv. 7,8).

Isaac probably knew that he was the sacrifice. He could have resisted because he was no longer a child. He was probably between 17 and 25 years of age. Physically, all the advantages were his. His father was old; he was young. However, God's Word says, "So they went both of them together." Thus, we see the father and son united in doing the will of God. As was the father's faith, so was the son's.

Here the Word of God introduces us to the submissive trait which seems to have been the strong factor in Isaac's life. He was characterized more by submissiveness than by aggressiveness. Abraham was the one with an aggressive faith, but Isaac had a submissive faith—willing to be what God wanted him to be. Even when he was offered as a sacrifice, Isaac submitted himself to his father because God had so willed it.

Isaac's submission was a picture of Christ's submission to the Father. Jesus Christ was the sacrifice for the sins of the world so that the holy standards of the Heavenly Father might be satisfied. Concerning Christ, I John 2:2 tells us that "he is the propitiation [satisfaction] for our sins: and not for our's only, but also for the sins of the whole world." Jesus was submissive to the Heavenly Father's will. The purpose of the Father and the Son was one. God the Father willed the sacrifice to be made and the Son willed to be the sacrifice. The life of the Lord Jesus Christ is summed up in the statement "I come . . . to do thy will, O God" (Heb. 10:7).

## The Triumph

Concerning Abraham and Isaac, the Scriptures say, "They came to the place which God had told him of; and Abraham built an altar there, and laid the wood in order, and bound Isaac his son, and laid him on the altar upon the wood. And Abraham stretched forth his hand, and took the knife to slay his son. And the angel of the Lord called unto him out of heaven, and said, Abraham, Abraham: and he said, Here am I. And he said, Lay not thine hand upon the lad, neither do thou any thing unto him: for now I know that thou fearest

God, seeing thou hast not withheld thy son, thine only son from me" (Gen. 22:9-12). This was the triumph of both Abraham and Isaac. Faith was now a proven fact. God said, "Now I know that thou fearest God." These are very important words—"Now I know." It had never before been proven to this extent. Abraham had passed the supreme test, and God's voice broke into the awful silence and said, "Now I know."

Faith is always proven by action. In his epistle, James said, "Was not Abraham our father justified by works, when he had offered Isaac his son upon the altar? Seest thou how faith wrought with his works, and by works was faith made perfect?" (2:21,22). James wrote this in answer to his previous question: "What doth it profit, my brethren, though a man say he hath faith, and have not works? can [that] faith save him?" (v. 14). Along with these statements, Romans 4:2,3 needs to be taken into consideration: "For if Abraham were justified by works, he hath whereof to glory; but not before God. For what saith the scripture? Abraham believed God, and it was counted unto him for righteousness." At first it may seem there is a contradiction in these statements about faith and works, but really there is not.

It is easy for people today to talk about faith. It is common to hear people say, "You must have faith." But faith itself is as rare as a true gem. The kind of faith that causes a man to launch out into the deep from the shore of present circumstances is practically missing. Where is our faith today? Perhaps you ask, What is faith? When taken in its most basic meaning, faith is believing what God says and then acting upon it. If we do not act upon what God says, this is an evidence that we really do not believe.

The lives of two men in particular illustrate that faith produces action. Hebrews 11:7 says, "By faith Noah, being warned of God of things not seen as yet, moved with fear, prepared an ark to the saving of his house; by the which he condemned the world, and became heir of the righteousness which is by faith." Faith produced an ark. God told Noah it was going to rain and that the world would be destroyed by a flood. He instructed Noah to build an ark to save himself and a few others. Noah took God at His word and built an ark. He acted upon his faith.

Verse 8 says, "By faith Abraham, when he was called out into a place which he should after receive for an inheritance, obeyed; and he went out, not knowing whither he went." God called Abraham to go, and Abraham took God at His word and went. Thus, we see that faith is believing what God says and then acting upon it.

In considering the statements made in Romans and James regarding faith and works, there are several important things to remember. Although Paul wrote Romans, and James wrote the book that bears his name, the Holy Spirit is the author of both. Because this is true, we may be assured that the statements in the two books are not contradictory. The Holy Spirit does not contradict Himself. In considering the two books closely, we observe that Paul referred to the inward principle of faith, whereas James referred to the outward development of this principle. Paul presented the hidden life; James, the manifested life. Both are needed. The inward cannot do without the outward, and the outward is valueless and powerless without the inward. Works alone are not sufficient.

Faith is proven by works. Paul said Abraham was justified when he believed God. This was inward faith. James said that Abraham was justified when he offered Isaac. This was the outward manifestation of his inward faith. In the former we have our standing—our position with God which is based on our faith. In the latter, we have our state—the manifestation of what we really are. Where there is a true inward principle of faith, there will also be an outward expression of it. If there is no outward expression, we must conclude that there is no inward faith.

## The Greatly Enlarged Blessing

As a result of Abraham's triumph of faith in being willing to offer Isaac, God announced a much greater blessing for him. The Scriptures say that "the angel of the Lord called unto Abraham out of heaven the second time, And said, By myself have I sworn, saith the Lord, for because thou hast done this thing, and hast not withheld thy son, thine only son: That in blessing I will bless thee, and in multiplying I will multiply thy seed as the stars of the heaven, and as the sand which is upon the sea shore; and thy seed shall possess the gate of his enemies; And in thy seed shall all the nations of the earth be blessed; because thou hast obeyed my voice" (Gen. 22:15-18).

Abraham had proven he was willing to sacrifice everything—even his son of promise. He evidenced that his greatest need was to know God. This reminds us of the Apostle Paul's statement: "That I may know him, and the power of his resurrection, and the fellowship of his sufferings, being made conformable unto his death" (Phil. 3:10).

Genesis 22:16 records God's words: "By myself have I sworn." Because there is no one greater, God could swear by no one greater than Himself. Absolute assurance was given to Abraham because his faith was proven by his works. God told Abraham that He would bless him and multiply his seed as the stars of heaven (spiritual seed), and as the sand on the seashore (earthly seed); and that his seed would possess the gate of his enemies. Much of this is yet future. The time is coming when the nation of Israel will possess the gate of her enemies—both her religious and earthly enemies. Abraham experienced the truth of the principle stated in Romans 8:31,32: "What shall we then say to these things? If God be for us, who can be against us? He that spared not his own Son, but delivered him up for us all, how shall he not with him also freely give us all things?" Abraham had graduated. His days of probation and testing were over. His diploma was inscribed with the words "Abraham, the friend of God and the father of the faithful."

After Abraham heard God's promises, he "returned unto his young men, and they rose up and went together to Beer-sheba; and Abraham dwelt at Beer-sheba" (Gen. 22:19).

This was a fulfillment of what Abraham had told the young men, as recorded in verse 5 of the same chapter. He had told them that he and Isaac were going to worship and that they would come again to them. Abraham dared to believe God, and God had proven faithful in every detail. Abraham was able to return to the young men, not only with his son Isaac, but also with the great promises of God for future blessing.

Chapter 14

# Isaac, the Man

Have you ever considered yourself so small in the sight of God that you thought He would never do for you what He has done for men like Abraham, Isaac or Jacob? I am sure you have. In our study of the life of Isaac, we find a man who was very common like most of us. Yet God chose to call Himself "the God of Isaac."

In contrasting Isaac's character with that of his father and that of his son, we see that Isaac experienced fewer of Abraham's triumphs of faith and fewer of Jacob's failures. Genesis 25:5 tells us that "Abraham gave all that he had unto Isaac." This was a beautiful foreshadowing of the believer's heavenly calling, for God has also given us many wonderful things. Ephesians 1:3 says, "Blessed be the God and Father of our Lord Jesus Christ, who hath blessed us with all spiritual blessings in heavenly places in Christ."

Romans 8:29-32 assures us: "For whom he did foreknow, he also did predestinate to be conformed to the image of his Son, that he might be the firstborn among many brethren. Moreover whom he did predestinate, them he also called: and whom he called, them he also justified: and whom he justified, them he also glorified. What shall we then say to these things? If [since] God be for us, who can be against us? He that spared not his own Son, but delivered him up for us all, how shall he not with him also freely give us all things?" We have all things of God in Christ Jesus. We are the principle heirs of Almighty God just as Isaac was the principle heir of his father, Abraham.

In this sense, the land of Canaan symbolizes the heavenlies; that is, the spiritual realm in which we have our citizenship. It is not a symbol of heaven—our future home—but of the heavenlies, for it is the place of spiritual warfare here and now. The believer's spiritual warfare is emphasized in Ephesians 6:12: "For we wrestle not against flesh and blood, but against principalities, against powers, against the rulers of the darkness of this world, against spiritual wickedness in high places." The present-day believer, living in the spiritual realm, has conflicts even as Abraham and Isaac did in the land of Canaan. Our faith is greatly tested even as Abraham and Isaac's faith was greatly tested.

Of the three patriarchs—Abraham, Isaac and Jacob—the only one who never left the land of Canaan was Isaac. He was born in the land of Canaan, and he died there without ever going outside the boundaries of the land. This was quite different from Abraham and Jacob. Perhaps this was because God realized Isaac had a weakness so great that if he had left the land he might not have returned. In light of this, God gave wisdom to Abraham regarding how to deal with his son. No doubt Abraham saw that his son did not have the kind of stability that was really needed. How wonderful it was that Isaac had a father like Abraham. In Genesis 18:19 God said concerning Abraham, "For I know him, that he will command his children and his household after him, and they shall keep the way of the Lord, to do justice and judgment; that the Lord may bring upon Abraham that which he hath spoken of him." God knew that Abraham would bring up his children in the way they ought to go.

After Abraham had given all that he had to Isaac, the Scriptures say that "unto the sons of the concubines, which Abraham had, Abraham gave gifts, and sent them away from Isaac his son, while he yet lived, eastward, unto the east country" (25:6). The "east country" is perhaps a reference to the land east of the Jordan River, which today is known as Jordan. The fact that Abraham sent the sons of his concubines away was perhaps because he knew the weakness of Isaac and did not want them to entice him with their wickedness.

Genesis 24:63 helps us to understand the kind of man Isaac was: "Isaac went out to meditate in the field at the eventide." Thus, we see that Isaac was a quiet and retiring man. He did not have the active, aggressive disposition of his eminent father, but he was deeply concerned about his relationship with God. He was gentle, retiring and unresisting in his relationship with God.

After Abraham's death, Isaac became heir to all things. God was careful, through Abraham, to see to it that Isaac was well taken care of. Genesis 25:11 says, "It came to pass after the death of Abraham, that God blessed his son Isaac; and Isaac dwelt by the well Lahai-roi." "The well Lahai-roi" means "the well of him that liveth and seeth me." It was a place of communion and fellowship with God. This fact about Isaac's life also emphasizes the kind of man he was.

## Isaac Tested

Genesis 26 tells us of an important test that Isaac experienced: "There was a famine in the land, beside the first famine that was in the days of Abraham. And Isaac went unto Abimelech king of the Philistines unto Gerar" (v. 1). Isaac forsook the place where he was living—the place of his fellowship with God. He went to Gerar and left behind the place of the altar. Isaac was headed toward Egypt—and possibly that is where he would have gone—but he stopped enroute at a place called Gerar. This city was in the land of Canaan, although it was well on the way toward Egypt. Because those who went to Egypt usually did so as a reliance on the flesh, Egypt became a symbol of the world. Those who live independently of God and rely on natural resources are spiritually in Egypt.

God was not going to allow Isaac to go into Egypt. His position on the outer fringes of the land certainly evidenced an advanced position of backsliding within the range of very dangerous influences. This was a test for Isaac and he failed it utterly. However, God remained true to His time-honored principle of not testing a believer beyond what he is able to bear but making a way of escape (I Cor. 10:13). God knew how much Isaac could stand, and He knows how much we can stand.

As Isaac was leaving the land of Canaan, "the Lord appeared unto him, and said, Go not down into Egypt; dwell in the land which I shall tell thee of: Sojourn in this land, and I will be with thee, and will bless thee; for unto thee, and unto thy seed, I will give all these countries, and I will perform the oath which I sware unto Abraham thy father; And I will make thy seed to multiply as the stars of heaven, and will give unto thy seed all these countries; and in thy seed shall all the nations of the earth be blessed; Because that Abraham obeyed my voice, and kept my charge, my commandments, my statutes, and my laws. And Isaac dwelt in Gerar" (Gen. 26:2-6).

This was the first appearance of God to Isaac, and God told him very precisely, "Don't go down to Egypt." God told Isaac to "sojourn in this land." The word "sojourn" means to "dwell temporarily."

Isaac had some basic weaknesses, and God knew that if Isaac once left the land he might be tempted never to return. Earlier in the Book of Genesis we saw how steps were taken to make sure that Isaac did not leave the land. When Isaac needed a bride, Abraham sent his servant to find one, but he did not permit Isaac to leave the country. Abraham told his servant, "Thou shalt go unto my country, and to my kindred, and take a wife unto my son Isaac" (24:4). The servant asked, "Peradventure the woman will not be willing to follow me unto this land: must I needs bring thy son again unto the land from whence thou camest?" (v. 5). Abraham's definite response was: "Beware thou that thou bring not my son thither again. The Lord God of heaven, which took me from my father's house, and from the land of my kindred, and which spake unto me, and that sware unto me, saying, Unto thy seed will I give this land; he shall send his angel before thee, and thou shalt take a wife unto my son from thence. And if the woman will not be willing to follow thee, then thou shalt be clear from this my oath: only bring not my son thither again" (vv. 6-8). Abraham was careful to make sure that Isaac did not leave the land. God did not stop Abraham from going out of the land because he knew what Abraham was like. He knew that Abraham would return after he had learned his lessons. Apparently this was not the case with Isaac, so God would not let him leave the land.

## Dwelling in Gerar

According to Genesis 26, Isaac stayed in the land but went to Abimelech, king of the Philistines. Immediately he had trouble. Even though he did not leave the land, he left his place of fellowship–an indication of his backslidden condition.

Verse 6 of this chapter tells us that "Isaac dwelt in Gerar." Earlier God had told him, "Sojourn in this land" (v. 3). To "sojourn" means to "dwell temporarily," whereas to "dwell" means to "stay or settle down." God had intended for Isaac to dwell temporarily in Gerar, but Isaac settled down and stayed there for a long time (v. 8).

One cannot settle down near the temptations of the world without being greatly tempted himself. Isaac was tempted to compromise. Lot also was tempted when he looked upon the riches of Sodom and Gomorrah and his heart was drawn away from the Lord. God's words to every believer are: "Wherefore come out from among them, and be ye separate, saith the Lord, and touch not the unclean thing; and I will receive you, And will be a Father unto you, and ye shall be my sons and daughters, saith the Lord Almighty. Having therefore these promises, dearly beloved, let us cleanse ourselves from all filthiness of the flesh and spirit, perfecting holiness in the fear of God" (II Cor. 6:17-7:1).

While Isaac was in Gerar, "the men of the place asked him of his wife; and he said, She is my sister: for he feared to say, She is my wife; lest, said he, the men of the place should kill me for Rebekah; because she was fair to look upon" (Gen. 26:7). Had Isaac not gone to Abimelech, he would not have had to lie about his wife. He lied about his wife just as his father, Abraham, had lied about his wife, Sarah. Isaac left his communion with God and ended up by sinning against the Lord.

This is the way sin works. It begins so simply and subtly. The progress of sin is set forth in James 1:14,15: "But every man is tempted, when he is drawn away of his own lust, and enticed. Then when lust hath conceived, it bringeth forth sin: and sin, when it is finished, bringeth forth death." This principle was seen in the life of Lot, who was tempted and fell. Although Isaac knew of the failures of Lot and of his father, Abraham, he also yielded to temptation. Because his wife, Rebekah, was a beautiful woman, he feared she might be taken by Abimelech. His fear caused him to commit the same sin his father had committed.

There are two important lessons we need to learn from Isaac's imitating his father's example. First, it is much easier for children to imitate the weaknesses or vices of their parents than to excel in their virtues. It is easier because it is natural. Second, while Abraham and Isaac were men of vastly different temperaments, each succumbed to the same temptation. When famine arose, they fled for help. While they were in the land of the enemy, they both became afraid and lied about their wives.

This proves that natural man is under the control of the same Adamic nature in which there is no good thing. The Apostle Paul recognized this and said, "For I know that in me (that is, in my flesh,) dwelleth no good thing: for to will is present with me; but how to perform that which is good I find not" (Rom. 7:18). Abraham and Isaac both had the Adamic nature, even as we do, and they yielded to temptation in similar situations. They had to realize that unless they applied the grace of God, they would inevitably fall into sin. This should also serve as a warning to us.

Isaac followed his father's footsteps toward evil when he should have learned from his father's experiences. We often warn our young people, trying to teach them by the experiences we have had. However, it seems so many of them have to learn the hard way. It is discouraging to see young people going their own way after we have told them what has happened to us as a result of our going our own way.

## Backslidden But Blessed

Even though Isaac was out of fellowship with the Lord, we find that the Lord blessed him. Genesis 26:12-14 says, "Then Isaac sowed in that land, and received in the same year an hundredfold: and the Lord blessed him. And the man waxed great, and went forward, and grew until he became very great: For he had possession of flocks, and possession of herds, and great store of servants: and the Philistines envied him."

How is it possible for God to bless a person who is out of fellowship with Him? God had permitted Isaac to go to Gerar to be tested. Isaac was yet too weak in the faith to be severely tested. Even when Isaac was in Gerar, God promised to bless him. God told Isaac, "Sojourn in this land, and I will be with thee, and will bless thee; for unto thee, and unto thy seed, I will give all these countries, and I will perform the oath which I sware unto Abraham thy father" (v. 3).

God's blessing was upon Isaac even though Isaac was out of the center of His will. God often brings His children back to Himself by showering unexcelled goodness upon them. Romans 2:4 emphasizes this as a principle of God's working when it says, "Or despisest thou the riches of his goodness and forbearance and longsuffering; not knowing that the goodness of God leadeth thee to repentance?" Or as we read in Romans 9:23: "And that he might make known the riches of his glory on the vessels of mercy, which he had afore prepared unto glory." God allows these things to happen for a purpose. Since Isaac was not able to endure ultimate testing, God permitted him to go as far as Gerar where He was able to teach him some valuable lessons.

Isaac was blessed of God and prospered, but this does not mean that every person who prospers is blessed of God. There are many in our day who are prosperous, yet they believe and live contrary to the teaching of the Word of God. Many leaders of false cults have been prosperous, but this is no indication they have been blessed of God. In Isaac's case, however, his prosperity did result from the blessing of God.

We should also observe that there is a vast difference between the Lord's presence and the Lord's blessing. The Israelites illustrated this fact: "They soon forgat his [God's] works; they waited not for his counsel: But lusted exceedingly in the wilderness, and tempted God in the desert. And he gave them their request; but sent leanness into their soul" (Ps. 106:13-15). While some look for signs from God to indicate His leadership, Moses was a great deal different. He stayed close to God and would not accept any means of leadership other than God's personal presence. After the people had sinned by making the golden calf, Moses made intercession for them. God told Moses, "Depart, and go up hence, thou and the people which thou hast brought up out of the land of Egypt, unto the land which I sware unto Abraham, to Isaac, and to Jacob, saying, Unto thy seed will I give it: And I will send an angel before thee; and I will drive out the Canaanite, the Amorite, and the Hittite, and the Perizzite, the Hivite, and the Jebusite" (Ex. 33:1,2).

God was saying to Moses that His presence was not going with them but that He would send an angel to fulfill what He said He was going to do. But notice the response of Moses: "If thy presence go not with me, carry us not up hence. For wherein shall it be known here that I and thy people have found grace in thy sight? is it not in that thou goest with us? so shall we be separated, I and thy people, from all the people that are upon the face of the earth" (vv. 15,16).

Moses refused to go unless God would assure him that His presence would go with them. He realized that if God did not go with them, the inhabitants of the land would not know that Israel had found grace in God's sight. Moses realized the Israelites could not be a testimony to those in Canaan if God's presence was not with them. The Lord answered Moses, "I will do this thing also that thou hast spoken: for thou hast found grace in my sight, and I know thee by name" (v. 17). Moses was concerned about the presence of the Lord and would not settle for anything less.

## Blessing and Presence

Many people confuse the blessing of the Lord with the presence of the Lord. How often we measure a man or his work by the outward appearance, rather than seeking to understand the inner essence of the man himself. "The Lord seeth not as man seeth; for man looketh on the outward appearance, but the Lord looketh on the heart" (I Sam. 16:7). Thus God tells us, "For my thoughts are not your thoughts, neither are your ways my ways, saith the Lord. For as the heavens are higher than the earth, so are my ways higher than your ways, and my thoughts than your thoughts" (Isa. 55:8,9). John 7:24 reminds us: "Judge not according to the appearance, but judge righteous judgment."

It is possible for a man to become very great and have many possessions and yet not have the full joy of the Lord's presence. Isaac was such a man.

In Genesis 26:3, when God told Isaac, "I will be with thee, and will bless thee," this was the same as saying, "I will never leave thee, nor forsake thee" (Heb. 13:5). This was the presence of God. Many times we are more concerned about the blessings of God than we are about the presence of God. Concerning David, God said that he was "a man after mine own heart, which shall fulfil all my will" (Acts. 13:22). David sought to please the Lord above all else. Moses was this kind of man also. When God saw how stiffnecked the children of Israel were, He told Moses, "Now therefore let me alone, that my wrath may wax hot against them, and that I may consume them: and I will make of thee a great nation" (Ex.

32:10). But Moses prayed that the Lord would not destroy the people, and his prayers were heard.

We must remember that flocks and herds are not the Lord. Even though Isaac had many possessions, this did not mean he had the blessing of the Lord's presence. The Philistines envied Isaac, not because they were convinced the Lord's presence was with him, but because of his possessions. The Bible says that Isaac "had possession of flocks, and possession of herds, and great store of servants: and the Philistines envied him. For all the wells which his father's servants had digged in the days of Abraham his father, the Philistines had stopped them, and filled them with earth. And Abimelech said unto Isaac, Go from us; for thou art much mightier than we" (Gen. 26:14-16). The Philistines would never have envied Isaac for the presence of God, because they could not have understood such a reality. However, they could see his possessions and they envied him for these.

Where do you stand in your relationship with the Lord? People often say, "God is good to me," by which they mean that they have experienced good health or prosperity. What a person possesses is not always a safe measure of his dedication to the Lord.

The Philistines gave Isaac much difficulty by filling up the wells he had dug, but God was with him. Philippians 1:6 shows God's principle of working with His own when it says, "He which hath begun a good work in you will perform it until the day of Jesus Christ." God had begun a good work in Isaac and He was gently, but definitely, leading Isaac back to his home and the altar. Little by little, God let the Philistines close Isaac's wells. This was a serious act in those days because the possession of a well indicated the possession of the land around it. However, the Philistines were being used of God to force Isaac out of their territory. Finally, Abimelech said, "Go from us; for thou art much mightier than we" (Gen. 26:16). This was really God speaking to Isaac from a distance. God spoke through Abimelech rather than speaking directly to Isaac.

## Isaac Departs

After Abimelech's command, the Bible says that "Isaac departed thence, and pitched his tent in the valley of Gerar, and dwelt there" (v. 17). Isaac left Abimelech, but he did not go very far. The Bible again refers to Isaac's digging wells when it says, "Isaac digged again the wells of water, which they had digged in the days of Abraham his father; for the Philistines had stopped them after the death of Abraham: and he called their names after the names by which his father had called them" (v. 18).

Isaac had to redig the wells his father had dug, but even this was used of God because the trouble that came to Isaac kept forcing him to move closer to his home and the place of the altar. At Gerar, he was only partway home and had pitched his tent where he should not have done so.

In this connection, there is a Scripture passage that has taught me something very important about obeying God when He says, "Get out" or "Leave." In the Book of Exodus, there are four major stages of separation emphasized concerning Moses' asking Pharaoh to let the children of Israel leave the land of Egypt. After the Lord had afflicted Pharaoh and the Egyptians with flies, "Pharaoh called for Moses and for Aaron, and said, Go ye, sacrifice to your God in the land" (8:25). This was the first compromise Pharaoh offered Moses. Pharaoh was willing to let the Israelites offer sacrifices "in the land." Moses was insistent that the children of Israel should leave the land of Egypt, for he said, "We will go three days' journey into the wilderness, and sacrifice to the Lord our God, as he shall command us" (v. 27).

Pharaoh then offered a second compromise: "I will let you go, that ye may sacrifice to the Lord your God in the wilderness; only ye shall not go very far away: intreat for me" (v. 28). Pharaoh was willing to let Moses and the children of Israel go, but he did not want them to go very far. He also asked that Moses entreat for him, obviously because of the troubles the land of Egypt was experiencing. However, after the swarms of flies had been removed from Pharaoh and the Egyptians, he refused to let the people go.

After the plague of the locusts on Egypt, Pharaoh offered a third compromise to Moses and the Israelites. Pharaoh said, "Go, serve the Lord your God: but who are they that shall go?" (10:8). When Moses made it clear that all the Israelites were going to go, Pharaoh said, "Let the Lord be so with you, as I will let you go, and your little ones: look to it; for evil is before you. Not so: go now ye that are men, and serve the Lord; for that ye did desire" (vv. 10,11). Pharaoh tried to get Moses to leave the families in Egypt while the men went into the wilderness to offer sacrifices to God. Moses refused this compromise also.

After the plague of darkness on Egypt that was so great that it could be felt, Pharaoh offered a fourth compromise. He told Moses, "Go ye, serve the Lord; only let your flocks and your herds be stayed: let your little ones also go with you" (v. 24). Moses answered Pharaoh, "Thou must give us also sacrifices and burnt-offerings, that we may sacrifice unto the Lord our God. Our cattle also shall go with us; there shall not an hoof be left behind; for thereof must we take to serve the Lord our God; and we know not with what we must serve the Lord, until we come thither" (vv. 25,26). Moses would accept no compromise. It had to be an all-out separation for the Israelites.

Just as Pharaoh offered compromises to the Israelites, the Devil tries to get present-day believers to compromise. He urges them not to get too excited about being Christians. He will try to convince you that if you want to be a Christian it is all right to go to church on Sunday, but you should not take Christianity too seriously during the week. Or he may try to get parents to think that it is all right for them to be Christians, but that they should let their children make their own choices and not force them to go to church. If the entire family becomes involved in church, Satan then tries to stir up their feelings concerning finances. He'll tempt them by saying, "All the church is interested in is your money. They want you to come to church so they can get your offerings."

However, we must realize that God wants our entire person—everything we are and have. We should not let Satan influence us to hold anything back. God wants us to be completely separated unto Him; no compromise is acceptable.

After Isaac had pitched his tent in the valley of Gerar, he redug several wells and the Philistines came behind him to fill them up. Each time he would move a little farther away and redig another of his father's wells. God was allowing more trouble to come to Isaac so he would return to his home.

Isaac was a weakling in this respect, but probably no weaker than most of us. Perhaps God has been speaking to you and you wonder why you have troubles. Maybe you have suffered a financial loss and you find it very difficult to understand. Is God speaking to you in an effort to bring you back to Himself? You need to face these matters squarely and be honest with God as He deals with you.

## Not Insisting on Rights

Isaac sought for satisfaction without a complete return, so he dug wells. However, there could be no real spiritual satisfaction until he completely returned to the Lord. God was forcing Isaac back to his homeland by permitting the Philistines to close up the wells he reopened. However, even in this, Isaac showed a very lovely trait in his life. He did not insist on his own rights. He simply moved to another place. First Peter 2:19,20 says, "For this is thankworthy, if a man for conscience toward God endure grief, suffering wrongfully. For what glory is it, if, when ye be buffeted for your faults, ye shall take it patiently? but if, when ye do well, and suffer for it, ye take it patiently, this is acceptable with God." The Philistines were treating Isaac wrongfully, but he did not insist on his own rights.

After there was strife over the well of Sitnah (Gen. 26:21), Isaac "removed from thence, and digged another well; and for that they strove not: and he called the name of it Rehoboth; and he said, For now the Lord hath made room for us, and we shall be fruitful in the land" (v. 22). Finally, Isaac was able to dig a well that the Philistines did not strive after. Little by little, Isaac had been moving back to where the Lord wanted him. Therefore, when he dug the well Rehoboth, the Lord did not allow the Philistines to further strive with him. The name "Rehoboth" means "an enlargement." Thus Isaac said, "For now the Lord hath made room for us." From this incident in Isaac's life we see that victory comes through yielding to God. One of the hardest lessons for Christians to learn is that they should not resist evil that is done to them personally. It is natural to want to stand up for our rights, but we must make room for God to work in our lives.

In I Peter 3:8,9 believers are exhorted: "Be ye all of one mind, having compassion one of another, love as brethren, be pitiful, be courteous: Not rendering evil for evil, or railing for railing: but contrariwise blessing." That is, we are to do good toward those who do us evil. God richly blesses the Christian who does this.

God rewarded Isaac for not insisting on his own rights. God patiently worked with Isaac until He had him in the place He desired him to be. This reminds us of Romans 8:28,29: "And we know that all things work together for good to them that love God, to them who are the called according to his purpose. For whom he did foreknow, he also did predestinate to be conformed to the image of his Son." This is the way God works. He deals with us as with children. Therefore, Hebrews 12:5-7 tells us, "Despise not thou the chastening of the Lord, nor faint when thou art rebuked of him: For whom the Lord loveth he chasteneth, and scourgeth every son whom he receiveth. If ye endure chastening, God dealeth with you as with sons; for what son is he whom the father chasteneth not?" This same chapter reminds us, "Now no chastening for the present seemeth to be joyous, but grievous: nevertheless afterward it yieldeth the peaceable fruit of righteousness unto them which are exercised thereby. Wherefore lift up the hands which hang down, and the feeble knees" (vv. 11,12). We should be encouraged when we realize the Lord is dealing with us, even though no chastening is joyful at the time we are passing through it.

### Isaac Returns to Fellowship

After Isaac dug the well Rehoboth, the Bible says that "he went up from thence to Beer-sheba" (Gen. 26:23). The name "Beer-sheba" means "the well of the oath [covenant]." Isaac's father, Abraham, had earlier made a covenant with Abimelech and gave him seven ewe lambs as a witness that he had dug the well (21:28-31). Isaac made things right with the Lord at this well of the covenant–he had had enough of the wrangling of the world. Isaac went back to his life of the altar.

How long does it take us to get back to the altar after we have backslidden? When we have left the place of fellowship with God, we need to return to the first works as Christ told the Church of Ephesus: "Remember therefore from whence thou art fallen, and repent, and do the first works; or else I will come unto thee quickly, and will remove thy candlestick out of his place, except thou repent" (Rev. 2:5). Let us not fool ourselves when we are out of fellowship with God. Our need is to return to fellowship with God, and the way back is Calvary itself. The Word of God promises that "if we confess our sins, he is faithful and just to forgive us our sins, and to cleanse us from all unrighteousness" (I John 1:9).

When Isaac returned to Beer-sheba, "the Lord appeared unto him the same night" (Gen. 26:24). Notice when the Lord appeared to him–the moment he came back to Beer-sheba, the place of the altar. There was no appearance of the Lord to Isaac while he was in the land of Abimelech. When the Lord appeared to Isaac, He said, "I am the God of Abraham thy father: fear not, for I am with thee, and will bless thee, and multiply thy seed for my servant Abraham's sake" (v. 24). God was going to bless Isaac "for [His] servant Abraham's sake." This was God's confirmation to Isaac that He would fulfill what He had promised to Abraham. This was God's second and last communication with Isaac. It is also the first time that God referred to Himself as "the God of Abraham." It is a phrase which appears many times in the rest of the Scriptures.

Blessings and wealth followed Isaac after the Lord appeared to him at Beer-sheba. Isaac's experience emphasizes the blessed presence of the Lord and the importance of being where He is. To enjoy His presence, we must be where He is.

Once when Abraham Lincoln was experiencing severe difficulties, some people advised him to ask the Lord to be on their side. Abraham Lincoln advised the people that what all of them needed to do was to get on the Lord's side. We need to be where the Lord is.

The question we must answer is the same question Moses asked the Israelites after they had sinned in making the golden calf: "Who is on the Lord's side?" (Ex. 32:26).

The Apostle Paul had a burning desire to know and experience the presence of God. As he reflected on the accomplishments of his past life, Paul said, "But what things were gain to me, those I counted loss for Christ. Yea doubtless, and I count all things but loss for the excellency of the knowledge of Christ Jesus my Lord: for whom I have suffered the loss of all things, and do count them but dung, that I may win Christ, And be found in him, not having mine own righteousness, which is of the law, but that which is through the faith of Christ, the righteousness which is of God by faith: That I may know him, and the power of his resurrection, and the fellowship of his sufferings, being made conformable unto his death" (Phil. 3:7-10). The power of God is where God is. We cannot have His power unless we are dwelling in fellowship with Him.

How did Isaac's life affect unbelievers while he was out of fellowship with God? There is a great deal of controversy these days as to what is the best way to appeal to those who are outside of Jesus Christ. Some suggest that it is necessary for us to speak and act like the unsaved in order for us to effectively reach them. However, from Isaac's life we see that he did not make an impression upon those with whom he was living while he was in poor fellowship with the Lord. Apparently he was living much like they were, yet they gave him nothing but trouble. Eventually his life did have an impact on the unbelievers around him, but it was only after he had reestablished his altar of communion with God. It is important that we discover what made the difference in his life so we can be sure we are following the right principles in our lives.

## Three Absolutes

If we want the power of God in our lives, we must observe the absolutes of God. There are three absolutes in particular that we must heed in order to have spiritual power. First, we must recognize that all power belongs to God. In this age, it is God the Holy Spirit who is responsible to direct the work of God. Thus, we must recognize the sovereignty of the Holy Spirit to direct all spiritual work.

Second, we must recognize the sovereignty of the Holy Spirit in delegating this power to anyone He chooses. It is the Holy Spirit's responsibility to give spiritual gifts to men as He desires so the work of God will be carried out. In I Corinthians 12:7 we learn that the "manifestation of the Spirit is given to every man to profit withal." The Word of God mentions various gifts and then says, "All these worketh that one and the selfsame Spirit, dividing to every man severally as he will" (v. 11).

The third absolute we must recognize in order to have spiritual power in our lives is that of absolute committal to the Holy Spirit. The Apostle Paul was exhorting all believers when he said, "I beseech you therefore, brethren, by the mercies of God, that ye present your bodies a living sacrifice, holy, acceptable unto God, which is your reasonable service. And be not conformed to this world: but be ye transformed by the renewing of your mind, that ye may prove what is that good, and acceptable, and perfect, will of God" (Rom. 12:1,2). It is only when we make this absolute committal to God that we will have spiritual power in our lives. Our witnessing for Christ will then have a great impact on the lives of others.

Just as Isaac had to go back to the place God intended him to be, present-day believers must live according to the absolutes of God and be in the place He wants them to be if they are to have spiritual power.

After Isaac had returned to Beer-sheba and the Lord had appeared to him, Isaac built "an altar there, and called upon the name of the Lord, and pitched his tent there: and there Isaac's servants digged a well" (Gen. 26:25). Notice particularly that when Isaac returned to the place where God wanted him, he built an altar and called on the name of the Lord. It was there also that he pitched his tent. The fact that he pitched his tent there indicated he was no longer attached to the world. He experienced the joy of God's presence and immediate progress took place in his spiritual life. He dug a well and no one bothered him as they had earlier.

As we read about the time Isaac spent in Gerar, there is no mention that he built an altar there. As a result, there was no progress in his spiritual life. Spiritual progress is only where the altar is. Spiritual progress begins with our communion with Almighty God. If God is not put first in every area of our lives, we cannot expect spiritual progress. Jesus Himself said, "Seek ye first the kingdom of God, and his righteousness; and all these things shall be added unto you" (Matt. 6:33). Jesus also said, "Abide in me, and I in you. As the branch cannot bear fruit of itself, except it abide in the vine; no more can ye, except ye abide in me. I am the vine, ye are the branches: He that abideth in me, and I in him, the same bringeth forth much fruit: for without me ye can do nothing" (John 15:4,5). If we are going to have spiritual fruit in our lives, we must put God first in everything and abide in Him.

When Isaac returned to the place where God wanted him, things began to happen. Genesis 26:26 says, "Then Abimelech went to him from Gerar." The word "then" is extremely important. It was not until Isaac had returned to the pathway of God's direct will that his former enemies sought him out and gave a wonderful testimony concerning Isaac's greatness and the evident presence of God with him. Three men came to Isaac—Abimelech, Ahuzzath and Phichol—and Isaac asked them, "Wherefore come ye to me, seeing ye hate me, and have sent me away from you?" (v. 27). It was then that the three men gave their testimony concerning Isaac and the Lord: "We saw certainly that the Lord was with thee: and we said, Let there be now an oath betwixt us, even betwixt us and thee, and let us make a covenant with thee; That thou wilt do us no hurt, as we have not touched thee, and as we have done unto thee nothing but good, and have sent thee away in peace: thou art now the blessed of the Lord" (vv. 27-29). The testimony of these men verified the principle set forth in the Word of God that "when a man's ways please the Lord, he maketh even his enemies to be at peace with him" (Prov. 16:7).

## How to Have an Impact for God

The only way the believer can act upon the hearts and consciences of the men of the world is to stand in decided separation from them while dealing in perfect grace and love toward them. The believer is not to stand aloof from the world and have a holier-than-thou attitude, nor is he to mix with the world so as to have an affinity with the unsaved. These are two extremes, but there are many proponents of both extremes. There are Christians who say, "We must not have anything to do with anyone who is unsaved or even with believers who are theologically liberal." On the other hand, there are Christians who say, "If you are going to win the lost, you have to become one of them. You have to sing like they sing and talk like they talk." Neither of these extremes is the method God has chosen. The believer is to be separated from unbelievers, but he is to deal in grace and love toward them.

As long as Isaac lived in Gerar, there was nothing but strife and contention. He was mixing with them even though he was not one of them. In witnessing there is no greater mistake than to imagine we can be one with the world and still be an influence for Christ. This cannot be done. For any who doubt, they need only to study the life of Lot. He learned the hard way that he could not be one with the world and also have a spiritual impact on the world.

The believer is to be *in* the world but he is not to be *of* the world. When Jesus prayed to the Heavenly Father concerning His followers, He said, "I pray not that thou shouldest take them out of the world, but that thou shouldest keep them from the evil [one]" (John 17:15). Then He said, "As thou hast sent me into the world, even so have I also sent them into the world" (v. 18). We are *in* the world, but we are not *of* the world.

The moment Isaac took his stand in separation from unbelievers, they immediately saw God's blessing on him and they sought him out to make a covenant with him. In order for believers to affect the stubborn hearts of the unsaved, the believers must first be right with God. Isaac returned to the altar and to his tent-life. He returned to the place of communion and prayer and dwelt as a pilgrim and stranger. The unbelievers had noticed Isaac's attitude when they closed up his wells. They saw that he did not insist on his rights. This had a profound effect on them. No matter what evil the unbelievers did to him, Isaac prospered. The people of the world were able to see that, in spite of everything, God's blessing was on Isaac.

In First Peter instructions are given to believers who are reproached. The Apostle Peter wrote: "If ye be reproached for the name of Christ, happy are ye; for the spirit of glory and of God resteth upon you: on their part he is evil spoken of, but on your part he is glorified. But let none of you suffer as a murderer, or as a thief, or as an evildoer, or as a busybody in other men's matters. Yet if any man suffer as a Christian, let him not be ashamed; but let him glorify God on this behalf" (4:14-16). The Lord Jesus Christ said, "Blessed are ye, when men shall revile you, and persecute you, and shall say all manner of evil against you falsely, for my sake" (Matt. 5:11). Christ also told believers, "Let your light so shine before men, that they may see your good works, and glorify your Father which is in heaven" (v. 16).

When we are abused by the unbelieving world, we need to remember the words of Psalm 37:5,6: "Commit thy way unto the Lord; trust also in him; and he shall bring it to pass. And he shall bring forth thy righteousness as the light, and thy judgment as the noonday." God will vindicate us if we are totally committed to Him and trust Him for everything. Our need is to entrust ourselves completely to Him by committing all of our ways to Him.

After Abimelech and the other men finished speaking to Isaac about the covenant they wanted to make with him, Isaac "made them a feast, and they did eat and drink. And they rose up betimes in the morning, and sware one to another: and Isaac sent them away, and they departed from him in peace. And it came to pass the same day, that Isaac's servants came, and told him concerning the well which they had digged, and said unto him, We have found water" (Gen. 26:30-32). Because Isaac dared to live the separated life, God poured out His blessing on him. Isaac was not offensive to the unbelievers, but he did that which was right in the sight of God. As a result, God blessed Isaac, and the well his servants had dug produced water.

I urge you to seriously consider the benefits of not insisting on your own rights. As a believer, you have friends and neighbors who are closely watching you. Are you the quarrelsome type who is driving them farther from the Lord? Even if they are saying things about you that are not true, why not suffer for the Lord's sake? Do not try to reach them by compromising your standards, but rather live a life that is separated unto God, and He will mightily use you in reaching others for Christ.

Chapter 15

# Isaac's Declining Years

When God said that He was the God of Abraham, the God of Isaac, and the God of Jacob, He was not saying that these men had perfect lives. There were many wonderful things about their lives in that they were stalwart men of faith, but they also had their weaknesses. This was especially true of Isaac. In his declining years, his carelessness and weaknesses became more prominent.

Genesis 26 tells of Isaac's son when it says, "And Esau was forty years old when he took to wife Judith the daughter of Beeri the Hittite, and Bashemath the daughter of Elon the Hittite; Which were a grief of mind unto Isaac and to Rebekah" (vv. 34,35). Esau married a Hittite and it deeply grieved his parents. Abraham, Isaac's father, had been careful to make sure that Isaac secured a wife from Mesopotamia, not from the people of Canaan. Abraham wanted Isaac's wife to come from his kindred land, not from Canaan. In examining the details of Isaac's marriage, we saw that God would not let Isaac leave the country, perhaps because he was too weak and would not have returned. Abraham exercised much concern for Isaac in refusing to let him go to Mesopotamia to get a wife. However, Isaac did not seem to be that concerned about his children and the wives they selected. In this matter, Isaac failed. He did not watch over his children properly to make sure they were what they should be.

Even though Isaac was grieved about Esau's marrying a Hittite, he did not rebuke him for what he did. This reminds us of Eli, the priest, of whom God said, "I have told him that I will judge his house for ever for the iniquity which he knoweth; because his sons made themselves vile, and he restrained them not" (I Sam. 3:13). These are sad accounts of both Eli and Isaac.

Isaac again revealed his carelessness and weakness when the time came to bestow his blessing on the proper heir of the promise. Of his two sons, Esau and Jacob, God had made it very clear that the youngest—Jacob—was His choice for the inheritance. It is true that they were twins, but because Esau was born first, the inheritance would naturally go to him. However, before the sons were born God said to Rebekah, "Two nations are in thy womb, and two manner of people shall be separated from thy bowels: and the one people shall be stronger than the other people; and the elder shall serve the younger" (Gen. 25:23). From the human standpoint the inheritance belonged to Esau, but from the divine standpoint the inheritance belonged to Jacob.

Esau despised the birthright because it was a spiritual thing—of value only as there was faith to apprehend it. In many respects, Esau was outwardly a more noble person than Jacob, but inwardly he despised that which was spiritual.

Isaac would have been fully aware that God had promised the blessing to Jacob, for God had said that "the elder shall serve the younger." However, when it came time for Isaac to give the blessing, we are told, "And it came to pass, that when Isaac was old, and his eyes were dim, so that he could not see, he called Esau his eldest son, and said unto him, My son: and he said unto him, Behold, here am I. And he said, Behold now, I am old, I know not the day of my death: Now therefore take, I pray thee thy weapons, thy quiver and thy bow, and go out to the field, and take me some venison; And make me savoury meat, such as I love, and bring it to me, that I may eat; that my soul may bless thee before I die" (27:1-4).

In weakness and carelessness, Isaac was preparing to perform the last religious act as a priest of the family, which was to bestow blessing on his son who was to be heir. We see no evidence, however, that he sought the Lord's guidance at this time. Rather, his mind was occupied with a feast of venison. Whereas Esau had sold his birthright for a mess of pottage, someone has said that Isaac sold the blessing for a mess of venison.

Isaac sought to reverse the express will of God and to bestow on Esau what the Lord had reserved for Jacob. Isaac loved the venison that Esau could prepare for him. So in preparation for the bestowing of the blessing on Esau, Isaac asked him to prepare some venison. Isaac acted in the energy of the flesh. As such, we need to remember the timeless principle that "whatsoever a man soweth, that shall he also reap" (Gal. 6:7). Because Isaac acted in the energy of the flesh, Rebekah and Jacob dealt with him on the same low level.

## Rebekah's Scheme

Rebekah had sufficient reason to mistrust her husband because previously he had been willing to jeopardize her honor in order to save his own life. He had told Abimelech that she was his sister, not his wife.

Rebekah realized that her husband might again resort to compromise or expediency when he faced the difficult situation of passing on the blessing. She thought she had to take matters into her own hands. In so doing, God was left out. She knew God's plan and purpose—that Jacob was to have the blessing—but she was unable to leave the matter to God.

Believers often face a similar problem. They know that God has promised to do certain things and, because of this, they are tempted to take the fulfillment into their own hands. However, if God has promised to do something, we can leave the fulfillment to Him. When the flesh tries to fulfill that which is spiritual, the result is nothing but trouble. Romans 8:8 makes it clear that "they that are in the flesh cannot please God." Verse 13 of this same chapter says, "If ye live after the flesh, ye shall die: but if ye through the

Spirit do mortify the deeds of the body, ye shall live." The Apostle Paul asked the Galatians, "Are ye so foolish? having begun in the Spirit, are ye now made perfect by the flesh?" (Gal. 3:3). Nothing good can come from that which is done in the energy of the flesh.

It was certainly true in Rebekah's case that good did not result from the efforts of the flesh. The plan she had carefully worked out resulted in her never again seeing her son Jacob.

Isaac had never concealed his preference for Esau. Now at the end of his life he was going to give the blessing to Esau even though God had instructed otherwise. The Scriptures say that "Rebekah heard when Isaac spake to Esau his son. And Esau went to the field to hunt for venison, and to bring it" (Gen. 27:5).

Rebekah was not going to allow Jacob to miss his God-given birthright and blessing. She had been thrown back on her own resources many times, and now in this critical hour she was not going to leave anything to chance. However, neither did she leave anything to faith. The principle stated in Hebrews 11:6 was just as true in Rebekah's time as it is in ours: "Without faith it is impossible to please him [God]." Verse 1 of this same chapter defines "faith" as "the substance of things hoped for, the evidence of things not seen." Such faith was not found in Rebekah. She left God out and schemed on her own to get the blessing for Jacob.

Rebekah told Jacob, "Go now to the flock, and fetch me from thence two good kids of the goats; and I will make them savoury meat for thy father, such as he loveth: And thou shalt bring it to thy father, that he may eat, and that he may bless thee before his death" (Gen. 27:9,10). Jacob responded to his mother, "Behold, Esau my brother is a hairy man, and I am a smooth man: My father peradventure will feel me, and I shall seem to him as a deceiver; and I shall bring a curse upon me, and not a blessing" (vv. 11,12). Even though Jacob himself was a schemer, he challenged the scheming of his mother. Jacob did not disapprove of the scheming because he knew it was a sin to deceive; he disapproved because he was afraid he would get caught.

Rebekah persuaded Jacob to leave the whole situation to her. She assured him that she would accept full responsibility. Rebekah's plan was to take advantage of her husband's physical limitations. She deceived him by capitalizing on his lack of sight and his emotional instability. She prepared the meat as Isaac loved it and "took goodly raiment of her eldest son Esau, which were with her in the house, and put them upon Jacob her younger son: And she put the skins of the kids of the goats upon his hands, and upon the smooth of his neck" (vv. 15,16).

### Jacob Before His Father

Rebekah "gave the savoury meat and the bread, which she had prepared, into the hand of her son Jacob. And he came unto his father, and said, My father: I am Esau thy firstborn; I have done according as thou badest me: arise, I pray thee, sit and eat of my venison, that thy soul may bless me" (vv. 17-19).

Isaac was puzzled and asked, "How is it that thou hast found it so quickly, my son?" Jacob answered, "Because the Lord thy God brought it to me" (v. 20). As Jacob sought to deceive his father, he referred to God in order to make everything sound right. How horrible are the depths to which some believers will go to make things seem what they are not.

Because of uncertainty, he said to Jacob, "Come near, I pray thee, that I may feel thee, my son, whether thou be my very son Esau or not" (v. 21). After Jacob had gone near so his father could feel him, Isaac said, "The voice is Jacob's voice, but the hands are the hands of Esau" (v. 22). Then the Scriptures comment that Isaac "discerned him not, because his hands were hairy, as his brother Esau's hands: so he blessed him" (v. 23).

In this incident we see another of Isaac's weaknesses. He depended on his natural senses for leadership instead of depending on God. How often this is also true of us. We go by our feelings, or by what our senses indicate, rather than by what God has said. Even though we know the Word of God promises certain things, we often refuse to believe because we do not feel such could be the case. Faith is not based on our senses; it is based on the Word of God.

What Jacob was doing was not of faith, and the Bible says that "whatsoever is not of faith is sin" (Rom. 14:23). The Bible also says, "Be sure your sin will find you out" (Num. 32:23). This is exactly what happened to Jacob. He had no more than left the room when Esau came in from his hunting (Gen. 27:30). When Esau discovered that Jacob had stolen the blessing, he wept over his failure to attain the blessing. Esau was reaping what he had sown. He had sold his birthright for a mess of pottage because he had despised it. He cared little about it in comparison to the desire of the moment—the gratification of his appetite. He was willing to throw away his religious privileges for a moment of satisfaction. Because of this, the Word of God refers to him as a "profane" person. Hebrews 12:16,17 warns believers: "Lest there be any fornication, or profane person, as Esau, who for one morsel of meat sold his birthright. For ye know how that afterward, when he would have inherited the blessing, he was rejected: for he found no place of repentance, though he sought it carefully with tears."

## Isaac Awakes to His Failure

Isaac also is suddenly awakened to his failure to heed God's plan. When Isaac learned that the last son to appear to him was actually Esau, he "trembled very exceedingly, and said, Who? where is he that hath taken venison, and brought it me, and I have eaten of all before thou camest, and have blessed him? yea, and he shall be blessed" (Gen. 27:33). Isaac "trembled very exceedingly," not just because he had been tricked, but because he suddenly realized how near he himself had come to upsetting God's plan. Before the sons were born, God had made it very clear that Esau, the older, was to serve Jacob, the younger. Thus, the younger was to receive the birthright and blessing. Even though Isaac knew this, he almost completely upset God's plan by attempting to give the blessing to Esau.

The fact that God had promised the blessing to Jacob causes some to say that Jacob was justified in what he did. However, the believer must never use unspiritual means to accomplish a spiritual end. Just because something is right, it should never be brought about in a wrong way.

Although Jacob had taken part in the scheme to get the birthright, he was not to enjoy its blessing until 30 years later. Rebekah and he thought they could hurry God's program by their scheming, but Jacob still had to wait.

When Isaac awakened to what he had done, he told Esau that he had blessed Jacob and said emphatically, "And he shall be blessed" (v. 33). Hebrews 11:20 comments on this incident by saying, "By faith Isaac blessed Jacob and Esau concerning things to come." This is all that God says about Isaac in the great faith chapter of Hebrews. In His grace, God passes over the weaknesses of Isaac and credits his faith.

The key to Isaac's faith is that after he realized what he had done, he emphasized that the blessing would remain Jacob's—"and he shall be blessed." Although we can never thwart God's plan, we can reap bitter results by sowing to the flesh. God's Word says that "he that soweth to his flesh shall of the flesh reap corruption" (Gal. 6:8).

Although Isaac did not upset the plan of God, he reaped serious results from what he had sown. Jacob had to flee from home as a result of his conniving. Rebekah never saw Jacob again because she died before he returned. Even though Isaac lived another 43 years after the incident of the blessing, nothing else is recorded about him except his death. After sending Jacob away, Isaac disappeared from the biblical scene. About 30 years later Jacob saw his father again, but his mother had already died. The entire family was affected because they had sown to the flesh. They had sought their selfish desires rather than seeking to please God.

In commenting on the life of Isaac, someone has said that instead of wearing out, he rusted out. How different he was from his father, Abraham. Abraham was still productive in his old age—as were such men as Moses, Joshua and Paul. Even Jacob was at his greatest peak in his last years—but not so Isaac. He was laid aside and for 43 years we know nothing about him. There is nothing recorded of him—good or bad. Doubtlessly he served God in quiet faith, even as he had done in his earlier years.

### Special Lessons

In review of Isaac's life of 180 years, there are some special lessons we should learn. It was not easy for Isaac to follow in the footsteps of his great father. In a sense, Isaac's life was made too easy because he occupied his father's position without having had his father's experiences. He passed into his inheritance without having passed through the various means of discipline that Abraham experienced. Thus, he did not realize the need of individuality of character and of the personal assertion necessary to do God's immediate will in extremely difficult situations.

There is the expression "Practice makes perfect." In an even more real sense it can be said, "Experience makes perfect." The suffering we experience in our lives brings about personal discipline. Even of the Lord Jesus Christ it is said, "Though he were a Son, yet learned he obedience by the things which he suffered" (Heb. 5:8). Jeremiah wrote: "It is good for a man that he bear the yoke in his youth" (Lam. 3:27).

Our youth today are experiencing what Isaac experienced. They find themselves living in an advanced age with advanced positions in life without having passed through the experiences of those who made these things possible. Although the younger generation does not need to experience everything we did, some extremely difficult experiences are essential for the kind of maturity God wants to produce.

Even though Isaac lacked the experience for his position, God chose to refer to Himself as "the God of Isaac." The common, everyday life of a person is precious to God. Because Isaac had faith in God and walked humbly before Him, God blotted out Isaac's mistakes and weaknesses. Those who walk humbly before God and confess their sins to Him are promised: "I will be merciful to their unrighteousness, and their sins and their iniquities will I remember no more" (Heb. 8:12).

God will also do the same for you. His Word promises: "If we confess our sins, he is faithful and just to forgive us our sins, and to cleanse us from all unrighteousness" (I John 1:9). When God forgives, He forgets. This was seen in Isaac's case, as we have noted, for when God referred to him in the New Testament, He did not mention his weaknesses—only his faith. Isaac's great mistake of seeking to pass the blessing on to Esau rather than Jacob is completely passed by in the New Testament. That sin had been covered over and removed through Christ's shed blood for the sins of the world.

In reviewing Isaac's life, we should also take special note of his spirit of meekness. All through his life his temperament was of a passive nature rather than of an active or aggressive nature. In childhood he was subjected to the insults of Ishmael, but there is no record that he became angry about them. As a young man he was taken to Mount Moriah to be offered as a sacrifice, and in meekness he surrendered and made himself available. He did not even choose his own wife, as she was chosen for him through his father's arrangements and the leading of the Holy Spirit. Isaac also accepted the rebuke of Abimelech in meekness. There were no reprisals. He and his men yielded whenever they were wrongly driven away from the wells they had redug. Isaac's meek spirit brought forth praise from even his enemies. They testified concerning his great power and might and their realization that the Lord was with him.

The world thinks little of meekness, yet it is the fruit of the Holy Spirit (Gal. 5:23). Christ Himself spoke of the reward of the meek when He said, "Blessed are the meek: for they shall inherit the earth" (Matt. 5:5). The Apostle Paul urged all Christians: "Let your moderation be known unto all men. The Lord is at hand" (Phil. 4:5).

Meekness involves the self-sacrifice of our own desires and interests. Because Isaac gladly gave up his own personal desires, it pleased God to refer to Himself as "the God of Isaac."

Chapter 16

# The God of Jacob

The account of Isaac's life merged into that of his two sons, Esau and Jacob. In these two sons was the beginning of two different nations who have had continuous conflict throughout the centuries. These two sons also represent the conflict of the flesh and the Spirit.

Esau represents that which is natural, whereas Jacob represents that which is spiritual. The conflict between the natural and the spiritual is present in every believer's heart. It is the conflict of the two natures. The Scriptures say, "The flesh lusteth against the Spirit, and the Spirit against the flesh: and these are contrary the one to the other: so that ye cannot do the things that ye would" (Gal. 5:17). However, believers are encouraged to realize that, because of the greatness of God, the Spirit will ultimately triumph and the flesh will be brought into subjection.

In Esau we see the profane nature which despises the riches and promises of God. In Jacob we see the desire for that which is godly, even though he used fleshly (carnal) methods to attain the benefit of the promises.

In comparing Abraham, Isaac and Jacob, the Scriptures present Abraham as a trailblazer—the pioneer of faith. He had an active faith and experienced many great triumphs of faith. Isaac was a totally different type of person. He had a passive faith. Although he had his weaknesses, he was a stern believer in God. When God revealed his weaknesses to him, Isaac became stalwart in faith. He was an unassuming type of man—meek, humble, submissive. Abraham was a leader; Isaac was a follower.

Jacob's life was one of conflict. In him we see the conflict between the flesh and the Spirit. This is the key to understanding his life. Jacob's life strikingly exhibits the power of the old nature, but it also exhibits the power of God's love and grace. In Jacob we see the utter worthlessness and depravity of the human nature, but we also see the deepest instruction as to God's purpose and infinite grace.

Have you sometimes wondered why God has been so careful to tell us the weaknesses of a man's character as well as his strengths? In the biblical record God has set forth both the good and the bad things about Jacob. He has done this to magnify the riches of divine grace and to admonish us not to follow in the carnal footsteps of this patriarch. God has not recorded Jacob's sins in order to perpetuate the memory of them, for He has blotted out Jacob's sins forever—even as He does those of the believer today who confesses his sins. God tells us both the good and the bad things about Jacob so we can see him as he really was.

By contrast, the majority of human biographers gloss over the errors and infirmities of those about whom they write. Their biographies often tend to discourage the reader rather than edify him, for the main characters are not believable—they do not seem to be real persons. I have read such biographies and have been greatly challenged to live like the persons I have read about, only to discover I was devoid of that which I needed. Human historians have mostly emphasized the wonderful things, not the discouragements, heartaches and trials, of their characters. Thus, they are histories of what men ought to have been, not of what they really were. Human biographers are not able to look into the souls of the men they write about and see the carnalities there. However, in the Bible God shows us both the strengths and the weaknesses of a man's character so that we can see the same struggles in his life as we have in ours.

Believers weary of the conflict between the flesh and the Spirit, and some wonder when there will no longer be the inner struggle. As long as we are in these earthly bodies, there will be the struggle of our two natures. As we walk with God we will learn what to expect of the old nature and how to cope with it, but the conflict will always be there. Thus, God gives us the whole picture of Jacob's life so that we might see this conflict and learn for ourselves. As God worked with Jacob, little by little He was able to instill in his heart the realization that the old nature is totally depraved and nothing good can be expected of it. This is true not only of Jacob but also of all men. Abraham lied to Abimelech when he was in Egypt, and Isaac lied about the same thing when he was in Gerar. Isaac succumbed to the scheming of Rebekah and Jacob. Nothing good can be expected of the old nature.

### Jacob's True Nature

In the biblical record, God reveals the true nature of Jacob—both his deep-seated, inner longing for God's best and his human scheming and carnal methods of attaining it. God's infinite grace is revealed to us as we see how He continued lavishing on Jacob His unwearied and uncompromising love. There was nothing in Jacob that merited all of this—even as there is nothing in us that merits God's love and grace. Although Jacob continued to abase his life with his fleshly actions, God continued to work with him in patient love. God continued to pour out His love on Jacob, while never once condoning the sins of Jacob. For many years God allowed Jacob to pursue the path he had chosen. Thus, Jacob learned better lessons because of his spirit of independence. He saw the cost of trying to live his life apart from God. Jacob wanted the things of God, but he wanted them in his own way and in his own time. Jacob found it almost impossible to wait for God to work out His will in His own time.

Jacob's selfishness, which manifested itself many times, became his own rod of chastening. In patient love, God always followed Jacob, until finally Jacob came to the end of himself.

God loved Jacob, but He hated the sin and carnality of Jacob. The life of Jacob is not a demonstration of man's perseverance with God as much as it is a demonstration of God's perseverance with man. God's perseverance with His own people is also evident in the way He worked with the nation, Israel. He was with His people for 40 years in the desert. After they had come into the land of Canaan they became engrossed in idol worship, and God had to send them into Babylonian captivity to teach them severe lessons. God was with them all the while, and by the time He was through with them they had learned their lessons well. After the Babylonian captivity, widespread idol worship was never again known among the Hebrew nation. God always finishes what He begins. The Word of God assures us, "Being confident of this very thing, that he which hath begun a good work in you will perform it until the day of Jesus Christ" (Phil. 1:6). God's principle of finishing what He begins is clearly seen in the life of Jacob.

If we had been choosing a man to head a nation, I am sure we would not have chosen Jacob. He was a schemer and crooked in so many ways as he sought to gain both material and spiritual blessings. However, we have to realize that Jacob's environment was not the best. Isaac loved Esau more, whereas Rebekah loved Jacob more. With such division in the family, it is understandable that the result would be serious conflict. Rebekah helped Jacob deceive his father—she felt the end justified the means. On the other hand, Esau belittled and despised that which was spiritual. What blessing can be expected from such a family of conflict?

### But God

It is in cases like Jacob's that God delights to work. He starts where there is no promise of anything and produces something for His glory. In His sovereign will, God laid His hand on Jacob for a special purpose, and when God undertakes something no one can defeat Him. It took 30 years for God to accomplish His purpose with Jacob, but when He finished He had the kind of man He desired.

God transformed Jacob into a prince. This is all the more significant when you realize the Bible refers to Jacob as a worm. Isaiah 41:14 says, "Fear not, thou worm Jacob, and ye men of Israel; I will help thee, saith the Lord, and thy redeemer, the Holy One of Israel." What is weaker and more worthless than a worm? This is what God thought of Jacob. But God stooped to associate Himself with one of the weakest and least attractive of our human race. God chose to transform Jacob from a worm into a prince. This gives us the key regarding God's choice of Jacob. The warped character of Jacob provided a suitable background for the display of God's grace.

If God chose only the strong, the noble, and the brilliant, the vast majority of us would be disqualified. But it pleases God to choose what the world considers foolish in order to confound the wisdom of the world. The Apostle Paul wrote: "Because the foolishness of God is wiser than men; and the weakness of God is stronger than men. For ye see your calling, brethren, how that not many wise men after the flesh, not many mighty, not many noble, are called: But God hath chosen the foolish things of the world to confound the wise; and God hath chosen the weak things of the world to confound the things which are mighty; And base things of the world, and things which are despised, hath God chosen, yea, and things which are not, to bring to nought things that are: That no flesh should glory in his presence" (I Cor. 1:25-29).

In Psalm 22, it is prophetically said of Christ, "I am a worm, and no man; a reproach of men, and despised of the people. All they that see me laugh me to scorn: they shoot out the lip, they shake the head, saying, He trusted on the Lord that he would deliver him: let him deliver him, seeing he delighted in him" (vv. 6-8). It was even prophesied of Jesus Christ Himself that He would be a worm in the eyes of the world, yet it was He who provided salvation for the sins of the world. The wisdom of the world was confounded by God.

None of us are worthy of God's grace and mercy, but it pleases Him to choose us so He might display His glory through us. This is why He chose Jacob—to make a prince out of a worm.

How wonderful it is that God condescends to be called "the God of Jacob." Only God could see the princely qualities in this unattractive man. Yes, He is the God of the misfit. He is the God of the warped personality. He delights to begin where others have given up in despair. Perhaps you do not see anything of value in your life. Give God a chance to make you into what He wants you to be. Perhaps you have too high a value on your life; thus, you do not realize your need of God. But if you see nothing in your life, then there is hope. It is in such a life that God delights to work. Yield yourself to God so He might do His perfect work in you.

Chapter 17

# Jacob's Birth

Jacob was a miracle child. Abraham and Sarah had waited 25 years for Isaac to be born, and Isaac and Rebekah waited 20 years for the birth of Jacob. Genesis 25:21,22 says, "Isaac intreated the Lord for his wife, because she was barren: and the Lord was intreated of him, and Rebekah his wife conceived. And the children struggled together within her; and she said, If it be so, why am I thus? And she went to enquire of the Lord." Rebekah did not know there were twins in her womb and she could not understand what the trouble was. God allowed this to happen to her so He could reveal His plan for the children she would bear.

God explained to Rebekah, "Two nations are in thy womb, and two manner of people shall be separated from thy bowels; and the one people shall be stronger than the other people; and the elder shall serve the younger" (v. 23). God told Rebekah that two nations would come into existence from her two children. These nations would have much conflict, just as there was conflict between the two sons in her womb.

Romans 9:13 makes a startling statement. It quotes God as saying, "Jacob have I loved, but Esau have I hated." Here the words "loved" and "hated" are not so much words of emotion as they are words of extreme comparison. They are used in the comparative way in Luke 14:26: "If any man come to me, and hate not his father, and mother, and wife, and children, and brethren, and sisters, yea, and his own life also, he cannot be my disciple." The word "hate" in this verse is used in a different way than it is commonly used today. The Lord was emphasizing that when our love for relatives and self is compared to our love for Him, our love for relatives and self should seem as though it were hate in comparison to our love for Him.

In Romans 9:13 the matter of choice seems to be emphasized also through the strong words of contrast. In God's sovereign grace and eternal purpose, He chose Jacob and the nation that would come into existence through him. The context of Romans 9 tells us, "And not only this; but when Rebecca [Rebekah] also had conceived by one, even by our father Isaac; (For the children being not yet born, neither having done any good or evil, that the purpose of God according to election might stand, not of works, but of him that calleth;) It was said unto her, The elder shall serve the younger. As it is written, Jacob have I loved, but Esau have I hated" (vv. 10-13).

This does not mean that Esau was damned before his birth, but it does emphasize the extreme contrast of God's dealing with these two men. Because God had chosen Jacob, His dealings with Esau seemed as hatred in comparison.

The choice between the two individuals involved the choice of nations, because nations were to be born of Jacob and Esau. God chose the Israelites, not the Edomites, to fulfill His plan. God's choice was not made on the basis of merit but according to His sovereign grace before the sons were born.

Faith, not merit, is the principle of sonship. God knew that Esau would be void of faith; therefore, he was not chosen. God is not arbitrary or biased in His choosing—nor can we charge Him with favoritism. God's choice between Jacob and Esau was not made out of favoritism but out of discernment.

Another of God's choices is also referred to in I Peter 1:2: "Elect according to the foreknowledge of God the Father." The word "elect" means "to choose." Election is according to the foreknowledge of God and is wholly of grace, apart from all human merit. Election proceeds from divine volition, for we are told in John 15:16, "Ye have not chosen me, but I have chosen you." Verse 19 of the same chapter records the words of Christ who said, "I have chosen you out of the world."

Election is the sovereign act of God whereby certain persons are chosen for distinctive services for Him. It primarily involves service, not salvation. Esau could have placed his faith in God and perhaps did, but the Scriptures do not indicate that he did. God knew Jacob and Esau before their birth.

### Jacob's Spiritual Conflict

In spite of all of Jacob's meanness and trickery, he had a genuine desire for spiritual things. He often violated his spiritual desires, but he persisted in spiritual things through God's dealing with him. It is one of the keys to his life to realize that in spite of his many weaknesses and failures, he had great aspirations for the deep and spiritual things of God.

By contrast, Esau was outwardly attractive and generous, yet inwardly he despised heavenly values. He preferred to gratify his sensual desires rather than setting his heart on spiritual values.

In God's foreknowledge, He knew all of this about Jacob and Esau before they were born. Thus, He was fully able to make a choice between them before their birth.

Even the birth of Jacob and Esau shows their great difference in character. The Scriptures record: "When her days to be delivered were fulfilled, behold, there were twins in her womb. And the first came out red, all over like an hairy garment; and they called his name Esau. And after that came his brother out, and his hand took hold on Esau's heel; and his name was called Jacob: and Isaac was threescore years old when she bare them" (Gen. 25:24-26).

Because the firstborn was hairy, he was called "Esau," which means "hairy." The second son was named "Jacob," which means "supplanter." When Jacob came out of the womb he took hold of Esau's heel. This was symbolic of his life, for Jacob went through life taking advantage of others—tripping them up so he could get ahead.

As to character, Esau was a shallow person. Hebrews 12:16 refers to him as a "profane person." The word "profane" means "impious" or "unhallowed." Esau lacked affinity for God. In Esau we see only the old nature—at times looking good outwardly but being totally corrupt inwardly. There is no record that Esau ever had an altar or that he was concerned about his spiritual relationship with God.

In Jacob we see both natures prominently, as well as the conflict that waged between them. Jacob not only had the old nature which he inherited from Adam, but he also had a new nature from God because of his faith in God. Hosea 12:3,4 emphasizes both natures of Jacob when it says, "He took his brother by the heel in the womb, and by his strength he had power with God: Yea, he had power over the angel, and prevailed: he wept, and made supplication unto him: he found him in Beth-el, and there he spake with us." Only the believer has two natures, because the new nature is received only by placing faith in God.

Man customarily looks at that which is worst in his fellowman, but God always searches out the best so that He might perfect it and release it through the person's life. God saw in Jacob tremendous spiritual possibilities and worked with him for 30 years to bring these about.

The difference between Jacob and Esau became more prominent as they grew older. Genesis 25:27 says, "And the boys grew: and Esau was a cunning hunter, a man of the field; and Jacob was a plain man, dwelling in tents." Esau loved the outdoors—he was "a man of the field." By contrast, Jacob was "a plain man, dwelling in tents."

The word "plain" is from a Hebrew word that is translated "perfect" nine times in the *King James Version*. It does not mean perfect in the sense of sinless perfection but refers to one who is right with God. However the word "plain" as used to describe Jacob seems also to emphasize a disposition that finds pleasure in the quiet life of home—in contrast to the wild hunter's life led by Esau. The context of

Genesis 25:27 indicates that the word "plain" emphasizes Jacob's personal desires rather than his spiritual character.

The significance of tent-dwelling has been pointed out in regard to Abraham's life. Hebrews 11:9,10 says of Abraham, "By faith he sojourned in the land of promise, as in a strange country, dwelling in tabernacles [tents] with Isaac and Jacob, the heirs with him of the same promise: For he looked for a city which hath foundations, whose builder and maker is God." A tent characterizes a person who realizes he is a stranger and pilgrim in a country. Spiritually, this was true of Abraham and Jacob but not of Esau. This points out to us again the spiritual desires Jacob had even though he fell so far short so many times. His spiritual aspirations provided God with the basis for His continued pursuit of Jacob and for the disciplines which were to shape his character. Despite Jacob's failures, there was always the undercurrent of faith. This also helps explain what is meant by God's statement: "Jacob have I loved, but Esau have I hated" (Rom. 9:13).

Chapter 18

# The Birthright

The first pact made between Esau and Jacob as grown men concerned the birthright. The boys had grown up in a home of conflict because the parents were guilty of favoritism. The Scriptures point out that "Isaac loved Esau, because he did eat of his venison: but Rebekah loved Jacob" (Gen. 25:28). Before the birth of the children God had told Rebekah that "the elder shall serve the younger" (v. 23). No doubt this was common knowledge in the family and resulted in more conflict because of the favoritism of the parents.

In Old Testament times the birthright was a most cherished possession. It consisted of the excellency of dignity and power. Usually it involved a double portion of inheritance, plus other special blessings. Concerning the birthright, C. I. Scofield noted: "The 'birthright' had three elements: (1) Until the establishment of the Aaronic priesthood, the head of the family exercised priestly rights. (2) The Abrahamic family held the Edenic promise of the Satan-Bruiser (Gen. 3:15)–Abel, Seth, Shem, Abraham, Isaac, Esau. (3) Esau, as the firstborn, was in the direct line of the Abrahamic promise of the Earth-Blesser (Gen. 12:3). For all that was revealed, in Esau might have been fulfilled those two great Messianic promises" (*Scofield Reference Bible*, p. 38).

Esau's sale of the birthright is recorded in Genesis 25:29-34: "And Jacob sod [boiled] pottage: and Esau came from the field, and he was faint: And Esau said to Jacob, Feed me, I pray thee, with that same red pottage; for I am faint: therefore was his name called Edom. And Jacob said, Sell me this day thy birthright. And Esau said, Behold, I am at the point to die: and what profit shall this birthright do to me? And Jacob said, Swear to me this day; and he sware unto him: and he sold his birthright unto Jacob. Then Jacob gave Esau bread and pottage of lentiles; and he did eat and drink, and rose up, and went his way: thus Esau despised his birthright."

Jacob had been waiting for an opportunity to get the birthright from Esau. It was noble and right that Jacob expected the birthright inasmuch as God had promised that the elder would serve the younger, but Jacob's methods of obtaining it were entirely wrong. Jacob sought the right thing in the wrong way. Using carnal methods to attain spiritual goals is never acceptable to God. Jacob felt that the end justified the means.

In this incident we see the value of waiting for God. The birthright was Jacob's by God's determinate will and, in due time, He was going to give it to Jacob. Although Jacob connived to get the birthright, it was 30 years later before he actually benefited from it. Jacob knew the importance of believing God, but he did not know the importance of waiting on God.

We also need to learn the discipline of patiently waiting on God to fulfill His will in His own time. God's Word says, "Cast not away therefore your confidence, which hath great recompence of reward. For ye have need of patience, that, after ye have done the will of God, ye might receive the promise" (Heb. 10:35,36).

Although Jacob schemed to get possession of the birthright, God did not permit him to receive its benefits until he first acknowledged Esau as the rightful owner from the human standpoint. How different Jacob's life would have been if he would have patiently waited on God to give him the birthright.

Jacob watched for his opportunity to catch his brother off guard so he could get the birthright from him. The time came. Esau came home from the field completely exhausted. Esau thought he was about to starve and he was willing to do almost anything to get something to eat. Jacob took advantage of the opportunity. He offered Esau something to eat if Esau would sell him his birthright.

### The Bargain of the Brothers

As Esau thought about Jacob's proposition, he said, "Behold I am at the point to die: and what profit shall this birthright do to me?" (Gen. 25:32). With an attitude like this, Esau was an easy victim to Jacob who said, "Swear to me this day; and he sware unto him: and he sold his birthright unto Jacob" (v. 33).

The Scriptures conclude the account of the sale of the birthright by saying, "Then Jacob gave Esau bread and pottage of lentiles; and he did eat and drink, and rose up, and went his way: thus Esau despised his birthright" (v. 34). The meal was served and eaten—and God's evaluation of Esau's action was recorded.

In selling his birthright, Esau revealed his true character. Notice especially his attitude as revealed by his words: "I am at the point to die: and what profit shall this birthright do to me?" (v. 32). Although at the time the threat of death seemed great to him, it is probably true that he also looked to the future and, knowing that all die sometime, he saw no value in the birthright. He was intent on those things that brought gratification for the moment—he set no value on that which was spiritual. As far as Esau was concerned, future blessings were intangible. He saw no need to grasp after a blessing that could not be enjoyed at the moment. Only the present time held reality for Esau.

Esau was supplanted by Jacob, but Esau really deceived himself. There is no excuse for what he did. The divine commentary on his action is given in Hebrews 12:16,17: "Lest there be any fornicator, or profane person, as Esau, who for one morsel of meat sold his birthright. For ye know how that afterward, when he would have inherited the blessing, he was rejected: for he found no place of repentance, though he sought it carefully with tears."

Esau would not have died from hunger—his parents were there, as well as other relatives who would have taken care of him. This also indicates that his concern about death had as much to do with the future as it did with the present. As he reflected on the fact that he would die someday, he thought the promises to the seed of Abraham were useless to him. In effect, he said, "I cannot live on promises. Give me something to eat and drink now. Tomorrow I die and nothing else will matter then."

Many Christians today are also more concerned about the present than they are about the future. They live for today only and are unconcerned about tomorrow. This was not true of Moses because when he considered the future he "refused to be called the son of Pharaoh's daughter; Choosing rather to suffer affliction with the people of God, than to enjoy the pleasures of sin for a season; Esteeming the reproach of Christ greater riches than the treasures in Egypt: for he had respect unto the recompence of the reward" (Heb. 11:24-26).

How different Esau was from Abraham and Isaac—even Jacob. Hebrews 11:13,14 says of Abraham and other men of God: "These all died in faith, not having received the promises, but having seen them afar off, and were persuaded of them, and embraced them, and confessed that they were strangers and pilgrims on the earth. For they that say such things declare plainly that they seek a country." This was not true of Esau. He lived for the present, not the future.

Both Jacob and Esau were at fault in the sale of the birthright. Jacob was in the wrong because he bought something that God had promised would eventually be his on the basis of faith. Esau was in the wrong because he sold something that was not really his to sell.

## The Believer's Birthright

The believer today also has a birthright. It is not material but spiritual. Romans 8:16,17 tells us, "The Spirit itself beareth witness with our spirit, that we are the children of

God: And if children, then heirs; heirs of God, and joint-heirs with Christ; if so be that we suffer with him, that we may be also glorified together." In verse 32 of this same chapter we are told, "He that spared not his own Son, but delivered him up for us all, how shall he not with him also freely give us all things?" From these verses we see that we are joint heirs with Christ; thus, we have a spiritual birthright, for we will inherit spiritual blessings.

In the first chapter of Ephesians, the Apostle Paul emphasized how the Christian is blessed, chosen, predestinated and accepted in Christ (vv. 3-7). Chapter 2 reminds us that "even when we were dead in sins, [God] hath quickened us together with Christ, (by grace ye are saved;) And hath raised us up together, and made us sit together in heavenly places in Christ Jesus" (vv. 5,6). We are seated with him so we might walk with Him, serve Him, and enter into spiritual warfare with Him.

Having received Jesus Christ as your Saviour, are you walking with Him today in service? Are you involved in the spiritual warfare? Even the spiritual warfare is part of what we inherit because of our spiritual birthright. Even though you are a Christian, perhaps you are only living for the pleasures of the moment and want no part of a spiritual warfare. If this is true, then you are as Esau, who despised his birthright and sold it for a mess of pottage. All that we have here on earth is nothing but a mess of pottage in comparison to what we will have throughout all eternity.

The birthright belongs to the one born first. Since Jesus Christ was "the firstborn from the dead" (Col. 1:18), the spiritual birthright belongs to Him. Having received Jesus Christ as Saviour, we become joint heirs with Him and inherit the blessings of the spiritual birthright.

Consider this One with whom we are joint heirs. Colossians 1 tells us that "by him were all things created, that are in heaven, and that are in earth, visible and invisible, whether they be thrones, or dominions, or principalities, or powers: all things were created by him, and for him: And he is before all things, and by him all things consist. And he is the head of the body, the church: who is the beginning, the firstborn from the dead; that in all things he might have the preeminence. For it pleased the Father that in him should all fulness dwell" (vv. 16-19).

Colossians 2:9,10 says, "For in him dwelleth all the fulness of the Godhead bodily. And ye are complete in him, which is the head of all principality and power." We have everything in Christ Jesus—we are complete in Him.

Believers are told in Ephesians 1:22,23 that God "hath put all things under his [Christ's] feet, and gave him to be the head over all things to the church, Which is his body, the fulness of him that filleth all in all." He that fills the whole universe also fills the body of every believer. In Christ Jesus we have this birthright.

It is important that we understand what is meant by being "in Christ." This expression refers to place or position in that everyone who receives Christ as Saviour is placed into the Body of Christ by the baptism of the Holy Spirit (I Cor. 12:13). Because our position is "in Christ" we are to be "in union with" Him—letting Him have control of our lives.

The believer's union with Christ is seen from the Apostle Paul's words in Galatians 2:20: "I am crucified with Christ: nevertheless I live; yet not I, but Christ liveth in me: and the life which I now live in the flesh I live by the faith of the Son of God, who loved me, and gave himself for me." Christ and the believer are united in one—Christ is the believer's life. The importance of Christ being in the believer is seen from Colossians 1:27: "Christ in you, the hope of glory."

### A Life of Faith

All of this refers to a life of faith. You cannot buy it as Jacob bought the birthright. Colossians 2:6 says, "As ye have therefore received Christ Jesus the Lord, so walk ye in him." How did we receive Christ? We received Him by faith. Therefore, we are to walk; that is, live the Christian life by faith. We are to be "rooted and built up in him, and stablished in the faith" (v. 7). Our need is to appropriate what we have in Christ Jesus. Do you want to appropriate the blessings of your spiritual birthright? If so, "set your affection on things above, not on things on the earth. For ye are dead, and your life is hid with Christ in God. When Christ, who is our life, shall appear, then shall ye also appear with him in glory" (3:2-4). When we appear with Christ in glory we will then fully possess all that He has for us.

Emphasizing this same truth, the Apostle John wrote: "Behold, what manner of love the Father hath bestowed upon us, that we should be called the sons of God: therefore the world knoweth us not, because it knew him not. Beloved, now are we the sons of God, and it doth not yet appear what we shall be: but we know that, when he shall appear, we shall be like him; for we shall see him as he is. And every man that hath this hope in him purifieth himself, even as he is pure" (I John 3:1-3).

We cannot buy that which is ours through union with the Lord Jesus Christ. It can only be appropriated through faith. Jacob desired the birthright and the accompanying blessings, but he utterly failed to realize that these could be his only by faith. Because he used carnal methods in seeking the birthright, God had to discipline him to bring him into submission. It took Jacob 30 years to learn the lesson God had for him.

## Esau's Attitude

After Esau had sold the birthright to Jacob and had finished eating and drinking, he "rose up, and went his way" (Gen. 25:34). God added the words "thus Esau despised his birthright." The word "despise" means "to look down on with contempt or aversion." It also means "to regard as negligible, worthless, or distasteful." Esau treated his birthright with contempt and, because he regarded it as nothing, he willingly sold it for the satisfaction of the moment.

What are you doing with the privileges you have as a result of being united with Christ? Are you regarding as nothing and treating with contempt the blessings you have because you are a joint heir with Christ? Part of the responsibility of this birthright has a ministry attached to it—the taking of the gospel to all the world. It is a responsibility that is ours because we are one in Christ—it is not an optional ministry.

The Scriptures refer to others besides Esau who despised God's provisions for them. The Israelites were promised the land of Canaan, but God's Word says, "Yea, they despised the pleasant land, they believed not his word: But murmured in their tents, and hearkened not unto the voice of the Lord. Therefore he lifted up his hand against them, to overthrow them in the wilderness" (Ps. 106:24-26). The Israelites were more concerned about that which had to do with the flesh than about that which had to do with the Spirit.

Not only did the Israelites despise the land, but they also despised the One who came to be their Messiah. The Book of Zechariah predicted their rejection of Christ: "If ye think good, give me my price; and if not, forbear. So they weighed for my price thirty pieces of silver. And the Lord said unto me, Cast it unto the potter: a goodly price that I was prised at of them. And I took the thirty pieces of silver, and cast them to the potter in the house of the Lord" (11:12,13). In particular, it was Judas who betrayed the Lord and later threw down the money in the temple, but it was the religious leaders who were responsible for this. They bargained for Christ—to get rid of Him for 30 pieces of silver. Even as Esau despised his birthright, they despised the blessing that could have come to them through the Messiah.

In the Gospel of Matthew we read of those who despised their invitation to the marriage feast. In chapter 22 Jesus spoke a parable and said, "The kingdom of heaven is like unto a certain king, which made a marriage for his son, And sent forth his servants to call them that were bidden to the wedding: and they would not come. Again, he sent forth other servants, saying, Tell them which are bidden, Behold, I have prepared my dinner: my oxen and my fatlings are killed, and all things are ready: come unto the marriage. But they made light of it, and went their ways, one to his farm, another to his merchandise: And the remnant took his servants, and entreated them spitefully, and slew them" (vv. 2-6). These "made light of" the invitation to the wedding feast. They regarded it as nothing—they despised it.

Have you despised God's invitation—especially His invitation for you to receive Christ as Saviour? If you have received Christ as Saviour, have you regarded as nothing His invitation for you to be a co-laborer with Him in a spiritual ministry here on earth? Those of us who know Him as Saviour will one day stand before Him to give an account for what we have done for Him. Second Corinthians 5:10 reminds every believer: "For we must all appear before the judgment seat of Christ; that every one may receive the things done in his body, according to that he hath done, whether it be good or bad."

Those who reject Jesus Christ as Saviour often look with contempt on the goodness of God. The Apostle Paul asked such unbelievers, "Despisest thou the riches of his goodness and forbearance and longsuffering; not knowing that the goodness of God leadeth thee to repentance?" (Rom. 2:4). The goodness, forbearance and long-suffering of God lead the unbeliever to repent of his sins and to receive Christ as Saviour. These attributes also cause the believer to change his mind about living for the things of the world and lead him to decide to begin living for the Lord.

We may be sure that our sins will find us out. God's Word assures us of this, and Jacob's life graphically portrayed this truth. As we carefully consider God's dealing with Jacob during the 30 years after he bought the birthright, we see the results of refusing to dare to walk with God. Jacob wanted God's best, but his error was in thinking he could obtain it by carnal means.

The God of Jacob is the God of long-suffering. Psalm 146:5 says, "Happy is he that hath the God of Jacob for his help, whose hope is in the Lord his God." God dealt with Jacob in long-suffering and He deals with present-day believers in the same way. How thankful we can be that our God is the God of Jacob, because we are in desperate need of His long-suffering.

Chapter 19

# The Stolen Blessing

One act of faithlessness leads to another. Having secured the birthright by his schemes, this led Jacob to deceive his father in order to secure the blessing, which was a vital part of the birthright. Jacob needed not only the birthright from Esau but also the blessing from his father. One was of no value without the other.

Consider the birthright and blessing of present-day believers. Our birthright, as we have indicated, is that which we have through our union with Jesus Christ. Our blessing is that which we have through the Holy Spirit. All that Christ is and shares with us is made real to us by the Holy Spirit. Before Christ ascended to heaven, He promised, "All things that the Father hath are mine: therefore said I, that he [the Holy Spirit] shall take of mine, and shall shew it unto you" (John 16:15). The birthright is ours because we are in Christ, and the blessing is ours because the Holy Spirit takes the things of Christ and makes them ours as we dare to believe Him.

The key to the Holy Spirit's blessing us is our attitude toward Christ. The Lord Jesus said, "If any man thirst, let him come unto me, and drink" (7:37). Jacob thirsted for the blessing of God. He longed to have what God wanted him to have. However, Jacob's problem was how to get what God wanted him to have. Jacob failed in his attitude toward God in that he failed to believe God for the blessings he was to have. As we have seen from the words of Christ in John 7:37,

His command for us to "drink" is a command for us to take by faith what He has made available for us. Faith is the basis for our receiving the blessing that goes along with our birthright in Christ.

Isaac's weakness led to a plot by Rebekah and Jacob which dishonored God. "It came to pass, that when Isaac was old, and his eyes were dim, so that could not see, he called Esau his eldest son, and said unto him, My son: and he said unto him, Behold, here am I. And he said, Behold now, I am old, I know not the day of my death: Now therefore take, I pray thee, thy weapons, thy quiver and thy bow, and go out to the field, and take me some venison; And make me savoury meat, such as I love, and bring it to me, that I may eat; that my soul may bless thee before I die" (Gen. 27:1-4).

Isaac loved Esau very much. The Scripture gives us the reason for this love when it says, "Isaac loved Esau, because he did eat of his venison" (25:28). In his old age, Isaac's love for Esau—because of the venison—became more prominent. This love for Esau took such preeminence in Isaac's life that he made preparations to act in direct opposition to the divine counsel that he was to give the birthright blessing to the younger son rather than to the older. God had made it clear to Isaac and Rebekah that "the elder shall serve the younger" (v. 23). Isaac's physical eyes were dim, and so were his spiritual eyes. Esau had sold his birthright for a mess of pottage, and Isaac was now about to give away the blessing for a mess of venison. Just as there was no excuse for Esau's act, there was no excuse for Isaac's.

Esau was quite willing to go along with his father's suggestion. Surely he also knew of the divine plan that the elder was to serve the younger. However, after pondering for some time his loss of the birthright because of Jacob's scheming, Esau was willing to do anything to reclaim his birthright. This provides a good illustration of reformation without regeneration. Esau was trying to change things by what he did, but there was no indication he had faith in God.

### Rebekah's Counterplot

Although Esau was the favorite son of his father, Jacob was the favorite son of his mother. Isaac was making plans to pass the blessing on to his favorite son, but Rebekah was not about to have Jacob left out—especially since God had indicated the blessing was to be Jacob's. Rebekah devised a counterplot. Her intent was to preserve for Jacob what God had intended for him. Her motive was a good one and was no doubt inspired by pure religious aspirations. To her, it seemed that God's purpose was in danger. She felt she must prevent great harm from coming to God's declared purpose concerning Jacob.

Genesis 27 says, "And Rebekah heard when Isaac spake to Esau his son. And Esau went to the field to hunt for venison, and to bring it. And Rebekah spake unto Jacob her son, saying, Behold, I heard thy father speak unto Esau thy brother, saying, Bring me venison, and make me savoury meat, that I may eat, and bless thee before the Lord before my death. Now therefore, my son, obey my voice according to that which I command thee. Go now to the flock, and fetch me from thence two good kids of the goats; and I will make them savoury meat for thy father, such as he loveth: And thou shalt bring it to thy father, that he may eat, and that he may bless thee before his death" (vv. 5-10).

Jacob had his doubts as to whether Isaac could be fooled, for he said, "Behold, Esau my brother is a hairy man, and I am a smooth man: My father peradventure will feel me, and I shall seem to him as a deceiver; and I shall bring a curse upon me, and not a blessing" (vv. 11,12). However, Rebekah counted the cost and told Jacob, "Upon me be thy curse, my son: only obey my voice, and go fetch me them" (v. 13). Rebekah was willing to suffer the curse herself if Isaac became wise to her plot.

Rebekah's sin was that she lacked faith in God's ability. She felt she had to help God accomplish His will. While the intended goal was legitimate, the means she used to accomplish the goal were not honoring to God. She thought

God must be frustrated concerning His plan and, therefore, needed her help. In this regard, Rebekah was like Sarah. Because Sarah was unable to bear children, she suggested that Abraham produce a child through her maid, Hagar. Sarah wanted to help God. Rebekah had the same lack of faith about God's being able to fulfill His plan.

Some people say, "The Lord helps those who help themselves." This is not true. The truth is that God helps those who come to the end of themselves. What we need is patience to wait on God. He is well able to do everything He has said He would do, and He will always do it on time. Even the Son of God Himself had to wait on the Father to fulfill His plan. The Father promised the Son, "Sit thou at my right hand, until I make thine enemies thy footstool" (Ps. 110:1). From the Scriptures we realize that such exaltation for the Son came only after His humiliation. Philippians 2 tells us how Christ willingly gave up the position He had with the Father and came to earth to die on the cross. Because of His willing humiliation, "God also hath highly exalted him, and given him a name which is above every name: That at the name of Jesus every knee should bow, of things in heaven, and things in earth, and things under the earth; And that every tongue should confess that Jesus Christ is Lord, to the glory of God the Father" (vv. 9-11). But even the Son of God had to wait. No doubt this element is also in view when we are told, "Let this mind be in you, which was also in Christ Jesus" (v. 5).

Jacob and his mother knew very little about waiting for God's time and God's way. They preferred their time and their way. They had not yet learned to depend on God to fulfill His own promises. Possibly this never was learned by Rebekah, and it took at least 30 more years for Jacob to learn it.

Consider how much trouble could be averted if we would learn to wait on God. It does not take a great mind to think of ways God could have prevented Esau from actually getting the blessing. God could have brought a serious illness on Isaac until he had time to think about what he was really doing.

There are many things God could have done, but Rebekah did not have faith that God's plan was going to work out without her help. She felt it was up to her to devise means to help God out of His dilemma.

Although Jacob hesitated in taking part in his mother's plot, he did not seem as concerned about the sinfulness of such an act as he was about being caught. He was afraid his father would feel him and he would "seem to him as a deceiver" (Gen. 27:12). Doing something that would dishonor God did not trouble Jacob as much as the thought that he might be caught in the act. Most people experience sorrow over sin when they are found out in their sin. However, it is usually that they are sorry they have been caught instead of sorry that they have sinned against God.

Jacob was afraid that he might "seem" to be a deceiver, but the facts were that by taking part in the plot he actually was a deceiver. He was refusing to call sin, sin.

In Rebekah and Jacob's plot we see their old natures seeking to take advantage of the old natures of Isaac and Esau. All of them were in the wrong and each was seeking his own good rather than God's will and purpose. God will not bless what He has destined should not be blessed. Rebekah and Jacob did not have faith to believe this. They did not have enough faith to trust God to abort Isaac's plan to bless Esau. God would have seen to it that His will was performed. After all, it was God who would do the blessing through human instrumentality. This incident shows us the seriousness of trying to run ahead of the Lord.

As Rebekah's plot unfolded, Jacob's true nature was revealed. Instead of shrinking back in horror from the sin of deception, he occupied himself with thinking about the possible unpleasant consequences of the sin.

After Rebekah had assured Jacob that the curse would be upon her if he were found out and had commanded him again to get the two young goats, Jacob "went, and fetched, and brought them to his mother: and his mother made savoury meat, such as his father loved. And Rebekah took goodly raiment of her eldest son Esau, which were with her in the house, and put them upon Jacob her younger son: And she put the skins of the kids of the goats upon his hands, and upon the smooth of his neck: And she gave the savoury meat and the bread, which she had prepared, into the hand of her son Jacob" (vv. 14-17).

The question arises, Who was more to blame—the mother or the son? Although we are not able to stand as judge, it is evident that Rebekah had direct communication from God that Jacob was going to receive the blessing (25:23). In light of this promise, she should have had enough faith in God to realize His plan would not be thwarted. Rebekah had reason to distrust her husband—he had been willing to sacrifice her chastity to save his own life—but she had no reason to distrust God. Although neither Rebekah nor Jacob could be excused for what they did, it seems that the greater responsibility was Rebekah's because of her communication from God.

## Sin Upon Sin

Once the plot was put into operation, Rebekah and Jacob kept heaping one sin onto another. Genesis 27:18-20 says of Jacob that "he came unto his father, and said, My father: and he said, Here am I; who art thou, my son? And Jacob said unto his father, I am Esau thy firstborn; I have done according as thou badest me: arise, I pray thee, sit and eat of my venison, that thy soul may bless me. And Isaac said unto his son, How is it that thou hast found it so quickly, my son? And he said, Because the Lord thy God brought it to me."

One lie always leads to another lie. Jacob kept adding sins to his previous sins. First, he impersonated his brother. Second, he lied to his father when he said, "I am Esau." Finally, he even went so far as to bring the name of the Lord into his deceit, for he said, "because the Lord thy God brought it to me." Jacob most probably did not anticipate all of his father's questions; therefore, he had to have quick answers, which caused him to get into deeper and deeper trouble with his lies.

We can be sure that the Devil was supplying him with answers and encouraging him even to invoke the name of God to make his deception seem plausible. In Psalm 1:1 we see the progression of sin: "Blessed is the man that walketh not in the counsel of the ungodly, nor standeth in the way of sinners, nor sitteth in the seat of the scornful." Notice the words "walketh . . . standeth . . . sitteth." How much we blame the Lord for things which are nothing but acts of the flesh—the reaping of what we have sown. How tragic it is when we blame the Lord for the works of the flesh.

As Jacob stood before his father, Isaac said, "Come near, I pray thee, that I may feel thee, my son, whether thou be my very son Esau or not. And Jacob went near unto Isaac his father; and he felt him, and said, The voice is Jacob's voice, but the hands are the hands of Esau. And he discerned him not, because his hands were hairy, as his brother Esau's hands: so he blessed him" (Gen. 27:21-23).

Jacob must have thought the scheme had worked. No doubt Rebekah was carefully listening to what was going on in Isaac's tent and also thought, It worked! So thought the flesh. The flesh prides itself on its achievements. But there were to be many sad results from the works of the flesh.

Isaac's lack of discernment was due partially to his reliance on feelings. His eyes were dim and he needed to rely on his sense of touch, but he also relied too much on his emotions. He was seeking to bless Esau because of his love for him rather than acting in accordance with what God had said about the elder serving the younger. We, too, are often guilty of acting in accordance with the way we feel rather than in accordance with "Thus saith the Lord."

After Isaac felt Jacob's hands, he said, "Art thou my very son Esau? And he said, I am. And he said, Bring it near to me, and I will eat of my son's venison, that my soul may bless thee. And he brought it near to him, and he did eat: and he brought him wine, and he drank" (vv. 24,25).

## Deceived by a Kiss

Isaac then said to his son, "Come near now, and kiss me, my son. And he came near, and kissed him: and he smelled the smell of his raiment, and blessed him, and said, See, the smell of my son is as the smell of a field which the Lord hath blessed: Therefore God give thee of the dew of heaven, and the fatness of the earth, and plenty of corn and wine: Let people serve thee, and nations bow down to thee: be lord over thy brethren, and let thy mother's sons bow down to thee: cursed be every one that curseth thee, and blessed be he that blesseth thee" (vv. 26-29).

A kiss was part of Jacob's deception of Isaac, even as a kiss was part of Judas' betrayal of Christ. Isaac was deceived and he pronounced the blessing on Jacob, but it was a long time before the blessing was fulfilled to Jacob. Because he had to reap what he had sown before he was ready to receive the benefits, 30 years passed before Jacob realized the benefits of the blessing. Again we are reminded of the words: "Be not deceived; God is not mocked: for whatsoever a man soweth, that shall he also reap" (Gal. 6:7). Jacob had sown to the flesh, and he reaped the results. Among the things he reaped were: his brother wanted to murder him; he had to flee from his father's house; he never saw his mother again; Laban deceived him for 20 years; he had to sneak away from Laban; some of his sons were wicked, and his own heart was broken later because his sons sold Joseph into Egypt. Jacob had many lessons to learn because of his reliance on the flesh to obtain spiritual blessing.

## Esau's Defeat

Jacob's deception had brought defeat to Esau. The Bible says, "And it came to pass, as soon as Isaac had made an end of blessing Jacob, and Jacob was yet scarce gone out from the presence of Isaac his father, that Esau his brother came in from his hunting. And he also had made savoury meat, and brought it unto his father, and said unto his father, Let my father arise, and eat of his son's venison, that thy soul may bless me. And Isaac his father said unto him, Who art thou? And he said, I am thy son, thy firstborn Esau" (Gen. 27:30-32).

Jacob was found out! God's Word warns: "Be sure your sin will find you out" (Num. 32:23). Although in some cases a person's sin is not evident for a long time, in Jacob's case it took only a short time. He was suddenly found out as the schemer. The Bible does not tell us how much Isaac knew about Rebekah's part in the scheming. Perhaps he later learned all the details, but Jacob was completely found out immediately.

There is no escape from God's all-seeing eye. In Hebrews 2:3 the question is asked, "How shall we escape, if we neglect so great salvation?" This verse refers to Christians who have, not just salvation, but a *great* salvation. It is a salvation that goes beyond the saving from hellfire and giving us a place in heaven. It is a salvation which also gives victory, abundant life and blessing while we are on earth. If we are viewing our salvation only as an escape from hell and neglecting the rest of it, we will not escape. The day is coming when every believer will give an account to Jesus Christ. Second Corinthians 5:10 assures us, "For we must all appear before the judgment seat of Christ; that every one may receive the things done in his body, according to that he hath done, whether it be good or bad." This does not have to do with salvation because only believers will stand before the Judgment Seat of Christ. Salvation will have already been determined. This will be a judgment for rewards, based on what we have done in this life for Jesus Christ. There will be no escaping having to answer for neglecting the abundant salvation Christ has provided for us.

## Isaac's Reaction

After Isaac realized he had been deceived, notice how he reacted: "Isaac trembled very exceedingly, and said, Who?

where is he that hath taken venison, and brought it me, and I have eaten of all before thou camest, and have blessed him? yea, and he shall be blessed" (Gen. 27:33). I believe this is the key verse concerning the life of Isaac. This was his turning point. Isaac "trembled very exceedingly" (literally, "trembled with a great trembling; great"). In horror Isaac suddenly realized how he had been pitting himself against God's express purpose and pronounced will. He realized how God had graciously overruled him in the wrong he had almost done. Isaac had great fear before God when he realized what had happened. This was self-judgment because Isaac was condemned in his own heart for what he had almost done. God did not condone Jacob's sin; nevertheless, He used it to awaken Isaac to his need.

At last faith found its true expression in Isaac. He came to his senses, for he really knew it was God's purpose and plan to bless Jacob, not Esau. What Isaac said when he realized all of this was one of the most crucial statements of his entire life: "Yea, and he shall be blessed." Isaac had no thought at this time of changing the blessing from Jacob to Esau. Of this incident, Hebrews 11:20 says, "By faith Isaac blessed Jacob and Esau concerning things to come." When Isaac was suddenly faced with his great mistake in endeavoring to bless Esau, he at once returned to fellowship with God and declared that the blessing was to remain on Jacob. God omits any reference to Isaac's weakness in the New Testament where it is simply recorded that "by faith Isaac blessed Jacob and Esau concerning things to come." How gracious God is!

The pronouncement of faith which Isaac made and which God honored in nowise indicated God's sanction of the sins that had been committed by the entire family. All four were guilty of sin. Esau had sold the birthright, Jacob had schemed to get it, Rebekah had planned and schemed with Jacob to get the blessing, and Isaac wanted to give the blessing to Esau. However, God forgives when confession is made. Isaac and Jacob's sins are not mentioned in the 11th chapter of Hebrews—God blotted out their sins. Genesis 27:33 indicates that Isaac made things right with God immediately. However, it took Jacob many years to realize his wrong. It was 20 years later when God asked him what his name was and he said, "Jacob" (32:27). By admitting his name was "Jacob," he was admitting he was a schemer and a deceiver. Because he admitted his name and his character, God changed his name to "Israel" (v. 28).

Esau probably never confessed his sins because the Scriptures refer to him as a "profane person" (Heb. 12:16). Neither do the Scriptures record whether Rebekah confessed her sin to the Lord, although quite possibly she did.

## Esau's Reaction

Observe how Esau reacted to his father's statement that Jacob would remain blessed: "When Esau heard the words of his father, he cried with a great and exceeding bitter cry, and said unto his father, Bless me, even me also, O my father" (Gen. 27:34). Isaac answered, "Thy brother came with subtilty, and hath taken away thy blessing" (v. 35). Esau retorted, "Is not he rightly named Jacob? for he hath supplanted me these two times: he took away my birthright; and, behold, now he hath taken away my blessing" (v. 36).

Esau was bitter toward his brother because he had taken advantage of him these two times. Desperate to have something, Esau asked his father, "Hast thou not reserved a blessing for me?" (v. 36). Isaac answered, "Behold, I have made him thy lord, and all his brethren have I given to him for servants; and with corn and wine have I sustained him: and what shall I do now unto thee, my son?" (v. 37).

Esau became more desperate as he said to his father, "Hast thou but one blessing, my father? bless me, even me also, O my father. And Esau lifted up his voice, and wept" (v. 38). Esau did not weep because he was concerned about spiritual values, but because he found no way to change his father's mind. Hebrews 12:17 says of Esau, "For ye know how that afterward, when he would have inherited the blessing, he was rejected: for he found no place of repentance, though he sought it [the blessing] carefully with tears." Esau was not repenting of his sin. He was trying to get his father to repent (change his mind) of having given the blessing to Jacob.

Isaac refused to change his mind about giving the blessing to Jacob, and he said to Esau, "Behold, thy dwelling shall be the fatness of the earth, and of the dew of heaven from above; And by thy sword shalt thou live, and shalt serve thy brother; and it shall come to pass when thou shalt have the dominion, that thou shalt break his yoke from off thy neck" (Gen. 27:39,40).

Esau was as much to blame for the loss of the birthright as Jacob was in securing it through deceit and cleverness. Had it not been for Esau's attitude toward his birthright, it would not have been as easy for Jacob to take it from him.

## The Reaping Begins

Having lost the blessing, the Bible says that "Esau hated Jacob because of the blessing wherewith his father blessed him: and Esau said in his heart, The days of mourning for my father are at hand; then will I slay my brother Jacob" (v. 41). Esau thought his father would soon die, but this was not the case. Isaac was 137 years of age when he gave the blessing to Jacob, and he lived another 43 years. However, this did not deter Esau in his plan to kill Jacob.

Rebekah learned of Esau's plot: "These words of Esau her elder son were told to Rebekah: and she sent and called Jacob her younger son, and said unto him, Behold, thy brother Esau, as touching thee, doth comfort himself, purposing to kill thee. Now therefore, my son, obey my voice; and arise, flee thou to Laban my brother to Haran; And tarry with him a few days, until thy brother's fury turn away; Until thy brother's anger turn away from thee, and he forget that which thou hast done to him: then I will send, and fetch thee from thence: why should I be deprived also of you both in one day?" (vv. 42-45).

Rebekah urged Jacob to flee to her brother and stay there until Esau forgot about the stolen blessing. Notice that Rebekah said to Jacob, "That which thou hast done to him" (v. 45). It is true that Jacob was guilty of stealing the blessing from Esau, but Rebekah was the one who devised the plan. Rebekah schemed again and decided it would be best for Jacob to go to her brother's place to live until Esau forgot about his plot against Jacob.

Rebekah did not expect that Jacob would have to stay long with Laban, for she instructed Jacob, "Tarry with him a few days, until thy brother's fury turn away" (v. 44). Esau was apparently very temperamental, and Rebekah assumed that even though he was so angry at the time, he would soon forget about the entire matter. Assuming that Esau would soon forget, Rebekah told Jacob, "Then I will send, and fetch thee from thence" (v. 45).

Rebekah did not realize all the sorrow that was to be reaped because of what she and Jacob had sown. After she sent Jacob away, she never saw him again. She died before he was able to return. Rebekah did not realize all the calamity that would come on her because of her disobedience to God. Like Rebekah, we sometimes think we can escape reaping what we have sown—but we may be sure that our sins will find us out.

To make it possible for Jacob to leave home, Rebekah went to Isaac with the excuse: "I am weary of my life because of the daughters of Heth: if Jacob take a wife of the daughters of Heth, such as these which are of the daughters of the land, what good shall my life do me?" (v. 46). The descendants of Heth were known as the Hittites. Earlier, Esau had taken two wives of the Hittites and this had caused much grief to Isaac and Rebekah (26:34,35). Rebekah posed the problem to Isaac and left the decision to him about what Jacob should do. It was a legitimate problem, but Rebekah used it as an excuse to help Jacob flee from Esau's wrath.

## The Bright Side

Up until now we have seen the gloomy side of Jacob's life—that which had resulted from his scheming—but there was also a bright side. This involved God's working with him to bring him back into fellowship. God had selected Jacob for a purpose, and what He had begun He was going to finish.

God is never defeated or frustrated when He sets out to accomplish His purpose. His ways of accomplishing His plan are beyond our comprehension. We must say with the Apostle Paul, "How fathomless the depths of God's resources, wisdom, and knowledge! How unsearchable His decisions, and how mysterious His methods! For who has ever understood the thoughts of the Lord, or has ever been His adviser? Or who has ever advanced God anything to have Him pay him back? For from Him everything comes, through Him everything lives, and for Him everything exists. Glory to Him forever! Amen" (Rom. 11:33-36, *Wms.*).

As we study Jacob's life in detail, we see that every time he was made to reap the fruit of his plotting and crookedness, God was bringing him back one step nearer to the place of fellowship. Jacob not only schemed to get his own way, but he also ran ahead of God. He wanted the things of God, but he wanted them in his own way and in his own time.

If we learn nothing else from Jacob's life, we should learn the importance of waiting on God. We are to wait expectantly on Him to fulfill His will in His own time. Although Jacob had sinned against God in his scheming, God caused His grace to abound over all of Jacob's sin and folly. Romans 5:20 tells us, "Where sin abounded, grace did much more abound." Does this mean that we should sin so grace can abound? The Apostle Paul anticipated this question and answered, "God forbid. How shall we that are dead to sin, live any longer therein? Know ye not, that so many of us as were baptized into Jesus Christ were baptized into his death?" (6:2,3). Paul emphasized that "our old man is [was] crucified with him, that the body of sin might be destroyed, that henceforth we should not serve sin" (v. 6). Although the grace of God is more prominent when seen against the backdrop of sin, this is no excuse for the believer to sin. God never condones sin, but makes provision for forgiveness and cleansing: "If we confess our sins, he is faithful and just to forgive us our sins, and to cleanse us from all unrighteousness" (I John 1:9).

## Lessons From Jacob

There are some extremely important lessons from Jacob's life that need to be underscored. We learn from him that we should never do evil in order that good might come. We should never try to win victories for Christ through unworthy means.

From Jacob we also learn the validity of the scriptural principle: Be sure your sin will find you out. This message is written in every line of the story of Jacob's life. Whereas every member of the family was guilty of sin, more is recorded about how the sin affected Jacob than how it affected the others. Jacob was God's man, so many details are given to show the way God worked with him.

If one lesson is emphasized more than others from the life of Jacob, it is that God is sovereign. It is futile to suppose that we can thwart God's program or purpose in any way. The Scriptures abound in evidence of this fact. Proverbs 19:21 says, "There are many devices in a man's heart; nevertheless the counsel of the Lord, that shall stand." The Book of Proverbs also declares: "A man's heart deviseth his way: but the Lord directeth his steps" (16:9). Emphasizing the same truth, the psalmist said, "The Lord bringeth the counsel of the heathen to nought: he maketh the devices of the people of none effect. The counsel of the Lord standeth for ever, the thoughts of his heart to all generations" (Ps. 33:10,11).

God Himself has exhorted, "Remember the former things of old: for I am God, and there is none else; I am God, and there is none like me, Declaring the end from the beginning, and from ancient times the things that are not yet done, saying, My counsel shall stand, and I will do all my pleasure" (Isa. 46:9,10). This should lead us to say as did Jeremiah, "O Lord, I know that the way of man is not in himself: it is not in man that walketh to direct his steps" (Jer. 10:23). The New Testament says, "So then it is not of him that willeth, nor of him that runneth, but of God that sheweth mercy" (Rom. 9:16). Isaac had his own will, but it came to nothing. Esau sought his own way, but he failed. God showed mercy unto Jacob because He had chosen him as His special vessel.

Chapter 20

# Blessing and Reaping

After Rebekah's plea to Isaac that Jacob not be allowed to take a wife from the Hittites, Jacob was sent away with Isaac's blessing. The Word of God says, "Isaac called Jacob, and blessed him, and charged him, and said unto him, Thou shalt not take a wife of the daughters of Canaan. Arise, go to Padan-aram, to the house of Bethuel thy mother's father; and take thee a wife from thence of the daughters of Laban thy mother's brother. And God Almighty bless thee, and make thee fruitful, and multiply thee, that thou mayest be a multitude of people; And give thee the blessing of Abraham, to thee, and to thy seed with thee; that thou mayest inherit the land wherein thou art a stranger, which God gave unto Abraham" (Gen. 28:1-4).

Isaac probably did not know that Esau had sworn to kill Jacob after the death of his father. However, Isaac lived 43 years after this time and nothing ever came of Esau's treacherous plot.

Rebekah and Isaac had one plan for Jacob, but God had quite another. God's ways are higher than our ways. While men are prone to point out another man's failures, God is concerned about bringing out that which is best in him. God is able to discern the true yearning of the heart and to bring about its realization. Basically, Jacob's desires were for the things of God—he wanted spiritual blessing. God knew this and He worked to bring out the best in Jacob, even though

Jacob often ran ahead and used carnal means to attain spiritual blessing.

Having blessed him, "Isaac sent away Jacob: and he went to Padan-aram unto Laban, son of Bethuel the Syrian, the brother of Rebekah, Jacob's and Esau's mother" (v. 5). Jacob had some great surprises in store for him. While he believed God and had a deep-seated faith, he knew little about the ways of God for his life. Jacob had a restless faith and it was very difficult for him to wait on God to work out His will. In the seven communications of God with Jacob, five of them were major communications in which Jacob was corrected and redirected into the path of God's will. In contrast, Abraham also had seven communications, but each involved a forward step of faith for him. However, Jacob had to be checked in the way he was going and directed back to the pathway of God's will. Although this correcting brought many difficult experiences for Jacob, he grew spiritually as a result. Jacob's restless faith was evident when he plotted to obtain the birthright and later the blessing because he was unable to wait on God. As a result, he had to flee for his life because of the wrath of his brother, Esau.

Genesis 28:10 says that "Jacob went out from Beer-sheba, and went toward Haran." On his way to Padan-aram, God made His first move to restore the fellowship that had been broken. God always does this. Even concerning salvation this is true. Jesus Christ Himself said, "No man can come to me, except the Father which hath sent me draw him: and I will raise him up at the last day" (John 6:44). No one can be saved apart from the Father's making the first move. So also, God initiated the move to restore the broken fellowship with Jacob.

### Jacob's Dream

Jacob was enroute to his uncle. It was on his first night away from home that God met him and dealt with him in a special way. Jacob "lighted upon a certain place, and tarried there all night, because the sun was set; and he took of the stones of that place, and put them for his pillows, and lay down in that place to sleep. And he dreamed, and behold a ladder set up on the earth, and the top of it reached to heaven: and behold the angels of God ascending and descending on it. And, behold, the Lord stood above it, and said, I am the Lord God of Abraham thy father, and the God of Isaac: the land whereon thou liest, to thee will I give it, and to thy seed" (Gen. 28:11-13). This was the second time God called Himself "the God of Abraham," and it is the first time He referred to Himself as "the God of Isaac."

God also promised Jacob, "Thy seed shall be as the dust of the earth, and thou shalt spread abroad to the west, and to the east, and to the north, and to the south: and in thee and in thy seed shall all the families of the earth be blessed. And, behold, I am with thee, and will keep thee in all places whither thou goest, and will bring thee again into this land; for I will not leave thee, until I have done that which I have spoken to thee of" (vv. 14,15). What a wonderful revelation God made to Jacob!

The Lord appeared to Jacob in great tenderness of heart, for He knew that beneath the surface Jacob really desired to please Him. God sought to bridge the gulf that existed between Jacob's thoughts of materialism and his concern for spiritual realities. Jacob began to learn the two sides of life: (1) Reaping the fruit of sin and (2) seeing the triumphs of divine grace. Jacob reaped what he had sown in his scheming and carnality, but God also satisfied his deep, inner longing for spiritual reality.

As Jacob lay under the stars while away from home that first night, he was alone with his own thoughts. No doubt he reflected on all that had happened. Perhaps he asked himself, Was it really worthwhile? Will I ever return to claim the birthright and blessing for which I schemed and successfully obtained? Jacob no doubt thought of these things and many more.

It was then that a dream came to him of a ladder that was set on earth and reached to heaven, with the angels going up and down it. Even this revealed the gulf that was between him and God at this time. God was at the top of the ladder; Jacob was at the bottom. However, in spite of the gulf that existed, there was communication between him and God. The ladder reached down to where he was—down to his deepest needs. Yet it also reached up to the very presence of God. What a revelation of God's mercy and loving compassion! God was molding Jacob into what He wanted him to be. At the top of the ladder was the God of Jacob's fathers—the God of Abraham and Isaac—and He promised to give the land on which Jacob was lying to him and his seed.

## The Personal God

On this first night away from home, Jacob had his first direct message from God. In speaking to Jacob, seven times God used the personal pronoun "I." First, He said, "I am"—emphasizing the ever-present One. Second, referring to the land, God said, "To thee will I give it." Third, God assured Jacob, "I am with thee, and will keep thee." Fourth, God promised, "[I] will bring thee again into this land." Fifth, God told Jacob, "I will not leave thee." Sixth, God assured Jacob He would be with him "until I have done that which [seventh] I have spoken to thee of." There were no conditions for Jacob to fulfill. There were no ifs or buts—it was all of grace. God had sovereignly willed what was to be done and His will would not be defeated—even by Jacob's carnality.

When God appeared to Jacob He gave him a fourfold assurance. There was the assurance of divine presence—"I am with thee." There was the assurance of divine protection—"I . . . will keep thee." There was the assurance of divine preservation—"I . . . will bring thee again into this land." There was also the assurance of divine promise—"I will not leave thee, until I have done that which I have spoken to thee of." This fourfold divine assurance is all recorded in verse 15.

God revealed Himself in His sovereign purpose to Jacob. God emphasized that He was ever-present—that Jacob could never get out of His sight. Jacob was experiencing the spiritual principle that "all things work together for good to them that love God, to them who are the called according to his purpose" (Rom. 8:28).

### Jacob's Eyes Are Opened

Jacob's inner eyes were suddenly opened, even as Paul prayed for the Ephesians "that the God of our Lord Jesus Christ, the Father of glory, may give unto you the spirit of wisdom and revelation in the knowledge of him: The eyes of your understanding being enlightened; that ye may know what is the hope of his calling, and what the riches of the glory of his inheritance in the saints, And what is the exceeding greatness of his power to us-ward who believe, according to the working of his mighty power" (Eph. 1:17-19).

When Jacob's inner eyes were opened, he was filled with awe, for he saw his undeserved prosperity and the wonderful promise that his seed should be a blessing to the whole world. This was too much for Jacob. The Scriptures say, "And Jacob awaked out of his sleep, and he said, Surely the Lord is in this place; and I knew it not" (Gen. 28:16). Jacob suddenly realized that his whole life was open to God—that he was completely found out because God had seen all of his sins. At the same time, Jacob saw God's mercy and grace revealed to him—that God was continuing to work in his behalf.

When Jacob realized all of this, "he was afraid, and said, How dreadful is this place! this is none other but the house of God, and this is the gate of heaven" (v. 17). Notice that Jacob called it a "dreadful" place even though he also referred to it as the "house of God" and the "gate of heaven."

This seems to be the time when Jacob experienced true conversion. One can know truth about God, as Jacob knew the truth, but not be identified with it. I, too, was reared in a godly home and knew much truth about God. I had gone through the catechism and had been baptized, but it was not until five years later that I came to the realization and significance of the truth of regeneration and received Christ as my Saviour.

Jacob's heart was not at home with God, as evidenced by the fact that he thought the place of the house of God and the gate of heaven was a dreadful place. His attitude at that time is a great contrast to David's attitude when he confessed his sin and cried out to God, "Against thee, thee only, have I sinned, and done this evil in thy sight. Hide thy face from my sins, and blot out all mine iniquities" (Ps. 51:4,9). Jacob had not made such statements to God, but on his first night away from home, on his way to Padan-aram, he began to realize that God is a personal God. Jacob was surprised to find that heaven was really so near. No wonder he was afraid. God is not someone far off, but immediately present. Jacob's life began to take on a new perspective when he came to the realization: "The Lord is in this place; and I knew it not" (Gen. 28:16).

## God Knows All About Us

God's house and God's presence are not dreadful to the soul who is in the habit of close communion with God. Nor does such a person fear the fact that God knows all about him. What is your first thought when you are reminded that God knows every detail of your life? Take time to meditate on Psalm 139, which records the psalmist's awareness of God's complete knowledge about every detail of his life. The psalmist said, "O Lord, thou hast searched me, and known me. Thou knowest my downsitting and mine uprising, thou understandest my thought afar off. Thou compassest my path and my lying down, and art acquainted with all my ways. For there is not a word in my tongue, but, lo, O Lord, thou knowest it altogether" (vv. 1-4). The psalmist realized that God knew what he was going to say even before he said it. As he pondered this truth, he said, "Such knowledge is too wonderful for me; it is high, I cannot attain unto it" (v. 6). With his finite mind, the psalmist could not comprehend the omniscience of God.

The psalmist continued, "If I say, Surely the darkness shall cover me; even the night shall be light about me. Yea, the darkness hideth not from thee; but the night shineth as the day: the darkness and the light are both alike to thee. I will praise thee; for I am fearfully and wonderfully made: marvellous are thy works; and that my soul knoweth right well" (vv. 11,12,14). The psalmist closed this beautiful psalm with this prayer: "Search me, O God, and know my heart: try me, and know my thoughts: And see if there be any wicked way in me, and lead me in the way everlasting" (vv. 23,24).

Are you willing to throw yourself wide open to God's searching eyes? Jacob suddenly realized that God knew all about him. God knew about his meanness, crookedness and scheming. But God also knew that deep within the heart of Jacob was a longing for spiritual realities; therefore, He undertook to make Jacob to the praise of His glory.

God knew every detail about Jacob's life, and He knows every detail about your life. He knows the good things, and He knows the ugly things. He knows when you are putting up a front—acting like you are something that you are really not. He knows how much of you is genuine—how much of what you say is really the truth.

How wonderful it is to know, however, that in spite of our shortcomings God loves us and will bring out the best in us if we will yield our lives to Him. Because God knew Jacob's inner longing for spiritual realities, He loved Jacob. Jacob was afraid when he suddenly realized God was in the place he was staying and he did not know it. Perfect love drives out fear, but fear precedes perfect love. God's holiness, followed by His love and grace, revealed Jacob's sin to him. God can reveal to us also exactly what we are. When we see God in His holiness, love and grace, we will realize how sinful we really are.

In Genesis 27:12 Jacob had said to his mother, "My father peradventure will feel me, and I shall seem to him as a deceiver." Jacob did not admit he was a deceiver at this time. But on his first night away from home, when he was fleeing for his life, Jacob saw the sinfulness of his scheming heart when he saw God in His holiness. Jacob realized that God knew he was a deceiver.

When we see ourselves as we really are, there will be dramatic results—even as there were when the Apostle Paul saw himself. "As he journeyed, he came near Damascus: and suddenly there shined round about him a light from heaven: And he fell to the earth, and heard a voice saying unto him, Saul, Saul, why persecutest thou me? And he said, Who art thou, Lord? And the Lord said, I am Jesus whom thou persecutest: it is hard for thee to kick against the pricks. And he trembling and astonished said, Lord, what wilt thou have me to do? And the Lord said unto him, Arise, and go into the city, and it shall be told thee what thou must do" (Acts 9:3-6). In effect, the Lord was saying to Saul, "I know all about you. I know that deep in your heart you are committed to doing what you believe is right. I know what you will be. I have checked you, Saul. Go into the city and you will be told what you are to do."

Job also was a wonderful man in the sight of God. However, there were certain things that neither he nor others realized concerning his life. God Himself described Job as "a perfect and an upright man" (Job 1:8). Job put God first in all that he did. However, after God was through dealing with him, Job said, "I have heard of thee by the hearing of the ear: but now mine eye seeth thee. Wherefore I abhor myself, and repent in dust and ashes" (42:5,6).

### Jacob's Memorial and Vow

After Jacob's exclamation that the place where he was staying was none other than the house of God and the gate of heaven, he "rose up early in the morning, and took the stone that he had put for his pillows, and set it up for a pillar, and poured oil upon the top of it. And he called the name of that place Beth-el" (Gen. 28:18,19). Jacob made a memorial to God because the place where he was staying suddenly had become a sacred place where he first met God. Have you met God? Where did you meet Him? When did you meet Him? Have you received Jesus Christ as your Saviour and yielded your life to Him to live through you as He pleases?

Then Jacob made a vow, saying, "If God will be with me, and will keep me in this way that I go, and will give me bread to eat, and raiment to put on, So that I come again to my father's house in peace; then shall the Lord be my God: And this stone, which I have set for a pillar, shall be God's house: and of all that thou shalt give me I will surely give the tenth unto thee" (vv. 20-22). Notice the conditions of Jacob's vow—"if God." God did not have any conditions in His promises to Jacob, but Jacob's heart was not yet at home in the presence of God. It is difficult to trust God completely and immediately when we have been accustomed to making our own plans and running our own lives. This was Jacob's problem. It was difficult to give up and all at once say, "Lord, I will leave everything to You." It takes time for such a decision.

Jacob wanted God's partnership, but he sought God's blessing on the things he had planned and what he wanted to do. Jacob failed to comprehend God's character and grace, so he met God's grace with an "if" and made a miserable bargain about food, raiment and journeying mercies. Then—and only then—would God be his God. How often we follow in Jacob's steps. Instead of appropriating God's unfailing grace, we bargain with Him with our stipulations and conditions. We should beware, because God will hold us accountable for our bargains.

Jacob had not yet found his rightful place in the presence of God; therefore, God used further circumstances to chasten him and bring him to Himself. Hebrews 12:5-11 indicates that chastening in the believer's life brings forth "the peaceable fruit of righteousness unto them which are exercised thereby." The purpose of God's chastening is so that the believer will bear more fruit.

Jacob was unable to enter into the reality and fullness of God. He still measured God by himself and thought of God only as a partner—someone he could call alongside to help him. It was utterly impossible for Jacob to comprehend who God really was. Jacob's God was small because Jacob measured Him by his own standards.

How big is your God? Most of us limit God because we confine Him to our ways. Jacob had to learn that God would have no part of his scheming attitude.

From his vision, Jacob learned that God was now taking him in hand and would not leave him until the work of grace was done. When Jacob awoke his real life was just beginning. During the next 20 years Jacob was allowed to experience many things to bring him to the end of himself. He bargained with one who was his equal in bargaining—Laban. Each tried to outwit the other and Jacob was finally brought to the end of himself.

God knows how and where to school His saints. Sometimes it takes many years. It took 40 years for Moses, 13 for Joseph, and 21 for David before they were ready to do the work God had chosen for them.

Do we really comprehend who God is and what He wants to do through us? As a believer, do you realize that Jesus Christ Himself lives within you? Do you realize the significance of Paul's statement: "I am crucified with Christ: nevertheless I live; yet not I, but Christ liveth in me: and the life which I now live in the flesh I live by the faith [faithfulness] of the Son of God, who loved me, and gave himself for me" (Gal. 2:20)? Can you say with the Apostle Paul, "I press toward the mark for the prize of the high calling of God in Christ Jesus" (Phil. 3:14)?

Chapter 21

# Twenty Years of Discipline

Bethel began a new life for Jacob. After he had established a memorial to God, "Jacob went on his journey, and came into the land of the people of the east" (Gen. 29:1). The phrase "Jacob went on his journey" is literally, "Jacob lifted up his feet." Jacob was probably light-footed—as if walking on clouds.

Remember the day you received Christ as Saviour? Or the day when you met God in a special crisis? Perhaps there was a great decision or a great victory. Did it not seem as if you were walking on a cloud—the birds sang sweeter and the stars looked brighter? No doubt that is the way Jacob felt with his new outlook. The revelation of God's presence and the assurance of blessing brought light and encouragement to his heart.

It was a long journey Jacob was making. It was about 450 miles, and he was making the entire journey on foot absolutely alone, through country he had never seen before.

Because God protected Jacob, he arrived without any trouble—not only in the area known as Padan-aram, but also at the very place where his uncle lived. Jacob came to a well where some men were watering sheep. He asked some of them where they were from and they told him they were from Haran. When Jacob asked if they knew Laban, they replied that they did. They assured him that Laban was well and said, "Behold, Rachel his daughter cometh with the sheep" (v. 6). What a unique meeting! God had promised Jacob He would be with him, and this meeting with Rachel was not by chance or accident. This is the way God also works in our lives. We may go a certain direction, but we never get out of God's sight. All that happened to Jacob was by divine appointment—there is no such thing as chance as far as God is concerned.

In seeking a wife, Jacob failed miserably in that he did not ask God for guidance. However, even though man fails, God remains faithful. As the Apostle Paul said in his letter to Timothy: "If we believe not, yet he abideth faithful: he cannot deny himself (II Tim. 2:13).

When Abraham had sent his servant to bring back a wife for Isaac, the servant had prayed for God's guidance (Gen. 24:12-14). This reveals how the servant of Abraham had depended on God for leadership, but this similar truth is not recorded regarding Jacob.

When Jacob met Rachel, it was love at first sight. "And it came to pass, when Jacob saw Rachel the daughter of Laban his mother's brother, and the sheep of Laban his mother's brother, that Jacob went near, and rolled the stone from the well's mouth, and watered the flock of Laban his mother's brother. And Jacob kissed Rachel, and lifted up his voice, and wept" (29:10,11).

Jacob told Rachel that her father, Laban, was his uncle. At once Rachel went to tell her father about Jacob. Then Laban "ran to meet him, and embraced him, and kissed him, and brought him to his house. And he told Laban all these things. And Laban said to him, Surely thou art my bone and my flesh" (vv. 13,14).

Laban invited Jacob to stay with him, and thus began 20 years of grueling discipline which eventually led to Jacob's complete transformation. Jacob had experienced the new birth, but he needed the transformation of his outward life also. During these 20 years God subjected Jacob to hard discipline so that He could make him a worthy instrument. His life reminds us of Proverbs 13:15: "The way of transgressors is hard." In Jacob's life we also see the truth: "Be not deceived; God is not mocked: for whatsoever a man soweth, that shall he also reap" (Gal. 6:7).

### Why Laban?

Although it seems to man that God sometimes moves slowly in His moral government, we can be assured that the moving of God and the working of God are absolutely sure. God's method for Jacob was to put him with a man who was harder, more grasping, more crooked and more cunning than Jacob himself. God's plan was to let Jacob see in another man all that was hateful about himself.

God still uses this method. Sometimes He places us in a position so that we will realize the position is not really for us. This has happened to me on numerous occasions. In my early years of ministry I thought I would like to teach the Bible in the classroom. For three months God allowed me to substitute for another teacher. The Lord gave me this experience to show me that the classroom was not His place for me.

God has many ways of showing us what our hearts are really like. If it were left to us, we would usually choose pleasant living conditions and congenial people to work with in whatever we do. But God is more concerned with our spiritual growth than with our temporal comforts. He will not spare us discomforts or pain if in the end it will mean eternal profit for us. God's love for us is strong and faithful. He has a purpose for every believer, and He uses the circumstances of life to accomplish that purpose and to make the believer more fruitful (Rom. 8:28).

What a disaster it would have been for Jacob if he had been put with some nice, reasonable person instead of Laban. Jacob's ego would have swollen and he would have become useless to God. Jacob had a longing for the things of God, so God worked patiently with Jacob to make him for His glory and to break him from the habits of his old life. Because God knows every detail of our lives, He knows the circumstances He needs to use to bring us to Himself.

Jacob wanted God's gifts and, in this, there was a great difference between Jacob and Esau. Esau despised the things of God and did not care to have anything to do with them. On the other hand, Jacob wanted the blessings of God so badly that he would even connive to obtain them. Although Jacob's methods were not right, they at least demonstrated how desperate he was to obtain the blessings of God.

God purposed to school Jacob by having him live with Laban. These men were similar in many ways, but there was also a great difference between them. Jacob was a believer in God, whereas Laban apparently was not, as evidenced by the fact that we are later told of his idols. However, God did not allow Laban to bring harm to Jacob. Laban would have sent Jacob away empty, but God was in control of the situation and He saw to it that Jacob received proper payment for his diligent work with Laban. Jacob must have been a hard worker, and God even blessed Laban because of Jacob. God wanted Jacob to have plenty, and He allowed Laban to have plenty also. When God undertakes for us, He always does the right thing.

God did the right thing for Jacob, and He will do the right thing for you also. Learn to trust God. I have been encouraged over and over again by Psalm 37:5: "Commit thy way unto the Lord; trust also in him; and he shall bring it to pass." I have gone to this verse hundreds of times and God has proven Himself absolutely faithful to His wonderful promise. If we will commit our way to Him—if we will simply trust Him for it—He definitely will bring it to pass.

## Jacob Endures

Jacob demonstrated great strength of character in not running away from God's discipline. It was not easy for Jacob, but he stayed with Laban until God decided he had had enough and gave him his release. This reminds us of I Corinthians 10:13: "There hath no temptation taken you but such as is common to man: but God is faithful, who will not suffer you to be tempted above that ye are able; but will with the temptation also make a way to escape, that ye may be able to bear it." It took 20 years for Jacob to learn his lesson and for God to allow him to leave Laban. Jacob had to work 14 years for his beloved wife, Rachel, and then 6 more years gaining possessions for himself.

We gain nothing by running away or trying to avoid God's dealings with us. This only means that more time is wasted. Let the Lord take control of your life. If He has to take you through some disciplinary action to get you to be what He wants you to be, let Him do so and have it over with because of the many blessings that will result for you. We will be the losers if we interfere with God's discipline in our lives. It is possible that God could have accomplished His purpose with Jacob in a shorter time if Jacob would have submitted to Him sooner. However, it took God 20 years to accomplish His purpose in Jacob's life.

During the 20 years that Jacob was with Laban, Jacob's dealings showed nothing of his Bethel experience. There was no evidence that he had really experienced a conversion. There did not seem to be any significant change in his life.

I was 20 years old when I received Jesus Christ as my Saviour and, as I look back now, I realize there were several years after that time that my life really did not evidence the change that had taken place inwardly. God had to work in my life, in some ways harshly, to bring out this new life in my everyday living. It was hard at the time, but I thank Him for it today.

## No Significant Differences

Like the unbeliever, Jacob struggled to gain worldly possessions. He seemed more concerned with accumulating property than with glorifying the Lord. Although Jacob was a believer and his uncle was an unbeliever, it is difficult to see the difference between the two. Both were greatly concerned with the possessions of life.

In our materialistic age it is also difficult to tell the difference between the believer and the unbeliever. Many Christians are so materialistically minded that they will make any kind of business agreement that will bring them gain.

Some even say, "I keep my religion out of my business dealings." That was exactly Jacob's problem. He had difficulty realizing that his relationship with God should permeate every area of his life.

For Jacob to really learn about God, he needed to go back and stay at Bethel. Because Jacob failed to comprehend the ways of God, God did something for him in Haran to teach him a valuable lesson. God, in His patience, taught Jacob what man really is. In his uncle, Jacob learned to see himself as he really was. His uncle was a greater schemer and more cunning than he was.

Although at Haran Jacob acknowledged God's presence and faithfulness, he did nothing without a scheme or a human plan. As one reads Genesis, chapters 29-31, he realizes it was a shame for Jacob to do some of the things he did. God would have brought him many blessings had he waited, but Jacob felt he needed to scheme and plot to make sure these blessings would be his. It became a contest between Jacob and Laban to see who could outscheme the other.

## Forced to Honor the Firstborn

Genesis 29:16-28 reveals at length how Jacob reaped what he had sown—how God allowed him to suffer from deceit. In this way God was able to teach him that there is no good thing in the flesh. Jacob made arrangements with Laban to work seven years for him so he could have his daughter Rachel for his wife. The seven years passed quickly for "they seemed unto him but a few days, for the love he had to her [Rachel]" (v. 20). At the end of the seven years, Jacob went to Laban and asked for Rachel.

Laban had another daughter, Leah, who was not as good-looking as Rachel. In those days it was the custom for the bride to wear a kind of veil that made it impossible to see her face. She was then given to her husband-to-be by her father. In his deceit, Laban gave Leah to Jacob instead of Rachel. Because Leah came to Jacob in the evening and was so heavily veiled, Jacob did not recognize her. Jacob discovered it was Leah only after the marriage had been finalized. The next morning, when Jacob discovered Laban had given Leah to him, he went to Laban and asked, "What is this thou hast done unto me? did not I serve with thee for Rachel? wherefore then hast thou beguiled me?" (v. 25).

Laban told Jacob, "It must not be so done in our country, to give the younger before the firstborn. Fulfil her week, and we will give thee this also for the service which thou shalt serve with me yet seven other years" (vv. 26,27). Jacob fulfilled the week of the celebrating of his marriage to Leah, and then he received Rachel for his wife. Jacob had been thoroughly cheated.

Back in his home country Jacob had refused to submit to God. He was now compelled to submit to a human master—he had to serve, not dominate. Jacob was the younger at home, but he had dominated the others, so God taught him a lesson by allowing him to go to Laban where he would be dominated.

Earlier, Jacob had not respected the rights of the firstborn, for he had schemed to get the birthright and the blessing away from Esau. Now, by the cunning of Laban, Jacob had to submit to the rights of the firstborn. In having to take Leah, the firstborn, as his wife before he could get Rachel, Jacob learned his lesson the hard way.

Jacob also learned the lesson about waiting on God. He had refused to wait on God's fulfillment of His promise that "the elder shall serve the younger" (25:23). Because he refused to wait for God to fulfill this promise in His own time, Jacob had to flee home to save his life. Because Jacob had such difficulty waiting on God, He taught him, through the incident of Leah and Rachel, the importance of waiting. He had to wait seven years for Rachel, and this in itself taught him many lessons in waiting. Although he most likely married Rachel a week after he married Leah, he still had to work another seven years for Rachel before he could receive any wages for himself—14 years of waiting before he began to accumulate possessions for himself. God has ways of teaching people how to wait.

### Laban Schemes to Keep Jacob

After 14 years with Laban, Jacob had had about all he could take he asked to be released. "It came to pass, when Rachel had born Joseph, that Jacob said unto Laban, Send me away, that I may go unto mine own place, and to my country. Give me my wives and my children, for whom I have served thee, and let me go: for thou knowest my service which I have done thee" (30:25,26). However, God was not through teaching Jacob some valuable lessons. Therefore, God allowed Laban to scheme ways for keeping Jacob from returning to his homeland.

Laban said to Jacob, "I pray thee, if I have found favour in thine eyes, tarry: for I have learned by experience that the Lord hath blessed me for thy sake. And he said, Appoint me thy wages, and I will give it" (vv. 27,28). This was a remarkable confession by Laban. He now realized that the blessing which had come to him was not due to his superior scheming but because of God.

The same principle applies to our salvation. We are not saved because of things we do, but because of what Jesus Christ has done for us. The Word of God says that Christ "is the propitiation [satisfaction] for our sins: and not for our's only, but also for the sins of the whole world" (I John 2:2). In the same chapter, the Apostle John wrote: "I write unto you, little children, because your sins are forgiven you for his name's sake" (v. 12). We are not saved from condemnation by any works we are able to do, but by receiving as Saviour the One who paid the penalty for our sins. God's Word assures us that "as many as received him, to them gave he power to become the sons of God, even to them that believe on his name" (John 1:12).

### Jacob Schemes to Deceive Laban

When Laban told Jacob to name his wages, this gave Jacob another opportunity to scheme and gain more blessings by deceit. Jacob told Laban, "Thou shalt not give me any thing: if thou wilt do this thing for me, I will again feed and keep thy flock. I will pass through all thy flock to day, removing from thence all the speckled and spotted cattle, and all the brown cattle among the sheep, and the spotted and speckled among the goats: and of such shall be my hire" (Gen. 30:31,32).

Jacob's wages had been changed several times, and during the next six years Laban changed them several times more. Altogether, Jacob's wages were changed 10 times during the 20 years he was with Laban. At this time, Jacob at least gave God credit, for he told Laban, "It was little which thou hadst before I came, and it is now increased unto a multitude; and the Lord hath blessed thee since my coming" (v. 30). But Jacob took full advantage of the opportunity to scheme ways to deceive Laban out of his possessions.

Although Jacob schemed and plotted, God did not let him out of His sight—and even continued to bless him. How marvelous was God's patience with His unworthy servant. God must have seen much in Jacob because of all the years He spent in disciplining him, leading him, overruling his mistakes and forgiving his sins.

Nothing is comparable to the patience and mercy of God! When we honestly examine our lives, we are unable to understand how God can be so merciful. We say with David, "Thy mercy, O Lord, endureth for ever" (Ps. 138:8).

None but God could have borne with such a person as Jacob. None but God would have undertaken such a task with such a person. But grace begins at the very lowest point—it takes man where he is and deals with him according to God's love and purpose. Truly, it is "amazing grace."

When God was finally through with Jacob and had forgiven all of his sins, it is said of God, "He hath not beheld iniquity in Jacob, neither hath he seen perverseness in Israel: the Lord his God is with him, and the shout of a king is among them" (Num. 23:21). Consider the grace of God that is revealed in this statement: "He hath not beheld iniquity in

Jacob." It is not said that there was no sin in Jacob, but God had forgiven it all and had blotted it from His mind.

What a marvelous God we have! Take time to examine your heart before God and confess any sin that is in your life. God has promised to forgive our sins when we confess them to Him (I John 1:9). Clear the record with God so that there is no unconfessed sin in your life. Because Christ shed His blood to pay the penalty for sin, it was possible for God to blot out Jacob's sin and it is possible for Him to blot out yours. Jesus Christ is the Lamb of God who has taken away the sins of the world.

Chapter 22

# Jacob's Departure From Haran

Jacob's years with Laban were years of testing. Because of Laban's deceit, Jacob had to spend 14 years working to obtain Rachel instead of 7. After those 14 years, Jacob wanted to return to his homeland, but Laban enticed him to stay by giving Jacob more opportunity to scheme for material possessions.

Jacob continued another six years with Laban, and during that time the sons of Laban became very jealous of him. Jacob overheard Laban's sons saying, "Jacob hath taken away all that was our father's; and of that which was our father's hath he gotten all this glory" (Gen. 31:1). In addition to what the sons were saying, "Jacob beheld the countenance of Laban, and, behold, it was not toward him as before" (v. 2).

The world does not like to see a believer prosper. God allowed Jacob to prosper because He loved him and saw that the basic desire of his heart was to please Him. But because of Jacob's prosperity, the sons of Laban were jealous of him and even Laban himself was changing in his attitude toward Jacob.

Believers who do not prosper in this world's goods should not be troubled about others who do. We are counseled in Psalm 37:7,8: "Rest in the Lord, and wait patiently for him: fret not thyself because of him who prospereth in his way, because of the man who bringeth wicked devices to pass. Cease from anger, and forsake wrath: fret not thyself in any wise to do evil."

After 20 years of silence, God communicated with Jacob and said to him, "Return unto the land of thy fathers, and to thy kindred; and I will be with thee" (Gen. 31:3). Jacob had gone through 20 years of heartbreaking experiences, but he was becoming prosperous in this alien land. Lest he also become satisfied and want to stay in this land, God appeared to him and commanded him to return to the land of his fathers. God assured Jacob that He would be with him—the same promise of protection God had given him previously.

Jacob had an inner desire to return to his country, as evidenced by his words six years earlier: "Send me away, that I may go unto mine own place, and to my country" (30:25). However, Jacob did not leave Laban until the Lord commanded: "Return unto the land of thy fathers" (31:3).

## How to Know the Will of God

An inner desire alone is not sufficient to determine the will of God. There are three factors that are essential in determining the will of God. First, there must be an inner desire. We have seen that Jacob had this, for he wanted to return to his homeland.

Second, there must be the command of God—the Word of God must agree in principle with the person's inner conviction. In verse 3 of chapter 31 Jacob had the direct command of God that he should return to the land of his fathers.

Third, circumstances must agree in that they must make the action possible. These three—an inner desire, a divine command, and agreeing circumstances—will all be in harmony when it is God's will that something should be done. If even one is not in agreement with the other two, then you should be very careful in making any move.

If there is an inner desire and a divine command, but not agreeing circumstances, perhaps the way is right but the time is wrong. However, if we have the indication of circumstances and perhaps the inner desire, but not divine command, we can be certain that the way is not right.

Too many Christians are led entirely by circumstances and desires. We must learn to wait on God. We must learn to trust Him completely. Psalm 37:5 says, "Commit thy way unto the Lord; trust also in him; and he shall bring it to pass." The psalmist prayed, "Lead me, O Lord, in thy righteousness because of mine enemies; make thy way straight before my face" (5:8).

We must also remember that "whatsoever is not of faith is sin" (Rom. 14:23). Concerning the will of God, Arthur W. Pink has written:

"If you are sincere and patient, and pray in faith, then, in His own good time and way, He will most certainly answer, either by removing the conviction or desire from your heart, and arranging your circumstances in such a manner that your way is blocked–and then you will know *His time* for you to move has not arrived–or, by deepening your conviction, so ordering your circumstances so that the way is opened up *without your doing anything yourself*, and by speaking definitely through His written word. 'Commit thy way unto the Lord, trust also in Him, and He shall bring it to pass' (Psa. 37:5)" (*Gleanings in Genesis*, p. 77).

Psalm 25 is a wonderful psalm to meditate on when you are seeking God's will. When you are faced with a difficult decision, you will find every verse of this psalm especially precious. The first eight verses emphasize the importance of being in right relationship to the Lord so He can speak to you. Verse 9 is especially important: "The meek will he guide in judgment: and the meek will he teach his way." The meek person is the one who totally relies on God for everything.

Verse 12 of this psalm says, "What man is he that feareth the Lord? him shall he teach in the way that he shall choose." The word "fear" is not used here as it is commonly used today. In this psalm it refers to a reverential trust which also involves a hatred for evil. To be led of the Lord, we must trust Him completely and have a hatred for being out of the will of God. If we fear the Lord in this way, He will teach us the way we should go.

The psalmist also said, "The secret of the Lord is with them that fear him; and he will shew them his covenant. Mine eyes are ever toward the Lord; for he shall pluck my feet out of the net" (vv. 14,15). In these verses we see both God's side and man's side. God will never fail to fulfill His part if man fulfills his part. The believer's responsibility is seen in the psalmist's words, "Mine eyes are ever toward the Lord." When this is true of us, we may be assured of God's leading in our lives.

The believer whose "eyes are ever toward the Lord" is the believer who has heeded Paul's exhortation: "I beseech you therefore, brethren, by the mercies of God, that ye present your bodies a living sacrifice, holy, acceptable unto God, which is your reasonable service. And be not conformed to this world: but be ye transformed by the renewing of your mind, that ye may prove what is that good, and acceptable, and perfect, will of God" (Rom. 12:1,2). This has to be done before we can ever know the will of God. We have to totally commit ourselves—and everything about us—to God. He is not going to show us His will if we are not totally committed to Him. We become transformed by the renewing of our minds as we turn our minds totally over to Him. When we do this, we will prove "what is that good, and acceptable, and perfect, will of God."

## God's Time for Jacob

The circumstances for Jacob's departure were now ripe. However, if Jacob had left Haran only because of the circumstances of personal hurt and resentment which he had earlier, he would have sinned. Many times we make this mistake. Circumstances go bad for us—perhaps people are talking about us or we are unable to get along with our employer, our pastor or the people we work with. In such adverse circumstances it is easy to feel that God is speaking to us to move elsewhere, but if we move without God's direct appointment we may find ourselves in far greater trouble.

In the record of Jacob's 20 years with Laban, there is not one mention of an altar at which he could find communion with God. There may have been some inner communion with God, but the kind of communion associated with an altar—the special place of fellowship—was completely missing.

After God had made it clear to Jacob that He wanted him to leave Haran for Canaan, Jacob talked with his family. The Word of God says that "Jacob sent and called Rachel and Leah to the field unto his flock" (Gen. 31:4). He called them to a place where he could talk to them without being overheard. He had a scheme. He said to them, "I see your father's countenance, that it is not toward me as before; but the God of my father hath been with me. And ye know that with all my power I have served your father. And your father hath deceived me, and changed my wages ten times; but God suffered him not to hurt me" (vv. 5-7). Jacob told his wives some of the details of the way their father had dealt with him and how God had commanded him to return to his own land.

Having been cheated by Laban, Jacob learned by experience the kind of person he himself was and how his dealings had affected others. God uses this kind of lesson to teach us also. Perhaps we have been guilty of speaking against someone and have not realized how it may have hurt them. Then when we are spoken against we suddenly realize how deeply such words hurt, and we become sensitive to what we have done.

Even though Laban had deceived Jacob in the bargains they had made, Jacob came out the better of the two because God purposed to bless Jacob in spite of Laban's scheming. Jacob told his wives that God had appeared to him and had said, "I am the God of Beth-el, where thou anointedst the pillar, and where thou vowedst a vow unto me: now arise, get thee out from this land, and return unto the land of thy kindred" (v. 13).

Because of the possibility that Jacob had even more possessions than Laban, some might ask, Was God partial and biased? No, because God knew the inner heart of Jacob. It cannot be impressed upon our minds too strongly that God knows the desires of our hearts. If you have been mistreated, cheated or deceived, and if your heart has been right all along, be assured that God knows your heart. The time is coming when God will vindicate you, but in the meantime you should be confidently aware that God knows the truth concerning what has happened to you. He knows if your heart has been right.

Rachel and Leah told Jacob, "Whatsoever God hath said unto thee, do" (v. 16). With their agreement to leave with him, Jacob plotted how he might flee from Laban.

## Jacob Flees

Jacob waited for the right time to flee from Laban. The right moment came when Laban had gone a three-days journey away from home to shear sheep (vv. 19-22).

Before Rachel fled, she "had stolen the images that were her father's" (v. 19). Thus, we see that Laban still had images. He was an idol worshiper. The word "images" is literally, *teraphim*. Traced from its Syrian root, it means "to inquire." When Rachel stole these gods, she was not planning to use them, but she wanted to prevent her father from inquiring of the gods where Jacob and his household had fled. No doubt the reason Laban suddenly missed his gods was because he was going to inquire of them immediately on learning that Jacob had fled.

There is another reason why Laban would have been greatly concerned about the missing household gods. According to the custom of the time, the son-in-law's possessing the household gods of the father-in-law indicated that the son-in-law would be the principal heir.

As to the use of the *teraphim* in Israel, they were only used when men turned away from Jehovah and worshiped the false gods of their heathen neighbors. So also, many in present-day Christendom have apostatized, for they have turned from the Holy Scriptures to seducing spirits, worshiping science and learning instead of the Lord. These apostates put their confidence in what man says rather than in "Thus saith the Lord."

Laban received the news "on the third day that Jacob was fled. And he took his brethren with him, and pursued after him seven days' journey; and they overtook him in the mount Gilead" (Gen. 31:22,23). Laban was seeking revenge but he had to contend with One who was stronger than either he or Jacob. "God came to Laban the Syrian in a dream by night, and said unto him, Take heed that thou speak not to Jacob neither good nor bad" (v. 24). God always watches over His own. He warned Laban not to harm Jacob.

How far Jacob had traveled by this time, we do not know. It was three days before Laban learned that Jacob had fled, and by the time he would have returned home another three days would have passed. Searching for his gods and preparing to pursue Jacob perhaps consumed another day. Then it took seven days for Laban to catch up with Jacob. So Jacob probably had been gone about 14 days by the time Laban caught up with him.

Laban overtook Jacob "in the mount Gilead" (v. 23). It is not certain where this was, but the land of Gilead was on the east side of Jordan. It was that part of the land of Israel which the two and a half tribes occupied. Most likely, the mount of Gilead was close to the border of the Promised Land. This is indicated also by the fact that it was not long after this that they crossed the brook Jabbok and entered into that part of the Promised Land.

### Jacob Vindicates Himself

Laban said to Jacob, "Though thou wouldest needs be gone, because thou sore longedst after thy father's house, yet wherefore hast thou stolen my gods?" (v. 30). Immediately, Jacob felt he had to vindicate himself. He said, "With whomsoever thou findest thy gods, let him not live" (v. 32). Jacob was not aware that Rachel had stolen the images.

Laban went from tent to tent looking for the gods. The Scriptures say, "Now Rachel had taken the images, and put them in the camel's furniture [saddle], and sat upon them. And Laban searched all the tent, but found them not. And she said to her father, Let it not displease my lord that I cannot rise up before thee; for the custom of women is upon me. And he searched, but found not the images" (vv. 34,35).

By this time Jacob was very angry. He said to Laban, "What is my trespass? what is my sin, that thou hast so hotly pursued after me? Whereas thou hast searched all my stuff, what hast thou found of all thy household stuff? set it here before my brethren and thy brethren, that they may judge betwixt us both" (vv. 36,37).

Then Jacob rehearsed some of the injustices that Laban had brought upon him: "This twenty years have I been with thee; thy ewes and thy she goats have not cast their young, and the rams of thy flock have I not eaten. That which was torn of beasts I brought not unto thee; I bare the loss of it; of my hand didst thou require it, whether stolen by day, or stolen by night. Thus I was; in the day the drought consumed me, and the frost by night; and my sleep departed from mine eyes. Thus have I been twenty years in thy house; I served thee fourteen years for thy two daughters, and six years for thy cattle: and thou hast changed my wages ten times. Except the God of my father, the God of Abraham, and the fear of Isaac, had been with me, surely thou hadst sent me away now empty. God hath seen mine affliction and the labour of my hands, and rebuked thee yesternight" (vv. 38-42).

The believer has no such need to vindicate himself. Psalm 37:5,6 makes this clear when it says, "Commit thy way unto the Lord; trust also in him; and he shall bring it to pass. And he shall bring forth thy righteousness as the light, and thy judgment as the noonday." God will take care of the believer and He will vindicate him.

### A Covenant of Separation

Because of their sharp disagreement, Laban suggested: "Let us make a covenant, I and thou, and let it be for a witness between me and thee" (Gen. 31:44). They gathered stones and heaped them together. Laban said, "This heap is a witness between me and thee this day. Therefore was the name of it called Galeed; And Mizpah; for he said, The Lord watch between me and thee, when we are absent one from another" (vv. 48,49).

This passage of Scripture is often used for a covenant of fellowship. However, the context clearly indicates that it was not a covenant of fellowship, but a covenant of separation. Laban said to Jacob, "This heap be witness, and this pillar be witness, that I will not pass over this heap to thee, and that thou shalt not pass over this heap and this pillar unto me, for harm" (v. 52).

This is the end result of two powerful schemers who clashed with each other. They could not trust each other, so they had to make a covenant and set up a pillar of stones to mark the spot over which neither of them would cross for the purpose of harming the other. Each was really saying, "I cannot trust you out of my sight. The Lord must be the Watchman between us if we and our goods are to be safe from each other." Visiting between the families was not prohibited, but Jacob and Laban agreed never to cross the line with the purpose of harming the other.

After having sworn himself to the covenant, Jacob "offered sacrifice upon the mount, and called his brethren to eat bread: and they did eat bread, and tarried all night in the mount. And early in the morning Laban rose up, and kissed his sons and his daughters, and blessed them: and Laban departed, and returned unto his place" (vv. 54,55).

Chapter 23

# The Carnal Man Becomes a Spiritual Man

Jacob, the schemer, has arrived at his most critical moment–he must face Esau, whom he had supplanted and cheated. Even more than that, he must meet himself face to face and see how filled he is with self. To do this, he must come to the end of himself and see God as He really is.

After Jacob and Laban had made their covenant not to cross over the boundary to harm each other, Laban returned to his place and "Jacob went on his way, and the angels of God met him. And when Jacob saw them, he said, This is God's host: and he called the name of that place Mahanaim" (Gen. 32:1,2). Jacob was finally free from his father-in-law, Laban, but he had a great danger ahead of him.

The Word of God tells us, "And Jacob sent messengers before him to Esau his brother unto the land of Seir, the country of Edom. And he commanded them, saying, Thus shall ye speak unto my lord Esau; Thy servant Jacob saith thus, I have sojourned with Laban, and stayed there until now: And I have oxen, and asses, flocks, and menservants, and womenservants: and I have sent to tell my lord, that I may find grace in thy sight. And the messengers returned to Jacob, saying, We came to thy brother Esau, and also he cometh to meet thee, and four hundred men with him" (Gen. 32:3-6).

God often has to bring us face to face with grave danger or a crisis before He can reveal His abundant strength to us. This was true also with the nation, Israel. When the Israelites were fleeing Egypt, they came to the Red Sea. The Red Sea was before them, the mountains were on one side, the desert was on the other side, and the Egyptians were behind them. What a critical moment! But in this crisis God appeared to the Israelites: "The angel of God, which went before the camp of Israel, removed and went behind them; and the pillar of the cloud went from before their face, and stood behind them: And it came between the camp of the Egyptians and the camp of Israel; and it was a cloud and darkness to them, but it gave light by night to these: so that the one came not near the other all the night" (Ex. 14:19,20). God brought darkness to the enemy and light to His own people—but it took this crisis for the Israelites to know the power of God.

As Jacob was now returning to Canaan and was face to face with his greatest crisis, the "angels of God met him" (Gen. 32:1). This was not the first time that angels appeared to him. That first night when he was fleeing from home, headed toward Haran, he saw a vision of a ladder with "the angels of God ascending and descending on it" (28:12). He also saw the Lord at that time, for the Lord stood above the ladder and spoke to Him (vv. 13-15).

Jacob had also met the angel of God in Haran who reminded him of God's promise at Bethel and beckoned him to return to Canaan (31:11-13). When the angels of God met Jacob as he was returning to Canaan, he said, "This is God's host" (32:2). These angels came to welcome Jacob back and to escort and protect him as he entered the land. He had already been protected from Laban, and now they would protect him from Esau who was coming with 400 men.

This is a similar situation to that recorded in II Kings 6:13-17. Elisha and his servant were in the city of Dothan and the enemy had surrounded it. When Elisha's servant saw all the horses and chariots of the enemy, he asked, "Alas, my master! how shall we do?" (v. 15). Elisha answered his servant, "Fear not: for they that be with us are more than they that be with them. And Elisha prayed, and said, Lord, I pray thee, open his eyes, that he may see. And the Lord opened the eyes of the young man; and he saw: and, behold, the mountain was full of horses and chariots of fire round about Elisha" (vv. 16,17). God was far more powerful than the enemy.

As Jacob was about to face Esau and his 400 men, it was of comfort to know that the host of God was on his side. Truly, there were more with Jacob than there were with Esau. Jacob called the name of the place "Mahanaim," which means "two hosts." It is not certain who the two hosts were. Jacob may have referred to the angels and considered one host as protection from Laban and the other host as protection from Esau. Or Jacob may have been referring to those who were with him as a visible host and to the angels of God as the invisible host.

### Jacob Instructs His Messengers

As Jacob prepared to meet Esau, it was evident that he still had not grasped what it is to really live by faith in God. Jacob still projected his own plans—he sent messengers to Esau and told them what to say. In instructing them Jacob said, "Thus shall ye speak unto my lord Esau" (v. 4). How interesting it is that Jacob used the word "lord" in referring to Esau. After 20 years with Laban, Jacob had a different language. Before he had fled from his home to go to Laban, Jacob had lorded it over Esau and had taken away his birthright and blessing. But he had now come to the place of recognizing Esau as lord. Humanly speaking, that was Esau's rightful place because he was the older. In referring to Esau as "lord," Jacob was putting himself in the place of a servant. From the human standpoint this was his proper place because he was the younger of the two. God had promised that the blessing would go to Jacob, but it was necessary for Jacob to realize, as did the Apostle Paul, "By the grace of God I am what I am" (I Cor. 15:10).

In instructing his messengers what to say to Esau, Jacob had them tell that he "sojourned with Laban, and stayed there until now" (v. 4). No reference was made to the fact that Jacob had fled from home earlier. Jacob had wronged Esau, and he could not have peace until he made things right with him. But there is nothing said at this time about the wrong Jacob had done nor about his desire to make things right with Esau.

Jacob was now willing to forfeit the blessing he had taken from Esau by deceit. He wanted Esau to know that he was not returning to the land to claim his birthright nor that portion of his father's inheritance. In effect, Jacob was saying to Esau, "I already have enough; God has given me plenty."

Great change had come over Jacob in his 20 years with Laban, but the change was not sufficient to meet God's standards. Jacob was still far from being a mature believer. There had been growth during the 20 years with Laban, but there had not been the maturity God desired. In Hebrews 6:1, believers are told, "Therefore leaving the principles of the doctrine of Christ, let us go on unto perfection [maturity]; not laying again the foundation of repentance from dead works, and of faith toward God." Jacob had not progressed on to maturity as God desired, but he had come to the place of recognizing Esau in his rightful place as the elder brother and himself as servant. Although God would change this later, up to this time God had not permitted Jacob to benefit from the birthright or blessing he had obtained through deceit.

Jacob told his messengers to tell Esau, "I have sent to tell my lord, that I may find grace in thy sight" (v. 5). Jacob's message indicated he was recognizing Esau's rightful place and that he himself was taking his rightful place, but the messengers returned with bad news. They reported: "We came to thy brother Esau, and also he cometh to meet thee, and four hundred men with him" (v. 6). Time had only intensified the hatred. Esau must have strutted with pride as he went forth to show his great power to Jacob. He had been beaten by Jacob's cunning, but now he would let Jacob know that he had power to humble him. Esau's attitude was, "I'll show him who's the better of the two."

Jacob was now in real trouble. What was he going to do? How often God has to bring us up against a wall of calamity before He can truly deal with our souls.

When Jacob learned that Esau was coming to meet him with 400 men, he "was greatly afraid and distressed: and he divided the people that was with him, and the flocks, and herds, and the camels, into two bands; And said, If Esau come to the one company, and smite it, then the other company which is left shall escape" (32:7,8). Jacob's first reaction was one of fear and distress—then he started making plans for survival. What about the heavenly host who was escorting him? What about the promise of God when He met Jacob at Bethel and said, "I am with thee, and will keep thee in all places whither thou goest, and will bring thee again into this land" (28:15)? Jacob's reactions revealed his imperfect faith and, in this regard, he was like so many of us.

### Jacob's Prayer

Because of Jacob's imperfect faith, he offered a prayer of panic and then resorted to his carnal planning. In fact, Jacob began to plan even before he prayed. He took time out of his planning to pray, then immediately returned to his carnal planning. There seemed to be no real trusting of God but only the asking of God to sanctify his plans.

How often we are guilty of the same thing. Like Jacob we go to God in prayer as a last resort. We do not have enough confidence to wait on God; we feel we must plot our own course if the work of God is to be salvaged. God has a perfect course of action for us to follow, and He can bless only as we follow His course. Paul said, "But none of these things move me, neither count I my life dear unto myself, so that I might finish my course with joy, and the ministry, which I have received of the Lord Jesus, to testify the gospel of the grace of God" (Acts 20:24).

When Jacob finally went to the Lord in prayer, his prayer evidenced the basic essentials of true prayer, but he lacked faith and true committal. He came short of doing what the psalmist said we should do: "Commit thy way unto the Lord" (Ps. 37:5). But the psalmist did not stop here. He added, "Trust also in him; and he shall bring it to pass."

Although Jacob did not have the Bible to guide him, he did have God's promise of protection.

When Jacob prayed, he said, "O God of my father Abraham, and God of my father Isaac, the Lord which saidst unto me, Return unto thy country, and to thy kindred, and I will deal well with thee" (Gen. 32:9). Jacob addressed his prayer to the God of a covenant relationship—the God of his fathers, Abraham and Isaac. Jacob appealed to God's faithfulness on the basis of His covenant with his fathers. This was very good. We, too, appeal to God the Father in the name of another. Our plea is based on our relationship to God which has been made possible through our faith in the Lord Jesus Christ.

Jacob called on the God of his fathers, but he failed to call on God as his own God. He failed to appropriate what he knew about the God of his fathers. The faith he had was genuine, but he did not have complete faith in the promises of God. His faith was inadequate.

When you realize that the God of Abraham, Isaac and Jacob is your God, it does something to your faith. This is what Jacob failed to comprehend. Jacob saw what had been accomplished in the lives of his fathers, but he failed to apply it to himself. He did not fully comprehend that the God of Abraham and Isaac was his God also.

There are four elements of faith that are extremely important: faith believes that God *can* do what we ask; faith believes that God *will* do what we ask; faith *expects* an answer; and faith *accepts* the answer. The last is crucial—unless we accept the answer, our faith falls short of what God intends it to be. This was Jacob's problem. He prayed and claimed the promises of God, but he did not accept the answer. He continued scheming, trying to help God bring the answer.

In his prayer Jacob referred to God as the One who said to him, "Return unto thy country, and to thy kindred, and I will deal well with thee" (v. 9). Jacob also recalled God's words when He said, "I will surely do thee good, and make thy seed as the sand of the sea, which cannot be numbered for multitude" (v. 12). Jacob was basing his prayer on the promises of God, and this is what God wants us to do. David prayed, "O Lord God, the word that thou hast spoken concerning thy servant, and concerning his house, establish it for ever, and do as thou hast said" (II Sam. 7:25). The believer is to claim God's promises and urge Him to "do as [He] hast said."

Concerning prayer, Philippians 4:6,7 says, "Be careful for nothing; but in every thing by prayer and supplication with thanksgiving let your requests be made known unto God. And the peace of God, which passeth all understanding, shall keep your hearts and minds through Christ Jesus." We are to expectantly ask God for the things He has laid upon our hearts to pray for. Our prayer and supplication is to be made "with thanksgiving." This is saying, "Thank you, Lord. I know You are going to answer. I accept the answer." The result of such a prayer is that God's peace, which passes all understanding, will keep our hearts and minds through Christ Jesus.

## A Lack of Mature Faith

Jacob could have had this peace of mind. He could have said, "This is God's doings. He is the One who has promised to bring me back into the land, and He has sent his angels to take care of me. Thank You, Lord. I know You are going to take care of my brother, Esau." But Jacob did not go that far in his prayer. Instead of committing the whole situation to God and saying, "Do as thou hast said," Jacob returned to his scheming to solve his problems.

This is a lesson all of us need to learn. As we pray for the salvation of our loved ones, we should not be overanxious and expect God to work immediately. We are to allow God to answer our prayers in His own time. It is not that God needs a lot of time, but the persons we are praying for may not be ready, or even we who are praying may not be ready. This is what Jacob so badly needed to learn.

The Lord Jesus Christ told His followers, "What things soever ye desire, when ye pray, believe that ye receive them, and ye shall have them" (Mark 11:24). In I John 5:14,15 we are told, "This is the confidence that we have in him, that, if we ask any thing according to his will, he heareth us: And if we know that he hear us, whatsoever we ask, we know that we have the petitions that we desired of him." We must come to the place of saying, "God, You said You were going to do it. I accept Your answer now, but I leave the time to You." When we do this, the peace of God will flood our hearts and minds.

Jacob's prayer was intense, earnest and good, but it was without the true or mature faith which would have accepted the answer then and there. His prayer was also marked by humility. Jacob said, "I am not worthy of the least of all the mercies, and of all the truth, which thou hast shewed unto thy servant; for with my staff I passed over this Jordan; and now I am become two bands" (Gen. 32:10).

Jacob admitted his own unworthiness and God's mercy and faithfulness. He took a low place before God. This indicates that Jacob had come a long way in his spiritual life. This showed the work of God in his heart.

It takes humility to receive the grace of God. James 4:6-10 says, "He gives us grace potent enough to meet this and every other evil spirit, if we are humble enough to receive it. That is why he says: God resisteth the proud, But giveth grace to the humble. Be humble then before God. But resist the devil and you'll find he'll run away from you. Come close to God and he will come close to you. Realize that you have sinned, and get your hands clean again. Realize that you have been disloyal, and get your hearts made true once more. As you come close to God you should be deeply sorry, you should be grieved, you should even be in tears. Your laughter will have to become mourning, your high spirits will have to become heartfelt dejection. You will have to feel very small in the sight of God before he will set you on your feet once more" (*Phillips*).

As Jacob prayed, he said, "Deliver me, I pray thee, from the hand of my brother, from the hand of Esau: for I fear him, lest he will come and smite me, and the mother with the children" (Gen. 32:11). What was the motive for Jacob's petition? At first, it might seem selfish, but verse 12 indicates Jacob was seeking the glory of God. Jacob was pleading God's promises when he said, "And thou saidst, I will surely do thee good, and make thy seed as the sand of the sea, which cannot be numbered for multitude."

We also need to check our motives when we are praying for the salvation of our loved ones. Are we praying for them only because they are loved ones, or are we truly concerned about the glory of God? Our chief concern should always be the glory of God. Whatever we do, we should "do all to the glory of God" (I Cor. 10:31).

Jacob still had fear, but it was an unnecessary fear. God had promised to bring him back to the land and to make his seed as the sand of the sea.

## The Rest of Faith

Jacob's faith—as evidenced by his prayer—was still very immature. When there is a lack of faith, things will not happen. Hebrews 11:1 says, "Faith is the substance of things hoped for, the evidence of things not seen." In reality, faith is having what you have asked for. But faith even goes beyond believing that you have what you have asked for—it produces something in your life. Hebrews 4:9,10 says, "There remaineth therefore a rest to the people of God. For he that is entered into his rest, he also hath ceased from his own works, as God did from his." The rest spoken of here is the rest of faith. Faith rests in God and allows God to take care of the problems. When a person does this, he ceases from his own works. Jacob had not come to this place because he had not ceased trying to solve his own problems.

The rest of faith is vividly seen in the life of the Apostle Paul. He was on a ship that had been blown about by the wind for many days. It looked as if all the sailors and Paul would be killed by the storm. As Paul prayed during the night, God spoke to him. The next day he told the sailors, "I exhort you to be of good cheer: for there shall be no loss of any man's life among you, but of the ship" (Acts 27:22). How did Paul know that? How could he say so firmly that there would be no loss of life? Note Paul's reason for such assurance: "For there stood by me this night the angel of God, whose I am, and whom I serve, Saying, Fear not, Paul; thou must be brought before Caesar: and, lo, God hath given thee all them that sail with thee. Wherefore, sirs, be of good cheer: for I believe God, that it shall be even as it was told me" (vv. 23-25).

What a tremendous encouragement this passage is! How different it is from the passages that tell us about Jacob. He prayed and told God all about his difficulty, but then he immediately began to scheme again. He could not believe, as did Paul: "I believe God, that it shall be even as it was told me." Jacob could have demonstrated the same faith because he had the same God. The promises of God were just as sure to him as they were to Paul.

Jacob had learned much during the 20 years he had spent with Laban, but his independent attitude still stood in his way. Reliance on self kept him from resting his faith completely in his God. He was still Jacob the schemer.

## A Plot to Appease

Genesis 32:13 tells how Jacob returned to his scheming immediately after his prayer: "And he lodged there that same night; and took of that which came to his hand a present for Esau his brother." Instead of trusting in God alone, Jacob plotted how he could appease Esau by giving of his possessions. Jacob substituted appeasement for deception. This shows some improvement, but his motives were still fleshly and debased in view of all the promises God had given him.

Jacob divided his livestock up into different droves, "and he delivered them into the hand of his servants, every drove by themselves; and said unto his servants, Pass over before me, and put a space betwixt drove and drove. And he commanded the foremost, saying, When Esau my brother meeteth thee, and asketh thee, saying, Whose art thou? and whither goest thou? and whose are these before thee? Then thou shalt say, They be thy servant Jacob's; it is a present sent unto my lord Esau: and, behold, also he is behind us. And so commanded he the second, and the third, and all that followed the droves, saying, On this manner shall ye speak unto Esau, when ye find him" (vv. 16-19).

Jacob realized that his plan was not foolproof, for he said, "I will appease him with the present that goeth before me, and afterward I will see his face; peradventure he will accept of me" (v. 20). Jacob's plot of appeasement was an uncertain venture which resulted from Jacob's refusal to rely totally on the sure word of God. What a great enemy self is! Jacob lacked confidence in God to the extent that he actually distrusted God. Jacob had to plot his own way because he did not have enough faith to believe that God could fulfill what He had promised. Psalm 37:5 says, "Commit thy way unto the Lord; trust also in him; and he shall bring it to pass." Jacob had committed his way unto the Lord, but he did not trust in Him; therefore, the Lord was not able to bring to pass what He had promised. When we commit our way to the Lord and trust in Him, our burdens are placed on Him. Because Jacob did not trust the Lord as he ought to have, he continued to carry the burden himself. Jacob leaned on his own plan more than on God's sure word of promise. This is a vivid illustration of the works of the flesh. The flesh is always in conflict with the Spirit. Galatians 5:17 says, "For the flesh lusteth against the Spirit, and the Spirit against the flesh: and these are contrary the one to the other: so that ye cannot do the things that ye would."

When we are in the habit of thinking that we provide for ourselves, it is hard to trust God completely. We feel that somehow we have to help God if our needs are to be taken care of. Instead of our fitting into God's plan, we expect Him to bless our plans.

Jacob's plan was to appease Esau. The old nature wants to appease rather than face the guilt. To be in fellowship with God, we have to face the guilt of our sins. Jacob was not willing to face and confess his guilt and to accept the judgment that God might mete out. The old nature, rather than seeking fellowship with God, seeks to advance its own desires by plotting its own course.

After Jacob had given instructions and the droves of animals had been sent off as presents for Esau, Jacob "lodged that night in the company. And he rose up that night, and took his two wives, and his two womenservants, and his eleven sons, and passed over the ford Jabbok. And he took them, and sent them over the brook, and sent over that he had. And Jacob was left alone" (Gen. 32:21-24).

Jacob still felt all depended on him, so he did more planning and sent his household across the brook of Jabbok for protection. It is admirable that Jacob made sure his loved ones were safe, but he was relying on his own plans for their safekeeping instead of relying on the promises of God. God had sent His angels to protect them, but Jacob was unable to completely trust God to do what He had promised.

### Jacob Is Left Alone

After Jacob's wives, womenservants and sons had been sent over the brook, "Jacob was left alone." He remained outside the land of Canaan to guard against any harm that might come. God permitted Jacob to do this so He could deal with him while he was alone.

This introduces us to the most important crisis in the life of Jacob. There are some battles that must be fought alone. There are times when no one is able to help us. This was just such a time in Jacob's life. Jacob's trouble was himself. There was self-will, self-purpose, self-defense, self-desire and self-righteousness. Jacob's self-life had to be dealt with, and God chose to deal with it while Jacob was alone.

The Bible says, "Jacob was left alone; and there wrestled a man with him until the breaking of the day" (v. 24). This was a decisive night—it was the turning point in Jacob's life. He was left alone with God, which is the only way of arriving at a true and just knowledge of ourselves and our ways. Away from the world, away from our thoughts about self, away from our reasonings and imaginations—alone with God.

There are many scriptural examples of how God works with men when they are alone. For 40 years Moses was alone with God in the desert. God took him there to teach him many valuable lessons. When Moses came out of the desert, he was a different man. He was then the man who could trust God for everything and was therefore qualified to lead the children of Israel out of Egypt. Without the great faith in God which he had acquired in the desert, Moses could never have accomplished this task.

David was also one who realized the importance of being alone with God. When David was living at Ziklag, he and his men were away from the city when the Amalekites invaded it and took the wives and children captive. The Bible says that "David was greatly distressed; for the people spake of stoning him, because the soul of all the people was grieved, every man for his sons and for his daughters: but David encouraged himself in the Lord his God" (I Sam. 30:6). David realized the importance of being alone with God and encouraging himself in God.

Jesus Himself made it a habit during His days on earth to spend time alone with His Father. If this was important for Him, it is much more important for us. There are many things that can be wrestled out and decided only when we are alone with God.

The fact that Jacob was alone with God is the first key to understanding the change that took place in his life that night.

### The Heavenly Wrestler

Jacob's plan was to stand guard against the possible night attack of his brother. He left nothing to chance; there was no sleep for him that night. This reveals his great concern for his family. As he stood watch, Jacob was suddenly assailed by a man who wrestled with him. Jacob was courageous and he sought to conquer his foe. No doubt it was dark, and Jacob did not at first realize with whom he was wrestling. God had appeared in the form of man and wrestled with him.

This passage of Scripture is often used to emphasize man's perseverance with God in prayer. However, we should observe that it was God, not Jacob, who began the wrestling match. Other passages of Scripture teach the importance of prevailing prayer, but it is not taught in this passage. Instead of persevering, Jacob was resisting continuously. He still felt competent to manage his own affairs apart from God, but the heavenly wrestler continued with him. This passage really teaches God's perseverance with His man until He can break and then make him.

Jacob was not a coward and, because he had succeeded at almost anything he had attempted, it was natural for him to think that he could win out against his powerful foe. It is a serious thing to resist God, whose only intent is to bless us. Jacob had to learn that he could never really gain the birthright, the blessing and the land of Canaan by his own cleverness. They were to be received as gifts from God—by faith alone.

God's time for a breakthrough had come. Jacob's most trying hour was ahead of him because Esau was coming with 400 men. This was a literal, physical struggle; yet in importance the physical was secondary to the spiritual. This is always true. This principle is seen in the life of the Apostle Paul, who had a thorn in the flesh and asked the Lord three times to take it from him. Paul wrote: "And he said unto me, My grace is sufficient for thee: for my strength is made perfect in weakness. Most gladly therefore will I rather glory in my infirmities, that the power of Christ may rest upon me. Therefore I take pleasure in infirmities, in reproaches, in necessities, in persecutions, in distresses for Christ's sake: for when I am weak, then am I strong" (II Cor. 12:9,10).

The most important lesson for Jacob to learn was that even though he was weak physically he could be strong spiritually. It took more than spiritual wrestling to convince Jacob of his need. God had been dealing with him in the spiritual realm for over 20 years, but Jacob had failed to learn. God now came to Jacob on a physical basis because this was something Jacob could comprehend. Jacob's spiritual level of discernment was not yet to the place where God could deal with him on a spiritual basis alone.

Sometimes God also has to deal with us on the physical level because this is the only thing that some of us really understand. It may be loss of wealth, health or family, but whatever it is, the loss is intended to draw us closer to the Lord. If we cannot be led spiritually, the Lord will communicate with us in a language we can understand by touching us in the physical realm. Let us become so sensitive to the leading of the Lord that He will be able to deal with us purely on a spiritual basis.

## Jacob Is Crippled

Genesis 32:25 says of the man who wrestled with Jacob, "And when he saw that he prevailed not against him, he touched the hollow of his thigh; and the hollow of Jacob's thigh was out of joint, as he wrestled with him." Because it was God who was actually wrestling with Jacob, the question arises, Why couldn't He prevail without wrestling with Jacob all night? Certainly God could have brought Jacob to the breaking point sooner. But as we consider God's wrestling with Jacob, we should ask ourselves the question, How long has God had to wrestle with us? Because God is patient, He has waited and worked with us for days, weeks, months, and possibly years to bring us to the point where He wants us to be. How thankful we should be that God is so patient with us. Have you thanked God recently for His long-suffering and patience with you?

God wanted Jacob to come to the end of himself on his own. He gave Jacob every opportunity, but Jacob could not break his self-will. Jacob was experiencing the long-suffering and patience of the Lord. The Word of God says that "the Lord is not slack concerning his promise, as some men count slackness; but is longsuffering to us-ward, not willing that any should perish, but that all should come to repentance" (II Pet. 3:9). Note especially that His long-suffering is to "us-ward." The purpose of God's patient waiting is also given in Isaiah 30:18: "Therefore will the Lord wait, that he may be gracious unto you, and therefore will he be exalted, that he may have mercy upon you: for the Lord is a God of judgment: blessed are all they that wait for him." The Lord waits that He may be gracious to His children.

God knows just the right hour to break His servant. The Lord had been waiting on Jacob for over 20 years, but Jacob had not come to the end of himself. Now was the right time for God to move in directly on His man. So the Lord appeared as a man to wrestle with Jacob. Even then He gave Jacob every opportunity to surrender, but Jacob would not. Jacob had never suffered defeat. Now, however, he was grappling with a different kind of foe—not man, but God.

Because Jacob would not surrender, the divine wrestler dislocated Jacob's thigh and lamed him for life. This shows us the seriousness of resisting God. The sentence of death had to be written on the flesh. Matthew 10:39 says, "He that findeth his life shall lose it: and he that loseth his life for my sake shall find it." Jesus said, "If any man will come after me, let him deny himself, and take up his cross daily, and follow me. For whosoever will save his life shall lose it: but whosoever will lose his life for my sake, the same shall save it" (Luke 9:23,24).

Jacob had to be broken of his reliance on the flesh—the ways of the old nature. Jacob depended too much on himself and his ability to accomplish what needed to be done. God had to touch his physical body to cause him to realize his need of depending on God. And God will have to do the same with us if we resist His working in our lives.

It is important for the Christian to recognize that the sentence of death must be passed upon the flesh. Judicially, this has been done by the death of Christ, but we need to appropriate it by faith. Romans 6:6 says, "Knowing this, that our old man is [literally, "was"] crucified with him, that the body of sin might be destroyed, that henceforth we should not serve sin." This is what took place when Jesus Christ died on the cross. But notice the need for our appropriation of this: "Likewise reckon ye also yourselves to be dead indeed unto sin, but alive unto God through Jesus Christ our Lord" (v. 11). We are to reckon it true because it is true. We are to consider it a fact. Verses 12 and 13 say, "Let not sin therefore reign in your mortal body, that ye should obey it in the lusts thereof. Neither yield ye your members as instruments of unrighteousness unto sin: but yield yourselves unto God, as those that are alive from the dead, and your members as instruments of righteousness unto God."

## At the End of Self

The first key to God's victory in Jacob's life is that Jacob was left alone with God. The second key is that Jacob had to be brought to the end of himself. His self-strength had to be broken. He had come to the end of his own resources. All confidence in his flesh had to be brought to an end, and this was done by crippling him. He had now come to realize his utter weakness.

Jacob could no longer fight his brother, Esau, in his own strength for his thigh was out of place. There were 400 men coming with Esau, and Jacob was completely powerless to do anything. Previously, he had resisted casting himself completely on the Lord, but now he had to because of his helplessness. He had been brought to the place where he had to depend upon God.

Because Jacob's faith would not come through God's promises, it had to come through his total helplessness. God had met him at Bethel and at Haran, and the heavenly host had met him when he was returning to the land. But all of these occurrences brought little response from Jacob. Therefore, God had to resort to doing something Jacob would understand in order to bring Jacob to Himself.

What all must God do to us to bring us to the end of ourselves? What must He do to us individually, organizationally, nationally and internationally in order to bring us to the end of ourselves? We struggle, strive, fight and resist, but we must realize that surrender to God is the only answer.

Self is the strongest internal antagonist we have to fight. But we cannot overcome self by strength alone. In ourselves, we cannot conquer self. This is evident from Romans 7 where the Apostle Paul wrote; "For I know that in me (that is, in my flesh,) dwelleth no good thing: for to will is present with me; but how to perform that which is good I find not. For the good that I would I do not: but the evil which I would not, that I do. Now if I do that I would not, it is no more I that do it, but sin that dwelleth in me" (vv. 18-20). In himself, the Apostle Paul did not have the strength to do that which was right. In desperation he cried out, "O wretched man that I am! who shall deliver me from the body of this death?" (v. 24). But praise God! There is victory in Jesus Christ. Although we cannot overcome self in the power of self, we are to recognize that "the law of the Spirit of life in Christ Jesus hath made me free from the law of sin and death" (8:2). That is why the old man was crucified with Christ (6:6) and our relationship to the old man is as death. On our part, the victorious life is possible only as we have faith in God to accomplish this for us in practice. Therefore, we are to consider ourselves dead to the old man but alive unto God.

After the power of Jacob was broken because his thigh was out of place, his entire attitude changed. As they wrestled, the angel of the Lord said to Jacob, "Let me go, for the day breaketh" (Gen. 32:26). Jacob answered, "I will not let thee go, except thou bless me." As the day dawned, Jacob no doubt realized who his assailant really was.

### Jacob Clings to the Lord

At last God had Jacob where He wanted him, but what a tremendous cost it was to Jacob! No longer able to wrestle, Jacob began to cling. He changed from cunning to clinging and from resisting to resting. Jacob had at last begun to wait upon the Lord and to rest in the promises of God. Hebrews 4:10 says that "he that is entered into his rest, he also hath ceased from his own works, as God did from his."

Jacob's clinging to the Lord is the third key to understanding the change in his life and walk. The first key is that Jacob was left alone, and the second is that the hollow of his thigh was touched and put out of place. This third key to the understanding of Jacob's life is that his attitude changed from independence to dependence. Jacob began to cling for his life.

All that Jacob had struggled for he had lost; all that he had trusted for he had gained. Like the Apostle Paul, Jacob had come to realize that in his flesh was no good thing. He came to realize that the only way out was God Himself. He was now in the position to which God had been leading him for 20 years. In patience, God had waited until Jacob had come to the end of himself and had begun to cling to Him.

Jacob won more through this one solitary defeat than he had won through his many years of walking according to the flesh. But before the fullness of blessing could come, there had to be a total collapse of his strong self-will. What was true of Jacob is also true of us—we must come to the end of ourselves.

Job was also an example of one who had to come to the end of himself before he could experience all that God intended for him. The first 31 chapters of the Book of Job show how Job grappled with his friends. He maintained his position against all of their arguments. He was a strong man; he stood for his rights. But in chapters 32-37 we have the record of how God began to bring Job to the end of himself through the words of Elihu. Finally, beginning with the 38th chapter, God Himself wrestled with Job and completely overwhelmed him with the display of His greatness and glory. All of this brought Job to cry out, "I have heard of thee by the hearing of the ear: but now mine eye seeth thee. Wherefore I abhor myself, and repent in dust and ashes" (42:5,6).

We also need a new vision of the Lord Himself in all of His holiness, majesty and power. We will see God in His glory as we study the Bible, which is His revelation to us.

Jacob had stolen the blessing from Esau; now he was clinging to the Lord for His blessing. Jacob had contended with Esau and Laban and had succeeded. But when he contended with God, he utterly failed.

Before Jacob could receive God's blessing, there was one more matter of extreme importance: Jacob had to confess. He had to humble himself before God. It was necessary for him to face up to the sin and shame of his previous life. The angel of the Lord asked Jacob, "What is thy name?" (Gen. 32:27). Jacob's name had haunted him everywhere he had gone. His name presented him as a fraud, a sham, a cheat, a supplanter, a contender and a deceiver. When Jacob answered that his name was "Jacob," he actually confessed to being all the things his name stood for. Jacob confessed the truth of it all. His entire life was characterized by what his name represented, but when confession was made to God, he was at once on his way to blessing that God alone could give him.

## From 'Jacob' to 'Israel'

The angel of the Lord told Jacob, "Thy name shall be called no more Jacob, but Israel: for as a prince hast thou power with God and with men, and hast prevailed" (v. 28). Jacob's name was changed and royal blessing was received.

Jacob prevailed in the sense that he capitulated. He ceased struggling with the Lord and submitted to Him.

Jacob's new name, "Israel," means "prince of God" or "prince with God." This gave recognition to Jacob's new character. Although Jacob was no longer to be known as a deceiver, his old nature remained in conflict with the new nature and occasionally the old nature gained prominence.

The name "Israel" indicated that Jacob was now one whom God would command. Jacob was to be God's fighter, no longer fighting for himself. As Jacob had once prevailed for self, now under God's command and power he (Israel) would prevail for God.

Present-day believers are also engaged in a spiritual warfare. The Apostle Paul wrote: "Finally, my brethren, be strong in the Lord, and in the power of his might. Put on the whole armour of God, that ye may be able to stand against the wiles of the devil. For we wrestle not against flesh and blood, but against principalities, against powers, against the rulers of the darkness of this world, against spiritual wickedness in high places" (Eph. 6:10-12). When we identify ourselves with Christ in the spiritual warfare, we can say with the Apostle Paul, "I can do all things through Christ which strengtheneth me" (Phil. 4:13).

Jacob's plan to meet Esau had all been perfected, but God took over. God took everything into His command, including Esau. It was no longer Jacob who was to arrange and order his life—it was God.

This was the third time God appeared to Jacob. The first time was at Bethel—the house of God—where God assured Jacob of His presence. Twenty years later, when Jacob was returning from Haran with his family and possessions, God appeared to him at Mahanaim, where the angelic host assured him of divine power and protection. The third time the Lord appeared to Jacob was at Peniel, where God brought Jacob into subjection.

### Fellowship With God

These three appearances of God were progressive steps in the life of Jacob. First, he was assured of the presence of God. Second, he was assured of the power and protection of God. Third, he was assured of the favor and fellowship of

God. At Peniel, Jacob could say as did Job, "I have heard of thee by the hearing of the ear: but now mine eye seeth thee."

That Jacob had come into the presence of God for fellowship is evidenced by the fact that he called the name of the place "Peniel," for he said, "I have seen God face to face, and my life is preserved" (Gen. 32:30).

The believer's life of fellowship and friendship with God is his highest spiritual privilege. Although some use the expression "coming into the Lord's presence" when they pray, actually the believer is in the Lord's presence all the time. The believer is to always be walking in fellowship with God and conscious of His presence. The believer is also to make a practice of talking with the Lord at all times, not just waiting until the end of the day to make confession of sin and bring requests to the Lord. We should be so sensitive to sin that we confess it as soon as we commit it.

The believer's greatest privilege is that of constant fellowship with God. Concerning this fellowship, the Apostle John wrote: "That which we have seen and heard declare we unto you, that ye also may have fellowship with us: and truly our fellowship is with the Father, and with his Son Jesus Christ" (I John 1:3). Christ Himself said, "Henceforth I call you not servants; for the servant knoweth not what his lord doeth: but I have called you friends; for all things that I have heard of my Father I have made known unto you" (John 15:15).

Jacob finally came to recognize God as his Commander in Chief. The Scriptures tell of many others who had to come to this same place. Joshua was such a person. He had taken over the leadership of Israel after Moses' death. The Israelites had crossed the Jordan River and were considering the conquest of Jericho.

"And it came to pass, when Joshua was by Jericho, that he lifted up his eyes and looked, and, behold, there stood a man over against him with his sword drawn in his hand: and Joshua went unto him, and said unto him, Art thou for us, or for our adversaries? And he said, Nay; but as captain of the host of the Lord am I now come. And Joshua fell on his face to the earth, and did worship, and said unto him, What saith my lord unto his servant? And the captain of the Lord's host said unto Joshua, Loose thy shoe from off thy foot; for the place whereon thou standest is holy. And Joshua did so" (Josh. 5:13-15). Joshua recognized the Lord as his Commander in Chief, and as long as Joshua obeyed the orders of God he was victorious.

Isaiah also had his life changed when he "saw also the Lord sitting upon a throne, high and lifted up" (Isa. 6:1). Seeing God in all of His holiness caused Isaiah to be willing to say, "Here am I; send me" (v. 8).

Others, too, were changed by a vision of God. Such was the case with Jeremiah (Jer. 1:4-9); Daniel (Dan. 10:8-10); and John (Rev. 1:13-19).

What a difference it makes when we see God in His fullness and walk in fellowship with Him. Do you know the Lord in this way? It is the highest privilege you can have, but it takes time and it takes seclusion. It will be necessary for you to give up self if you are going to experience all that God wants you to have.

## 'The Sinew Which Shrank'

After Jacob's experience at Peniel, the Scriptures say that "as he passed over Penuel the sun rose upon him, and he halted upon his thigh. Therefore the children of Israel eat not of the sinew which shrank, which is upon the hollow of the thigh, unto this day: because he touched the hollow of Jacob's thigh in the sinew that shrank" (Gen. 32:31,32). Notice the beautiful expression "the sun rose upon him." After Jacob had come to the end of himself and had settled things with God, the sun rose on his life. Peniel was the turning point in Jacob's life, for it was there that he turned in another direction. The fellowship that Jacob had with God as he left Peniel was just as real as the sun that rose on him that day. Jacob experienced a new abundant life with God.

The present-day believer also has in his heart the Son of God, who produces new life within. Christ is the life in the believer. The Apostle Paul told of the "mystery which hath been hid from ages and from generations, but now is made manifest to his saints: To whom God would make known what is the riches of the glory of this mystery among the Gentiles; which is Christ in you, the hope of glory" (Col. 1:26,27). What a wonderful truth it is for the believer to realize that the eternal God actually indwells him. Christ is our life. Our responsibility is to submit to Him so that He can live out His life through us. He will take charge of every aspect of our lives as we appropriate what He has made possible for us through His death and resurrection.

Genesis 32:31 says that Jacob "halted upon his thigh." He was now a broken man, and this brokenness was evident to all who saw him. Verse 32 refers to the "sinew which shrank." A doctor explained the sinew of the thigh as the strongest part of the human body. If pulled straight out, a horse could hardly tear away the limb. Only by being twisted can it be disjointed, and in wrestling this is easily done.

The sinew was not removed; it shrank. The sinew is representative of the flesh. It is impossible to remove or eradicate the flesh (Adamic nature) from the believer. Neither can the flesh be subdued; it must be withered. Its power must be broken and held in the place of death. Romans 6 makes it clear that the old man (flesh) has been crucified with Christ. Because the believer has died with Christ to the old nature, he is to live unto God by the indwelling, resurrected Christ.

That which had made Jacob the strong man that he was had shrunk to the extent that he was now a helpless man—completely dependent upon God. Jacob's old nature was not eradicated, for as he went forth to meet Esau—and during the next few years after—it is evident that the old Jacob was still very much alive.

Jacob's new life was characterized by his new name, Israel. From the time of Jacob's experience at Peniel onward, we see less and less of Jacob (the old nature) and more and more of Israel (the new nature). Jacob's attitude was now as that expressed by John the Baptist, who said, "He must increase, but I must decrease" (John 3:30).

Chapter 24

# After Peniel

After God changed his name, Jacob began to live a new life. But he learned very slowly. God is patient, but He is also firm. The conflict between Jacob's two natures became more prominent. In Jacob, God gives us a picture of the desperate struggle between the two natures which takes place in every believer's life. In Jacob's conflict, he was guilty of unbelief.

Unbelief is to be distinguished from disbelief. Those guilty of unbelief are those who know the truth but do not follow it. They do not appropriate by faith what is available to meet their needs. This was Jacob. He knew the truth but did not appropriate it. Disbelief, on the other hand, is true of those who simply do not believe the truth; therefore, there is nothing for them to appropriate.

In recording Jacob's life, a typical human biographer would emphasize the glowing victories that Jacob had after Peniel. The tendency would be to omit the failures which were due to his still-functioning old nature. Jacob's name had been changed to Israel, but after Peniel he is referred to as Jacob 45 times in the Book of Genesis and as Israel only 23 times. It is also true that when referring to him God called Himself "the God of Jacob," not "the God of Israel." If God had said, "I am the God of Israel," many of us would have difficulty depending on such a God for our victories because we are too much like Jacob in his old nature. It is "the God of Jacob" who we realize we need. In effect, God says, "I am Jacob's God. I am willing to be called the God of any man if deep in his heart there is a yearning for Me. I will see that kind of man through to the end."

There were others in the Scriptures who had their names changed. Abram's name was changed to Abraham. Saul's name was changed to Paul. Simon's name was changed to Peter. With only a few exceptions in Peter's case, he was thereafter referred to by his new name. The reason this was not true of Jacob is that at first he acted more like Jacob than Israel. He continued to supplant and deceive rather than to be commanded and ruled by God.

It is one thing to be privileged with a special visitation or manifestation of God, but it is quite another to live in the power of it. This, however, is the privilege the present-day believer has. Colossians 2:6,7 tells us, "As ye have therefore received Christ Jesus the Lord, so walk ye in him: Rooted and built up in him, and stablished in the faith, as ye have been taught, abounding therein with thanksgiving." Also, as we are told in Ephesians 6:10: "Be strong in the Lord, and in the power of his might."

## Needless Fear

After Peniel there were four distinct steps of backsliding in Jacob's life. The first was that of needless fear. Genesis 33:1,2 says, "And Jacob lifted up his eyes, and looked, and, behold, Esau came, and with him four hundred men. And he divided the children unto Leah, and unto Rachel, and unto the two handmaids. And he put the handmaids and their children foremost, and Leah and her children after, and Rachel and Joseph hindermost [last of all]." Jacob had just experienced a wonderful night with God which resulted in his becoming the new man, Israel. But now as he saw the danger—Esau coming with 400 men—fear gripped his heart.

Perhaps you say, "But it was only human for Jacob to react this way." That is exactly the point. It was a human reaction. God had assured Jacob that He would protect him, so Jacob really had nothing to worry about. His name had been changed to Israel and he was to be God's fighter. God was in complete charge of all circumstances and Jacob was to walk in that victory.

Jacob had already experienced how God could take care of him when Laban caught up with him after he had fled. God could also take care of Esau, but Jacob would have to bow to God's command of the situation. Jacob was not to do the planning; he was to believe God and walk in the victory that God would bring about.

The Christian who believes God is also assured of triumph in the Lord Jesus Christ. Paul wrote the Corinthian believers: "Thanks be to God, which giveth us the victory through our Lord Jesus Christ. Therefore, my beloved brethren, be ye stedfast, unmoveable, always abounding in the work of the Lord, forasmuch as ye know that your labour is not in vain in the Lord" (I Cor. 15:57,58). God does not always remove the obstacles from our pathway, but He always gives power to triumph over them.

Jacob could not believe as he ought to have, but God was faithful because He could not deny Himself. God was in command even though Jacob did not believe. The Scriptures tell us, "If we believe not, yet he [God] abideth faithful: he cannot deny himself" (II Tim. 2:13). Jacob's life illustrates the truth of this verse.

Jacob was slow to appropriate and order his life according to the new name God had given him. But consider how slow we are to do the same. God calls us "saints," which refers to godly, holy, pure, clean persons. This is what God has made us in His sight, and He says in effect, "You can walk accordingly, and I will give you the strength to do so." God also calls us "sons." This is not something to be realized in the future; it is true even now. The Scriptures say, "Beloved, now are we the sons of God" (I John 3:2).

God also calls us "heirs." Romans 8:17 says, "If children, then heirs; heirs of God, and joint-heirs with Christ; if so be that we suffer with him, that we may be also glorified together." God does everything for the believer. He indwells, empowers, commands, leads and fulfills—if we will but believe Him. The Christian life is a walk—it is lived a step at a time. The Christian life is not a magic carpet which suddenly transports us from one place to another. God provides all we need, but we must walk a step at a time.

Great experiences do not guarantee constant faithfulness. Jacob's great experience at Peniel was a stepping-stone to greater living, but it did not guarantee faithfulness on his part. He had made significant progress during his 20 years with Laban, but he was not yet all that God intended him to be. Even Paul wrote: "Brethren, I count not myself to have apprehended: but this one thing I do, forgetting those things which are behind, and reaching forth unto those things which are before, I press toward the mark for the prize of the high calling of God in Christ Jesus" (Phil. 3:13,14).

Experiences that result from crises are like open doors that make it possible for us to enter a newness of walk in the Christian pathway. Thus, Jesus said, "If any man will come after me, let him deny himself, and take up his cross daily, and follow me" (Luke 9:23). We are to daily take our position in Christ and follow Him. Galatians 5:16 assures us that when we walk in the Spirit we will not fulfill the lust of the flesh. When we commit ourselves to following Him, the Holy Spirit controls our lives and God lives the Christian life through us.

## Jacob Meets Esau

Jacob had tried to purchase Esau's favor earlier when he sent the various droves of animals out to meet him (Gen. 32:13-20). After his experience at Peniel, Jacob attempted to do the same thing. We do not have to be cowardly before those who might harm us. We are to stand courageous with God. In the New Testament, believers are instructed to "put on the whole armour of God, that ye may be able to stand against the wiles of the devil" (Eph. 6:11). This same passage of Scripture exhorts, "Wherefore take unto you the whole armour of God, that ye may be able to withstand in the evil day, and having done all, to stand" (v. 13). We need to stand, not haughtily, but boldly in Him.

Jacob had earlier revealed that he was willing to take the place of the younger before Esau when he referred to him as "lord" (Gen. 32:4,5,18). Now Jacob revealed this attitude again. Having divided the children and the mothers, Jacob "passed over before them, and bowed himself to the ground seven times, until he came near to his brother" (33:3).

When Jacob came near, "Esau ran to meet him, and embraced him, and fell on his neck, and kissed him: and they wept. And he lifted up his eyes, and saw the women and the children; and said, Who are those with thee? And he said, The children which God hath graciously given thy servant" (vv. 4,5). Jacob referred to himself as Esau's servant. He admitted that Esau was the elder and that as such the birthright belonged to him.

It was no longer necessary for Jacob to fear Esau because God had everything in hand. God had control of Esau even as He did of Jacob. No one could harm God's chosen one. Even though men rebel against God, God's Word assures us, "The king's heart is in the hand of the Lord, as the rivers of water: he turneth it whithersoever he will" (Prov. 21:1).

Jacob could finally say, as did the psalmist, "In God I will praise his word, in God I have put my trust; I will not fear what flesh can do unto me. In God have I put my trust: I will not be afraid what man can do unto me" (Ps. 56:4,11). In Hebrews 13:5,6 we have the same thought: "For he hath said, I will never leave thee, nor forsake thee. So that we may boldly say, The Lord is my helper, and I will not fear what man shall do unto me."

All of Jacob's planning was to no avail. God had subdued his enemy. Not only did God subdue Esau, but He also changed his heart attitude. What an unexpected reunion Jacob and Esau had. With this background, Psalm 46:7-10 is especially meaningful: "The Lord of hosts is with us; the God of Jacob is our refuge. Selah. Come, behold the works of the Lord, what desolations he hath made in the earth. He maketh wars to cease unto the end of the earth; he breaketh the bow, and cutteth the spear in sunder; he burneth the chariot in the fire. Be still, and know that I am God: I will be exalted among the heathen, I will be exalted in the earth."

## Jacob Lies to His Brother

After Jacob and Esau's reunion, Esau said, "Let us take our journey, and let us go, and I will go before thee" (Gen. 33:12). Esau offered to protect Jacob and those with him. Esau could easily have done this because there were 400 men with him. But Jacob answered, "My lord knoweth that the children are tender, and the flocks and herds with young are with me: and if men should overdrive them one day, all the flock will die. Let my lord, I pray thee, pass over before his servant: and I will lead on softly, according as the cattle that goeth before me and the children be able to endure, until I come unto my lord unto Seir" (vv. 13,14). Jacob indicated he would meet Esau at Seir. But the account continues, "And Esau said, Let me now leave with thee some of the folk that are with me. And he said, What needeth it? let me find grace in the sight of my lord. So Esau returned that day on his way unto Seir. And Jacob journeyed to Succoth, and built him an house, and made booths for his cattle: therefore the name of the place is called Succoth" (vv. 15-17).

God had clearly instructed Jacob that he was to return to his father and to Bethel. Jacob knew this, but he failed to testify to Esau by letting him know that he was following God's plan. Instead, Jacob led Esau to believe that he would follow him slowly and meet him in Seir. This was Jacob's second major step in backsliding after Peniel. Because of weakness and fear he lied to Esau. Jacob was afraid of what Esau might do, so he resorted to deceit. He feared Esau's temper more than God's disfavor.

Consider what Esau must have thought later when Jacob did not come as he had said. This supposedly spiritual leader had lied to his brother because he did not have the courage to tell him he was following God. Words that are not supported by actions turn many people away from the gospel. This is one of the reasons that the present-day church has lost rapport with the world. We are not direct in making our position with God known, and because of half-truths and timidity we are not winning people to the Lord as we should.

## Jacob Stops Short

Jacob's third major step in backsliding after Peniel was that he did not completely obey what God had instructed him to do. He was to return to Bethel, but he stopped at Succoth. He stopped short of the perfect will of God—short of Bethel. Jacob sought earthly advantages even as Lot did. Perhaps the grazing at Bethel was not as good for his livestock, and perhaps the environment was not as good for his children. Whatever the reasons, there was no excuse for disobeying God's instructions.

Jacob should have realized that seeking earthly advantages as Lot did would only bring on more trials. At Succoth, Jacob "built him an house" (v. 17). His tent-life was temporarily abandoned. There is nothing sinful about a house or earthly possessions; it is our attitude toward earthly possessions that constitutes sin. God was not going to give Jacob rest until he arrived at the place where He wanted him. Thus, God caused Jacob to leave Succoth.

## Farther, But Still Short

Genesis 33:18-20 says, "And Jacob came to Shalem, a city of Shechem, which is in the land of Canaan, when he came from Padan-aram; and pitched his tent before the city. And he bought a parcel of a field, where he had spread his tent, at the hand of the children of Hamor, Shechem's father, for an hundred pieces of money. And he erected there an altar, and called it El-elohe-Israel."

The word translated "Shalem" is literally "peace." Thus, the verse could read: "Jacob arrived safely and in peace at the city of Shechem." Although "Shalem" means "peace," Jacob did not have peace for long at that place. Again he purchased property so he might settle down. He was still short of returning to Bethel even though perhaps he planned to return to Bethel later.

Jacob actually bought a piece of property that was his by promise. It was his by faith, but his faith was too small. Perhaps he reasoned that this was a good place to settle down to rear his growing family. In this place he saw all the advantages that made it attractive to settle there instead of returning to Bethel.

Jacob built an altar, but not in the place where God had told him to build it. He was to have built it in Bethel, but in self-will he built it at Shechem. Many people are like this today. Attending church and having family devotions are very good things—and to be desired by all—but they are never substitutes for complete obedience.

I have heard some say, "I can serve the Lord here just as well as in some other place; there are many opportunities here." There are opportunities everywhere, but you cannot serve the Lord just as well in one place as in another. The only place where we can serve God as He intends is the place to which He has called us. God's fullest blessing is found only in the place of His choice for us. Unfaithfulness in this regard will not be offset by attending church or having a family altar.

Jacob called his altar "El-elohe-Israel." This name means "God, the God of Israel." No doubt Jacob was referring to himself and to the new name God had given him, because at this time there was no nation of Israel. Also, Jacob was probably referring to the vow he had made to God when he was fleeing from Esau: "If God will be with me, and will keep me in this way that I go, and will give me bread to eat, and raiment to put on, So that I come again to my father's house in peace; then shall the Lord be my God" (28:20,21). But neither Jacob nor the altar was where God ordered them to be.

Partial obedience is unsatisfactory to God. The account of King Saul vividly portrays what God thinks of partial obedience. Saul was to completely destroy the Amalekites and all of their possessions (I Sam. 15:3). However, Saul did not completely obey. He kept the best of the sheep and cattle and even spared the life of the king. When God, through Samuel, confronted Saul with his disobedience, Saul said, "The people spared the best of the sheep and of the oxen, to sacrifice unto the Lord thy God; and the rest we have utterly destroyed" (v. 15). Samuel said, "Hath the Lord as great delight in burnt-offerings and sacrifices, as in obeying the voice of the Lord? Behold, to obey is better than sacrifice, and to hearken than the fat of rams" (v. 22).

God did not accept Jacob's sacrifices and altar as long as Jacob was not in complete obedience. Let us learn this most important lesson. God is in command, and He expects total and unreserved obedience. Only then will He bless.

### Jacob Reaps Through His Family

Jacob did not completely obey God, and he began to reap what he had sown. This reaping was particularly through his children, for whose advantage he had probably settled in Shechem. One cannot stop short of God's will, purpose and place of service without reaping some bad fruit.

This truth has a direct application to America. Under God's hand it has had much protection and prosperity, but today even American Christians are failing God and turning to materialism. God's hand of blessing and protection is thus being lifted from America. We are beginning to reap what we have sown.

The true Church is the restraining force against evil, but when believers become like the rest of the world their restraint is nullified. Such Christians will also reap what they have sown. Too many Christians travel and move to places that will give their families mere earthly advantages without considering the proper environment of home, church, school and God's place of service for them. It has become the custom for both the father and mother to be employed outside the home so that many children are reared by baby-sitters. We may be sure that home life eventually affects national life. As far as the believer is concerned, his home life also affects his church life. Someone has said, "As goes the home, so goes the church and the nation."

Many parents and pastors are in anguish of soul because of the worldliness of their children. Such parents frequently blame circumstances for what their children are like even though the circumstances were probably of the parents' making. We must do more than blame the circumstances—we must correct the situation. There was no progress in Jacob's life until he corrected what he had done wrong.

How sad it is to realize that even Jacob's children experienced the tragic effects of Jacob's unfaithfulness. Genesis 34:1 says, "And Dinah the daughter of Leah, which she bare unto Jacob, went out to see the daughters of the land." Dinah was the only daughter, and I believe she may have felt her parents were too narrow-minded in the standards they had set for her. The result was a debasing experience, for "when Shechem the son of Hamor the Hivite, prince of the country, saw her, he took her, and lay with her, and defiled her" (v. 2). Jacob was reaping the results of incomplete obedience—his daughter was defiled. What a heartbreaking experience this must have been for Jacob.

In our day we have lost the concept of how desecrating and defiling this sin really is. The New Testament gives us clear instructions about defiling the body. First Corinthians 3:16,17 says, "Know ye not that ye are the temple of God, and that the Spirit of God dwelleth in you? If any man defile the temple of God, him shall God destroy; for the temple of God is holy, which temple ye are." The sixth chapter of this same book tells us, "Now the body is not for fornication, but for the Lord; and the Lord for the body. Know ye not that your bodies are the members of Christ? shall I then take the members of Christ, and make them the members of an harlot? God forbid. What? know ye not that he which is joined to an harlot is one body? for two, saith he, shall be one flesh. But he that is joined unto the Lord is one spirit. Flee fornication. Every sin that a man doeth is without the body; but he that committeth fornication sinneth against his own body" (vv. 13,15-18).

The reason the sin of fornication is so serious for the believer is that it is committed against his body, which is a temple of the Holy Spirit. The following two verses of this passage say, "What? know ye not that your body is the temple of the Holy Ghost which is in you, which ye have of God, and ye are not your own? For ye are bought with a price: therefore glorify God in your body, and in your spirit, which are God's."

## A Satanic Suggestion

After Shechem had defiled Dinah, "his soul clave unto Dinah the daughter of Jacob, and he loved the damsel, and spake kindly unto the damsel. And Shechem spake unto his father Hamor, saying, Get me this damsel to wife" (Gen. 34:3,4). Shechem tried to remedy the situation by offering marriage. Observe that Satan, who brought about the fall of man, suggested a remedy of a mixed marriage—a believer with an unbeliever. Satan always fosters mixture, not separation. Verses 8-12 of this chapter give us the account of how Hamor presented the case for further coexistence with Jacob and his people. Hamor said, "Make ye marriages with us, and give your daughters unto us, and take our daughters unto you" (v. 9).

Jacob had not come to this serious situation in one great fall. It was by a series of steps that he had now come to this despicable situation. First, there was compromise. God had told him to go to Bethel, which involved a separation from the world. Second, there was only partial obedience. Jacob had only come as far as Shechem—there was not total separation. Third, this situation caused their only daughter to be tempted to go and see the world around her. Fourth, she became defiled by Shechem, the son of Hamor. Fifth, there was the offer by the Hivites to intermarry and coexist with the Israelites. Sixth, all of this led to further sin within Jacob's own family.

The Bible says, "Jacob heard that he [Shechem] had defiled Dinah his daughter: now his sons were with his cattle in the field: and Jacob held his peace until they were come. And the sons of Jacob came out of the field when they heard it: and the men were grieved, and they were very wroth, because he had wrought folly in Israel in lying with Jacob's daughter; which thing ought not to be done" (vv. 5,7).

### The Plot for Revenge

Jacob's sons plotted a way of revenge against Shechem and the Hivites. "The sons of Jacob answered Shechem and Hamor his father deceitfully, and said, because he had defiled Dinah their sister: And they said unto them, We cannot do this thing, to give our sister to one that is uncircumcised; for that were a reproach unto us: But in this will we consent unto you: If ye will be as we be, that every male of you be circumcised; Then we will give our daughters unto you, and we will take your daughters to us, and we will dwell with you, and we will become one people. But if ye will not hearken unto us, to be circumcised; then will we take our daughter, and we will be gone" (vv. 13-17).

In God's moral order there is no allowance for compromise with evil. James 4:4 says, "Ye adulterers and adulteresses, know ye not that the friendship of the world is enmity with God? whosoever therefore will be a friend of the world is the enemy of God." Through the Apostle Paul, God also tells us, "Be ye not unequally yoked together with unbelievers: for what fellowship hath righteousness with unrighteousness? and what communion hath light with darkness? And what concord hath Christ with Belial? or what part hath he that believeth with an infidel? And what agreement hath the temple of God with idols? for ye are the temple of the living God; as God hath said, I will dwell in them, and walk in them; and I will be their God, and they shall be my people. Wherefore come out from among them, and be ye separate, saith the Lord, and touch not the unclean thing; and I will receive you" (II Cor. 6:14-17).

God's principle is that there can be no possession without there first being dispossession. God wanted the Israelites to possess the land of Canaan without compromising with the ungodly peoples around them, and today He wants the believer to live in the world but not to be a part of the world.

Coexistence with evil is in direct opposition to the principles of God. However, it has always been Satan's trick to get the believer to compromise with evil. Satan accomplished a significant victory in the fourth century when Constantine joined his empire with the church. And Satan is gaining an even greater victory through the present-day emphasis of the ecumenical church. It offers so-called union at the expense of spiritual separation.

The sons of Jacob were deceitful. As was the father, so were the sons. Jacob was now able to see himself in his sons. He could now see the results of his own scheming. However, his sons went a step further by using a purely religious covenant for a fleshly means to an end, which they felt was justifiable. They knew that what Shechem had done to their sister was a horrible sin, but what they plotted was not going to solve the problem.

Jacob's sons used a religious covenant as a cover for premeditated murder. Their proposition "pleased Hamor, and Shechem Hamor's son" (Gen. 34:18). Hamor and Shechem went back to their people and urged them to consent to the religious covenant: "Hamor and Shechem his son came unto the gate of their city, and communed with the men of their city, saying, These men are peaceable with us; therefore let them dwell in the land, and trade therein; for the land, behold, it is large enough for them; let us take their daughters to us for wives, and let us give them our daughters. Only herein will the men consent unto us for to dwell with us, to be one people, if every male among us be circumcised, as they are circumcised. Shall not their cattle and their substance and every beast of their's be our's? only let us consent unto them, and they will dwell with us" (vv. 20-23).

Compromise always seems to bring gain. Lot entered Sodom for gain, and history has recorded the tragic results of his compromise. Genesis 34 proves to us that even unbelievers will compromise and agree to religious vows if they think they will profit.

Genesis 34:25-29 says, "And it came to pass on the third day, when they were sore, that two of the sons of Jacob, Simeon and Levi, Dinah's brethren, took each man his sword, and came upon the city boldly, and slew all the males. And they slew Hamor and Shechem his son with the edge of the sword, and took Dinah out of Shechem's house, and went out. The sons of Jacob came upon the slain, and spoiled the city, because they had defiled their sister. They took their sheep, and their oxen, and their asses, and that which was in the city, and that which was in the field, And all their wealth, and all their little ones, and their wives took they captive, and spoiled even all that was in the house." Such treachery in the name of religion! Some of the blackest crimes in history have been committed in the name of religion. When the Hivites were unable to defend themselves, they were slain. Satan does not protect his own; therefore, it never pays to compromise.

Not only did the sons of Jacob commit murder, but they also sacked the city, taking captive the children and wives of the men and carrying off the wealth of the city. The women were perhaps put to use as slaves, and some possibly became wives of the captors. How cruel can men be? How far can they fall into sin? When a person is out of the will of God and compromises with the world, he may be surprised at the things he finds himself doing.

## Jacob's Rebuke

Jacob was not a part of the plot of his sons. However, he was reaping what he had sown. Finally, Jacob spoke up. He said to Simeon and Levi, "Ye have troubled me to make me to stink among the inhabitants of the land, among the Canaanites and the Perizzites: and I being few in number, they shall gather themselves together against me, and slay me; and I shall be destroyed, I and my house" (v. 30).

Jacob's rebuke was completely based on the human aftermath of what Simeon and Levi had done, not on the sin and dishonor it had been to God. All that Jacob seemed to be concerned about was what the people would do to him. Not only was Jacob overlooking the sin of his sons, but he was also completely forgetting God's promise to protect him and to bring him into the land again. God had told Jacob, "I am with thee, and will keep thee in all places whither thou goest, and will bring thee again into this land; for I will not leave thee, until I have done that which I have spoken to thee of" (28:15). When Jacob rebuked his sons he was speaking as Jacob, not Israel. He was speaking as a supplanter and deceiver, not the prince of God who was to be God's fighter.

Jacob had compromised. He had settled in Shechem, not Bethel. Now the old fears came back to haunt him. However, the Bible says, "There is no fear in love; but perfect love casteth out fear: because fear hath torment. He that feareth is not made perfect in love" (I John 4:18). Referring to Jesus Christ, Hebrews 2:14,15 tells us, "Forasmuch then as the children are partakers of flesh and blood, he also himself likewise took part of the same; that through death he might destroy him that had the power of death, that is, the devil; And deliver them who through fear of death were all their lifetime subject to bondage." God has overcome Satan; therefore, there is no reason to fear if we are walking in fellowship with God. Jacob feared because he was not separated unto God and completely obedient to God's will. One begins to wonder how much more Jacob would have to endure before he would see his need of complete reliance on and obedience to God.

After Jacob rebuked his sons, they asked, "Should he deal with our sister as with an harlot?" (Gen. 34:31). Simeon and Levi tried to justify their actions. At times, do we not also think it is all right to do evil in order that good may come? Jacob's sons were right—it should never have happened. And it would not have happened if Jacob had gone to Bethel as God had instructed him. Jacob compromised, and his sons compromised with him. The sin of Shechem was an awful sin, but the sins of deceit and murder did not correct anything. One sin is not made right by committing another.

Jacob never forgot the deeds of his sons. Later he said, "Simeon and Levi are brethren; instruments of cruelty are in their habitations. O my soul, come not thou into their secret; unto their assembly, mine honour, be not thou united: for in their anger they slew a man, and in their selfwill they digged down a wall. Cursed be their anger, for it was fierce; and their wrath, for it was cruel: I will divide them in Jacob, and scatter them in Israel" (49:5-7).

## Worldliness

The lesson that stands out from this incident involving Jacob, Simeon and Levi is the danger of worldliness. Worldliness is hard to define, but it is easy to detect and describe. It is an atmosphere that is lowering, poisoning, deadening and disastrous to the soul, and *always* dishonoring to God. It leads to deeper and deeper sin. Worldliness prevents spiritual blessing. Jacob could have no testimony among the Gentiles where he lived because of his compromise and worldliness.

Both Abraham and Isaac were guilty of lying about their wives, but both of them made things right with God and brought honor to Him by the way they lived. As a result, they were respected by those around them. How different it was, however, with Lot in Sodom and now with Jacob.

Worldliness can be prevented only by complete separation. In Christ's prayer, recorded in John 17, there is revealed the only safeguard against the insidious peril of worldliness. First, as Christ prayed to the Father, He said, "I have manifested thy name unto the men which thou gavest me out of the world" (v. 6). God took them out of the world and gave them to Jesus. Second, Jesus said, "Now I am no more in the world, but these are in the world" (v. 11). Third, Christ said, "I have given them thy word; and the world hath hated them" (v. 14). Fourth, Christ said that the world hated them "because they are not of the world, even as I am not of the world" (v. 14). The believers were in the world but they were not to be of the world. Fifth, Christ said, "I pray not that thou shouldest take them out of the world, but that thou shouldest keep them from the evil [one]" (v. 15). Sixth, Christ prayed, "As thou hast sent me into the world, even so have I also sent them into the world" (v. 18). Seventh, the reason Christ prayed that the believers would be sent into the world but kept from the world was so "the world may know that thou hast sent me, and hast loved them, as thou hast loved me"(v. 23). They were to witness *to* the world but not be *of* the world.

### Jacob Reaches the Bottom

God allowed Jacob to go to the depths of sin. Worldliness completely overwhelmed him. He could not go any lower, and his family could not go any lower. They were now in disrepute with the nations around them. They were guilty of murder because of their desire to right a wrong against their family. Even though Jacob had fallen to the depths of sin, God never gave up working with him. God did not leave Jacob alone until Jacob was back in the center of His will. God commanded him, "Arise, go up to Beth-el, and dwell there: and make there an altar unto God, that appeared unto thee when thou fleddest from the face of Esau thy brother" (Gen. 35:1). Even though Jacob often turned his back on God, it could never be said that God was unfaithful to Jacob. It is wonderful to know that the God of Jacob is our God also. How long-suffering and merciful God is to His own! With Jeremiah, every believer can say, "It is of the Lord's mercies that we are not consumed, because his compassions fail not. They are new every morning: great is thy faithfulness" (Lam. 3:22,23).

Chapter 25

# Bethel at Last

Jacob had spent 20 years with Laban under the disciplining hand of God. All of this time God was working with Jacob to make him into the kind of man He wanted him to be. During those 20 years Jacob sowed both good and bad, and reaped as he had sown. For the most part, however, his life during that time was lived in the energy of the flesh. Then, at Peniel, Jacob met God and had his name changed to Israel. Jacob knew the importance of returning to Bethel, but for 10 years after his experience at Peniel he lived in a backslidden condition.

Just as Christ told the Church of Ephesus to "remember therefore from whence thou art fallen, and repent, and do the first works" (Rev. 2:5), so God instructed Jacob to return to Bethel. It was only about 30 miles from Shechem to Bethel, but Jacob tarried at Shechem for nearly 10 years. There he reaped what he had sown to the flesh. The way back to God is repentance and faith. The two always go together. Jacob was still not living in complete fellowship with God. Although he had been back in the land 10 years, he was still short of Bethel. But at Shechem, God shut Jacob up to Himself.

Because of what his sons had done, Jacob needed to flee Shechem. But where could he go? He could not go back to Laban. Neither could he go back to Esau, for he had deceived him on the other side of the Jordan. Jacob had said he would follow slowly after Esau and meet him in Seir, but instead Jacob went to Succoth and then on to Shechem. God had

Jacob where He wanted him. Jacob was hemmed in on all sides. He had no place to flee but to God Himself.

In God's fourth communication with Jacob, He said, "Arise, go up to Beth-el, and dwell there: and make there an altar unto God, that appeared unto thee when thou fleddest from the face of Esau thy brother" (Gen. 35:1). Each previous communication that God had had with Jacob was for the purpose of establishing and restoring him. Jacob had a restless faith and he needed to become established in his faith. In God's fourth communication with Jacob, He gave him the final call for complete separation. There was no other place Jacob could go. His only alternative was to flee to God. But to flee to God is to go forward with God.

God's call for Jacob to return to the land of his fathers was given on several occasions. After Jacob had spent 20 years with Laban, God told him, "Return unto the land of thy fathers, and to thy kindred; and I will be with thee" (31:3). When Jacob was returning and was on the border of the land, God appeared to him and said, "I am the God of Beth-el, where thou anointedst the pillar, and where thou vowedst a vow unto me: now arise, get thee out from this land, and return unto the land of thy kindred" (v. 13). In Genesis 35:1 God once more, and with great emphasis, commanded Jacob to return to Bethel.

Jacob's experience at Shechem, when he had no place to turn but to God, was similar to the experience the nation of Israel had later. Under the leadership of Moses the nation was fleeing Egypt, but they became hemmed in on all sides. The Red Sea was in front of them, the mountains on one side, the desert on the other, and the Egyptians were pursuing behind. They had only one way to go and that was to follow God and cast themselves completely on Him. As a result, He led them through the Red Sea without casualty.

## Jacob Makes Haste

For Jacob, the patient chastening of a loving Heavenly Father had achieved its purpose: Jacob made haste to do as

God had told him. God had met Jacob at Peniel and had changed his name and had made great promises to him. There were some great advances in Jacob's life at Peniel, but a great time of crisis was still to follow. Jacob fell into deep sin after the mountaintop experience at Peniel. It was extremely difficult for him to learn the lessons of God, so God had to allow him and his family to fall into great reproach to cause them to see the need of returning to Bethel.

God's purpose had been accomplished—Jacob did not linger any longer. In God's command for Jacob to return to Bethel, He reminded him that it was the place where He had met him when he was fleeing from Esau. Once Jacob fully remembered Bethel, he also realized how far he had really fallen. In Shechem he could not realize this because he had grown too accustomed to sin. His backslidden condition and the unregenerate people around him had clouded his vision so that he could not see the standards of God.

Today, much of Christianity is in the same condition. We have our local churches and we attend them regularly, but somehow we are blinded to the way we are going. The age of secularization has affected us to the extent that we cannot see the time we are wasting which could be profitably spent for God.

Once Jacob had a renewed vision of the God of Bethel, it stirred him to quick action. The memory of past sins and what he had reaped from them drove him toward Bethel.

Perhaps this is the way God is working in your life. Has He had to bring many difficulties and much suffering into your life to cause you to want to return to fellowship with Him? If you have not yet come to this place, how much more distress is God going to have to bring on you before you turn completely to Him? It is not necessary that all of these things come to you. Jacob could have gone directly to Bethel from Peniel, but he spent 10 years enroute even though it was only about 30 miles in distance.

When God gave His call for complete separation—His command for Jacob to return to Bethel—Jacob lived up to his new name, Israel. "Then Jacob said unto his household, and to all that were with him, Put away the strange gods that are among you, and be clean, and change your garments: And let us arise, and go up to Beth-el; and I will make there an altar unto God, who answered me in the day of my distress, and was with me in the way which I went" (vv. 2,3). Jacob's family obeyed: "They gave unto Jacob all the strange gods which were in their hand, and all their earrings which were in their ears; and Jacob hid them under the oak which was by Shechem" (v. 4). Jacob's family, including the sons who had committed murder, were suddenly obedient to him instead of rebellious. What had made the difference? The difference was that Jacob was now speaking with the authority of God. God was now in command and was speaking through Jacob to his family.

### Strange Gods Put Away

In preparation for their leaving Shechem for Bethel, Jacob asked for three things. First, he asked that the strange gods be put away (v. 2). It would be impossible to have these and the altar of God at the same time. Jacob made it clear to his family that his intent was to go up to Bethel and build an altar to God there (v. 3).

Because Jacob asked for the strange gods, they gave him their gods and also their earrings. It was the custom of the day to use earrings in godless ceremonies. Aaron asked for the golden earrings when he made the golden calf (Ex. 32:2). In referring to adulterous Israel, God said, "I will visit upon her the days of Baalim, wherein she burned incense to them, and she decked herself with her earrings and her jewels, and she went after her lovers, and forgat me, saith the Lord" (Hos. 2:13).

Remember, Rachel had stolen the gods of her father, Laban. There is no record that Jacob had said anything about these gods previously, but now he said, "Put away the strange gods." During the time he was out of fellowship with God, Jacob was so weak spiritually that he did not have a clear-cut witness for God. Our testimony will also be weak before the world if we are not in fellowship with God and speaking with His authority.

After the strange gods had been given to Jacob, he "hid them under the oak which was by Shechem" (Gen. 35:4). Jacob knew he never dared to go back to Shechem again, so he buried the gods there. The things of Satan are never to be used in the service of God. Certain things in connection with the natural life must be entirely given up and destroyed. It is impossible to consecrate and sanctify them to God's service. Have you had a burial service for the unholy things in your life?

The Bible speaks strongly against those who follow after gods and idols. The word "idol" refers to that which is wholly seen. Whenever we are living for that which is seen instead of that which is unseen, we are idol worshipers. Thus, we see how easy it is to make idols out of our work, recreation, family, etc. If our lives are devoted to God, who is not seen, then we will have the right relationship to those things which are seen. The attitude of believers should be: "We look not at the things which are seen, but at the things which are not seen: for the things which are seen are temporal; but the things which are not seen are eternal" (II Cor. 4:18).

## Cleansing Commanded

Jacob not only demanded his household to put away the strange gods, but he also commanded them: "Be clean" (Gen. 35:2). This command was in preparation for meeting God. Jacob realized there had to be a cleansing if they were to meet God and have real fellowship with Him. For Jacob this did not have to do with the cleansing of salvation, for he had met God 30 years earlier at Bethel, which was probably the time of his salvation. But now Jacob was coming back to Bethel to meet God, and it was important for him to be clean as he did so. What was necessary for Jacob, he also demanded of his family.

The means of cleansing for present-day Christians is found in I John 1:9: "If we confess our sins, he is faithful and just to forgive us our sins, and to cleanse us from all unrighteousness." These sins may be sins of omission as well as sins of commission, but verse 7 of the same chapter assures us, "If we walk in the light, as he is in the light, we have fellowship one with another, and the blood of Jesus Christ his Son cleanseth us from all sin."

Do you really desire fellowship with God? If you do, meditate on Psalm 139. It is a psalm which you should read over and over again. This psalm shows how God can look into our hearts. He sees everything; He knows everything. God even knows the words you are going to speak before you speak them. Because of this, the Psalmist David prayed, "Search me, O God, and know my heart: try me, and know my thoughts: And see if there be any wicked way in me, and lead me in the way everlasting" (vv. 23,24). David was asking God to put him to the test—to try him. If there was anything in his life that was grievous or injurious to God in any way, David was determined to confess it and be cleansed from it.

Psalm 56:13 has been a blessing to me many times. The psalmist told God, "For thou hast delivered my soul from death: wilt not thou deliver my feet from falling, that I may walk before God in the light of the living?" If you have received Jesus Christ as Saviour, you can say with the psalmist, "Thou hast delivered my soul from death." As you live the Christian life, you need to make the rest of this verse your prayer: "Wilt not thou deliver my feet from falling, that I may walk before God in the light of the living?"

## 'Change Your Garments'

In addition to Jacob's commanding that his household put away the strange gods and be clean, he also commanded: "Change your garments" (Gen. 35:2). This is most important in its spiritual application. There were garments of self-righteousness which Jacob's household had to put aside. New Testament believers are commanded: "Put off concerning the former conversation the old man, which is corrupt according to the deceitful lusts; And be renewed in the spirit of your mind; And that ye put on the new man, which after God is created in righteousness and true holiness. Wherefore putting away lying, speak every man truth with his neighbour: for we are members one of another" (Eph. 4:22-25).

We who know Christ as Saviour have died with Him to the old self, and our need is to appropriate the benefits of His death for our lives. Christ not only died for our sins, but we died with Him to sin. Therefore, the believer is to "put off" the things concerning the old man, the flesh. This is done by an act of faith as seen in Romans 6:6,11-13.

After Jacob's instructions had been followed, the Scriptures say, "They journeyed: and the terror of God was upon the cities that were round about them, and they did not pursue after the sons of Jacob. So Jacob came to Luz, which is in the land of Canaan, that is, Beth-el, he and all the people that were with him" (Gen. 35:5,6). Because God was in command, He took all evil intent from the enemies of Jacob so that Jacob and those with him were not harmed. God has sovereign control, and when we obey Him we reap the blessings of that control. There is not a hand that can be raised against God's saints when they are in the center of His will. "When a man's ways please the Lord, he maketh even his enemies to be at peace with him" (Prov. 16:7).

## Jacob Builds an Altar

God protected Jacob and he arrived safely at his destination. Bethel at last! Then Jacob "built there an altar, and called the place El-beth-el: because there God appeared unto him, when he fled from the face of his brother" (Gen. 35:7). This was in fulfillment of what Jacob had told his household when they were making preparations to go to Bethel: "Let us arise, and go up to Beth-el; and I will make there an altar unto God, who answered me in the day of my distress, and was with me in the way which I went" (v. 3). At that time, Jacob was saying to his family, "I am going back to where I found God, and there I am going to set up an altar to the God who has protected me these 30 years and has now led me back." That is exactly what Jacob did. On arrival at Bethel he built an altar unto God.

When Jacob built his new altar at Bethel he called it "El-beth-el." Previously at Shechem he had built an altar and called it "El-elohe-Israel." His name for the altar at Shechem meant "God, the God of Israel." Israel was Jacob's spiritual name. In this we see the importance of recognizing God as our personal God. But when Jacob built the new altar at Bethel he called it "El-beth-el," which means "the God of Beth-el." The word "Beth-el" means "the house of God." So "El-beth-el" is literally "the God of the house of God." Jacob saw the Heavenly Father as the God of the whole house of God. Jacob saw Him as his personal God and he also realized that He was the God of every believer, for He is the ever-present God of the house of God.

This truth has its parallel in the New Testament. Ephesians 1:22,23 says, "And hath put all things under his feet, and gave him to be the head over all things to the church, Which is his body, the fulness of him that filleth all in all." Every believer is baptized into the Body of Christ. First Corinthians 12:12,13 says, "For as the body is one, and hath many members, and all the members of that one body, being many, are one body: so also is Christ. For by one Spirit are we all baptized into one body, whether we be Jews or Gentiles, whether we be bond or free; and have been all made to drink into one Spirit."

There is just one Head—Jesus Christ—and every believer is a member of His Body. Ephesians 4:15,16 emphasizes this truth: "But speaking the truth in love, may grow up into him in all things, which is the head, even Christ: From whom the whole body fitly joined together and compacted by that which every joint supplieth, according to the effectual working in the measure of every part, maketh increase of the body unto the edifying of itself in love."

In Genesis 28:19, after Jacob had a vision of the ladder which reached to heaven, he called the name of the place "Beth-el," the house of God. But after he returned to Bethel, he built an altar and called it "El-beth-el," the God of the house of God. The latter was a far higher view of God. The first name emphasized the place or house of God, whereas the latter emphasized God Himself. God had become more real to Jacob. His desire had become like the Apostle Paul's of the New Testament: "That I may know him" (Phil. 3:10).

When Jacob returned to Bethel, he found things as he had left them. It was here, 30 years earlier, that Jacob had felt so small in the sight of God. Now he had been brought back to that place where he had earlier found real fellowship with God. During his years away from Bethel, Jacob thought he had attained so much by outscheming others. He had become too big to realize his need of God.

When a person first enters God's service, he feels exceedingly small. He realizes he is nothing in the sight of God. But after much success there is the temptation to feel self-sufficient. Remember King Saul. Samuel told him, "When thou wast little in thine own sight, wast thou not made the head of the tribes of Israel, and the Lord anointed thee king over Israel?" (I Sam. 15:17). Many of God's servants have to be set aside by Him because they do not remain small in their own sight.

James 4:6-10 is a passage of Scripture on which every believer ought to meditate frequently: "But he giveth more grace. Wherefore he saith, God resisteth the proud, but giveth grace unto the humble. Submit yourselves therefore to God. Resist the devil, and he will flee from you. Draw nigh to God, and he will draw nigh to you. Cleanse your hands, ye sinners; and purify your hearts, ye double minded. Be afflicted, and mourn, and weep: let your laughter be turned to mourning, and your joy to heaviness. Humble yourselves in the sight of the Lord, and he shall lift you up."

When Jacob came back to Bethel, he was returning to the joy of his salvation. His years away from God had brought great agony of soul, even as David's sin had brought great anguish to him and caused him to pray, "Restore unto me the joy of thy salvation" (Ps. 51:12).

### God Appears to Jacob

After Jacob built the altar unto God, "God appeared unto Jacob again, when he came out of Padan-aram, and blessed him" (Gen. 35:9). Jacob received a new revelation from God when he returned to Bethel. Reconciliation had been completed. This was the fifth communication God had with Jacob. In it, He ratified the covenant He had made with Abraham and had later confirmed to Isaac. God told Jacob, "Thy name is Jacob: thy name shall not be called any more Jacob, but Israel shall be thy name: and he called his name Israel. And God said unto him, I am God Almighty: be fruitful and multiply; a nation and a company of nations shall be of thee, and kings shall come out of thy loins; And the land which I gave Abraham and Isaac, to thee I will give it, and to thy seed after thee will I give the land" (vv. 10-12).

The princeliness of Jacob was restored! God called him Israel instead of Jacob. Ten years earlier God had changed Jacob's name to Israel, but Jacob had not appropriated his position. So also, when we received Jesus Christ as Saviour we were called "saints" and "sons of God," but it is possible we have never appropriated the provisions God has made for our lives. Positionally, Jacob had a new name, but he had been living in a backslidden state. Then he came back to Bethel.

From this time forward Jacob did not backslide to his old life of scheming and deception. He applied faith and appropriated the provisions of God. As a result, in Hebrews 11 his name is mentioned in the gallery of the men of faith, alongside those of Abraham and Isaac (vv. 17-21).

When Jacob returned to Bethel, his communion and prayer life were reestablished. Genesis 35:13 says, "And God went up from him in the place where he talked with him." After Jacob had made things right in his life, he was able to talk freely and commune with God.

Have you also experienced the dryness of life that comes from a lack of communion with God? Are there things in your life that need to be confessed to God? If so, apply I John 1:9, and as you appropriate His forgiveness and cleansing, you will again know the sweetness and blessing which come from talking and communing with God. How wonderful it is to be on good speaking terms with our God!

### A Divine Ebenezer

After God had gone up from the place where He and Jacob had talked, "Jacob set up a pillar in the place where he talked with him, even a pillar of stone: and he poured a drink-offering thereon, and he poured oil thereon. And Jacob called the name of the place where God spake with him, Beth-el" (vv. 14,15). Out of gratitude Jacob established a memorial to God—a divine Ebenezer. God had recovered His wayward child; Jacob had now become established in God. God knew from the beginning that this would be the result. That is why He was long-suffering and continued to work with Jacob.

The outworking of God's purpose for all of our lives is seen in Romans 8:28,29: "And we know that all things work together for good to them that love God, to them who are the called according to his purpose. For whom he did foreknow, he also did predestinate to be conformed to the image of his Son, that he might be the firstborn among many brethren."

God predestinates in the sense that He undertakes to see something through to its end. Certainly this was true concerning Jacob. Nothing about Jacob was wasted as far as being used to accomplish God's purpose in his life. Even Jacob's failures were used by God to accomplish His desired end. Each of Jacob's failures had an important educative value. The supreme lesson we can learn from Jacob is that no failure need be final. There is always hope in God.

There is no past failure that makes it impossible for you to have the approval of God. Failures are to be confessed to

God, and then you are to step out in faith for Him. The Apostle Paul said, "Forgetting those things which are behind, and reaching forth unto those things which are before, I press toward the mark for the prize of the high calling of God in Christ Jesus" (Phil. 3:13,14). When a person receives Jesus Christ as his Saviour, God begins to do a work in him, and nothing deters Him from performing and finishing that work.

The principle by which God works in our lives is faith. That which is important about faith is not its quantity but its object. Faith in itself is valueless, but faith in God is invaluable. God always honors faith, regardless of how feeble and trembling it may be.

It was faith in God that marked the difference between Jacob and Esau. God never pursued after Esau to accomplish a great work in his life because Esau despised the things of God. Faith in God was not evident in Esau's life. Even Lot, who was a child of God, did not desire the deep things of God, so God did not do a great work in his life either.

God did not follow after these men, but in long-suffering He pursued Jacob because deep down in his heart there was a longing for the things of God—even though he often tried to obtain them by carnal means.

## God Is Just

It must be remembered, however, that even though God is a God of patience and love, He is also a God of justice. In bringing Jacob back to Himself, God made no allowance for His servant's sin. In fact, Hebrews 12:5-11 indicates that God is more strict with His own children because He wants to bring out the best in them. Because God is holy and just, He cannot overlook sin.

Jacob had made a solemn vow when he had been at Bethel earlier: "If God will be with me, and will keep me in this way that I go, and will give me bread to eat, and raiment to put on, So that I come again to my father's house in peace; then shall the Lord be my God: And this stone, which I have set for a pillar, shall be God's house: and of all that thou shalt give me I will surely give the tenth unto thee" (Gen. 28:20-22). God had completely fulfilled His part, yet much of Jacob's part had not yet been fulfilled. Jacob's need was to "repent, and do the first works," even as Christ instructed the Church of Ephesus (Rev. 2:5).

When Jacob returned to Bethel, it was his pleasure to make things right with God. Jacob set up "a pillar of stone" (Gen. 35:14), which no doubt reminded him of his vow and the pillar of stone at Bethel previously. Then Jacob "poured a drink-offering thereon, and he poured oil thereon." All of this indicates that he now had the pleasure of fellowship with God. Jacob was fully restored, and he began to appropriate the provisions of God and to live in accordance with his name, Israel.

God performed a great work in Jacob. What has God been able to do with you? The following poem emphasizes God's loving patience:

He came to my desk with a quivering lip–
The lesson was done.
"Dear teacher, I want a new leaf," he said–
I have spoiled this one."
In place of the leaf so stained and blotted
I gave him a new one all unspotted.
And into his sad eyes smiled–
"Do better now, my child."

I went to the throne with a quivering soul–
The old year was done.
Dear Father, hast Thou a new leaf for me?
I have spoiled this one."
He took the old leaf, stained and blotted,
And gave me a new one all unspotted,
And into my sad heart smiled–
"Do better now, My child."

–Author Unknown

Chapter 26

# The School of Sorrow

Sorrow is one of God's means to make permanent in our lives the lessons of grace He has taught us. God had been dealing with Jacob for 30 years, and now, back at Bethel Jacob was where God wanted him to be. Now God began to make permanent—to press deep into his heart—the lessons He had taught him during those 30 years.

From the day Jacob fulfilled his vow at Bethel to the day he learned Joseph was alive and the ruler in Egypt, Jacob was scarcely out of the furnace of affliction.

God makes no mistakes. He knows what He is doing. Sorrow is not necessarily punishment, but it strengthens us in Him by perfecting our faith and confidence in Him. Sorrow is often used for spiritual training. Through the process of chastening, God makes us into the kind of sons He wants us to be. Sorrow is intended to yield the peaceable fruit of righteousness: "Now no chastening for the present seemeth to be joyous, but grievous: nevertheless afterward it yieldeth the peaceable fruit of righteousness unto them which are exercised thereby" (Heb. 12:11). The peaceable fruit of righteousness only comes "afterward"—after the chastening.

### Rebekah's Nurse Dies

Jacob felt the chastening hand of God even while he was at Bethel. After returning to Bethel, "Deborah Rebekah's nurse died, and she was buried beneath Beth-el under an oak: and the name of it was called Allon-bachuth" (Gen. 35:8). Deborah was probably the nurse who went with Rebekah when she left home to marry Isaac (24:59). Deborah must have been dear to Jacob since she had likely been his nurse as a child. She may have come to Jacob earlier to inform him of his mother's death. Doubtlessly she had filled a vacant spot in his heart after the death of his mother.

Deborah's death was the final separation of Jacob from his unregenerate life at home. The last link had been broken. There was no one left now to remind him of his past unregenerate life. Back at Bethel, Jacob was now ready for God to deal the death blow on anything that could link his life to the old ways and keep him from God.

This truth is also important for us today. Colossians 3:1-4 says, "If [since] ye then be risen with Christ, seek those things which are above, where Christ sitteth on the right hand of God. Set your affection on things above, not on things on the earth. For ye are dead [have died], and your life is hid with Christ in God. When Christ, who is our life, shall appear, then shall ye also appear with him in glory." Galatians 2:20 says, "I am [have been] crucified with Christ: nevertheless I live; yet not I, but Christ liveth in me: and the life which I now live in the flesh I live by the faith of the Son of God, who loved me, and gave himself for me."

### Jacob's Wife Dies

Then Rachel, Jacob's beloved wife, died while they were enroute to Ephrath (Bethlehem). "Bethlehem" means "the house of bread." Jacob was traveling from the house of God (Bethel) to the house of bread (Bethlehem). Genesis 35:16 says, "And they journeyed from Beth-el; and there was but a little way to come to Ephrath: and Rachel travailed, and she had hard labour." Note that there was only "a little way" between Bethel and Bethlehem. Although these were literal cities, they point out a principle to us. The house of God and the house of bread are closely connected. When we put God first in everything, He provides the needs of our lives. Christ Himself told His disciples, "Seek ye first the kingdom of

God, and his righteousness; and all these things shall be added unto you" (Matt. 6:33).

When Rachel "was in hard labour, . . . the midwife said unto her, Fear not; thou shalt have this son also. And it came to pass, as her soul was in departing, (for she died) that she called his name Ben-oni: but his father called him Benjamin. And Rachel died, and was buried in the way to Ephrath, which is Beth-lehem" (Gen. 35:17-19).

Rachel named the child "Ben-oni," which means "son of sorrow." However, Jacob named the child "Benjamin," which means "son of my right hand." Rachel's death was one of Jacob's deepest sorrows. She died sorrowing, but he triumphed in faith and called the child "son of my right hand," which was the same as calling him "the victorious one."

Jacob took a victorious stand for God in spite of the fact that this had touched upon the most precious thing in his life. Rachel's death and burial broke Jacob's main link with his past carnal life at Haran. He had gone there to get a wife and had been guilty of many carnal things. "Jacob set a pillar upon her grave: that is the pillar of Rachel's grave unto this day" (v. 20). Jacob established a pillar near the house of bread in remembrance of this one who had been so very precious to him.

Because Jacob had returned to Bethel and had been fully restored to fellowship with God, he was now able to fulfill the second part of God's command: "Return . . . to thy kindred" (31:3). Thus, Jacob was on his way to his father, Isaac, who lived in Mamre. That is where Jacob was going when Rachel died in childbirth along the way.

## Reuben's Sin

As Jacob and his family continued on their way to Mamre, his firstborn, Reuben, committed a great sin. The Bible says, "And Israel journeyed, and spread his tent beyond the tower of Edar. And it came to pass, when Israel dwelt in that land, that Reuben went and lay with Bilhah his father's concubine: and Israel heard it" (vv. 21,22). Three times in these two verses Jacob is referred to by his new name, Israel. Jacob's life was now characterized by his new name.

When Reuben committed fornication with the concubine, it says that "Israel heard it." Before, when "Jacob" had learned of his sons' wickedness, he did nothing about it. But in Reuben's case, "Israel" was concerned about the things of God and did not let the sin go unpunished. Although it is not recorded in Genesis 35 how Jacob judged Reuben's sin, what he did was recorded later. Jacob said, "Reuben, thou art my firstborn, my might, and the beginning of my strength, the excellency of dignity, and the excellency of power: Unstable as water, thou shalt not excel; because thou wentest up to thy father's bed; then defiledst thou it: he went up to my couch" (49:3,4). Reuben, as the firstborn, had rightful possession to the birthright, but Jacob said, "Thou shalt not excel." Jacob thoroughly judged Reuben's sin and took away his birthright.

Reuben's birthright was given to Joseph. This is evident from I Chronicles 5:1,2: "Now the sons of Reuben the firstborn of Israel, (for he was the firstborn; but, forasmuch as he defiled his father's bed, his birthright was given unto the sons of Joseph the son of Israel: and the genealogy is not to be reckoned after the birthright. For Judah prevailed above his brethren, and of him came the chief ruler; but the birthright was Joseph's)."

## Isaac Dies

Finally, Jacob arrived at his father's home in Mamre: "Jacob came unto Isaac his father unto Mamre, unto the city of Arbah, which is Hebron, where Abraham and Isaac sojourned" (Gen. 35:27). Jacob had not seen his father for at least 30 years. What a reunion they must have had! During the next 13 years Jacob cared for his father. Then we are told, "The days of Isaac were an hundred and fourscore years. And Isaac gave up the ghost, and died, and was gathered unto his people, being old and full of days: and his sons Esau and

Jacob buried him" (vv. 28,29). The death of Isaac meant the separation of Jacob from the past generation. The responsibility of the family was now placed entirely on Jacob. He had deceived Esau out of the birthright and had stolen the blessing 43 years earlier, but now the birthright was his by divine appointment—and so was the responsibility.

It was also a sobering experience for me the day of my father's funeral. I was suddenly overwhelmed with the thought that the previous generation was gone. As the oldest in the family and the only son, I realized there was a special responsibility to carry on in behalf of the family. One of the last things my father said to me was, "There is Mother, and there are your younger sisters." Thus I, too, inherited special responsibility at the death of a father.

In the account of Isaac's death, it is precious to see that Esau and Jacob had been reconciled: "His sons Esau and Jacob buried him." Death is often a great reconciler. Esau had said 43 years earlier, "The days of mourning for my father are at hand; then will I slay my brother Jacob" (27:41). But Isaac did not die at that time, as was expected, and by the time he did, Esau and Jacob were reconciled.

Concerning Esau, Genesis 36:6-8 says, "And Esau took his wives, and his sons, and his daughters, and all the persons of his house, and his cattle, and all his beasts, and all his substance, which he had got in the land of Canaan; and went into the country from the face of his brother Jacob. For their riches were more than that they might dwell together; and the land wherein they were strangers could not bear them because of their cattle. Thus dwelt Esau in mount Seir: Esau is Edom." Esau completely separated himself from the birthright heritage which now belonged to Jacob. Now Jacob (Israel) experienced total separation unto God. Up until this time it was a separation *from* the things of the world, but now it was a separation *unto* God.

Consider all that Jacob buried as recorded in Genesis 35. First, he buried the strange gods that were yielded up by his household (v. 4). Second, he buried Deborah—the last link with his unregenerate life. Third, he buried Rachel—his major link with his past carnal life. Fourth, he buried Isaac—the last link with the past generation. DEATH was written across this whole scene.

If we want to have true communion with God and serve Him in newness of power, we, too, must have the sentence of death written on our members. This is evident from Romans 6:11-14: "Likewise reckon ye also yourselves to be dead indeed unto sin, but alive unto God through Jesus Christ our Lord. Let not sin therefore reign in your mortal body, that ye should obey it in the lusts thereof. Neither yield ye your members as instruments of unrighteousness unto sin: but yield yourselves unto God, as those that are alive from the dead, and your members as instruments of righteousness unto God. For sin shall not have dominion over you: for ye are not under the law, but under grace." The sentence of death must be passed upon the self-life if we are to be conquerors. This is an act of faith based on the already accomplished work of Christ (Rom. 6:6).

Afflictions such as Jacob had are not to be viewed as judgments from God which result from divine anger. God does not act in such a way toward His own children. However, we are told, "Whom the Lord loveth he chasteneth, and scourgeth every son whom he receiveth" (Heb. 12:6). Even afflictions are among the love gifts of God, sent in faithfulness for our blessing and to exercise our hearts thereby. They are intended to wean our affections from the things of the earth so that we will cast ourselves completely on God to learn and experience His sufficiency. These afflictions are some of the "all things" of Romans 8:28. They are what yield "the peaceable fruit of righteousness unto them which are exercised thereby" (Heb. 12:11).

God usually deals with His children on the tenderest spots in their lives so there will be no rival to Him. Later, Jacob also experienced a severe trial concerning Joseph (Rachel's firstborn), who was taken from him and sold into Egypt.

When we humbly submit, God usually returns what He has taken from us or gives us something better. This principle was seen in the life of Abraham. God called on Abraham to offer up Isaac, but God gave Isaac back to him. Jacob was now experiencing this principle in his own life through the loss of loved ones. All of these experiences were used to mold Jacob into the man God intended him to be. Like John the Baptist, Jacob came to the place of saying, "He must increase, but I must decrease" (John 3:30). The following song emphasizes this so beautifully:

O the bitter pain and sorrow,
That a time could ever be,
When I proudly said to Jesus,
All of self and none of Thee.

Day by day His tender mercies,
Helping healing full and free,
Brought me lower while I whispered,
Less of self and more of Thee.

Higher than the highest heaven,
Deeper than the deepest sea,
Lord, Thy love at last has conquered,
None of self and all of Thee.

—Theodore Monroe

A. J. Gordon said, "In every man's heart there is a throne and a cross. If Christ is on the throne, then self is on the cross. If self is on the throne, then Jesus is still on the cross."

Chapter 27

# Victorious Faith in the Retiring Years

In his retiring years, Jacob might well have been described by the words, "For which cause we faint not; but though our outward man perish, yet the inward man is renewed day by day. For our light affliction, which is but for a moment, worketh for us a far more exceeding and eternal weight of glory; While we look not at the things which are seen, but at the things which are not seen: for the things which are seen are temporal; but the things which are not seen are eternal" (II Cor. 4:16-18).

Jacob's retiring years evidenced the triumphs of God's grace in transforming a nearly impossible person. These latter years were the results of God's working in his life during all those previous years. God always showed Himself as a God of mercy, long-suffering and grace.

In considering the grace of God, it is impossible to know which is the greater—the grace of God, which gives the believer a perfect standing in Christ; or the grace of God, which ever bears with the believer in his failure to make his state (behavior) correspond with his standing (position in Christ). As we consider both of these aspects, we will be overwhelmed with the realization that Christ died for our sins so that we could receive Him as Saviour, and that God has been so long-suffering, merciful and gracious to us throughout the years. How patiently God works with us until we produce the kind of fruit He desires.

Verses that especially emphasize the long-suffering and goodness of God toward us are Psalm 103:10-14: "He hath not dealt with us after our sins; nor rewarded us according to our iniquities. For as the heaven is high above the earth, so great is his mercy toward them that fear him. As far as the east is from the west, so far hath he removed our transgressions from us. Like as a father pitieth his children, so the Lord pitieth them that fear him. For he knoweth our frame; he remembereth that we are dust."

## Joseph Is Sold

Concerning Jacob, the Word of God says that he "dwelt in the land wherein his father was a stranger, in the land of Canaan" (Gen. 37:1). Although Jacob was in the land of his fathers, he still experienced the heartaches of reaping what he had sown. His son Joseph was sold into Egypt, but Jacob was made to think differently by his sons.

Jacob's sons had "sold Joseph to the Ishmeelites for twenty pieces of silver" (v. 28). Then "they took Joseph's coat, and killed a kid of the goats, and dipped the coat in the blood; And they sent the coat of many colours, and they brought it to their father; and said, This have we found: know now whether it be thy son's coat or no. And he knew it, and said, It is my son's coat; an evil beast hath devoured him; Joseph is without doubt rent in pieces. And Jacob rent his clothes, and put sackcloth upon his loins, and mourned for his son many days. And all his sons and all his daughters rose up to comfort him; but he refused to be comforted; and he said, For I will go down into the grave unto my son mourning. Thus his father wept for him" (vv. 31-35). The apparent death of Joseph again struck one of Jacob's tenderest spots, and victory was slow in coming.

Joseph had risen to a place of rulership in the land of Egypt and was responsible for conserving food in the time of famine. "Now when Jacob saw that there was corn in Egypt, Jacob said unto his sons, Why do ye look one upon another? And he said, Behold, I have heard that there is corn in Egypt: get you down thither, and buy for us from thence; that we may live, and not die" (42:1,2).

Jacob's action stood in great contrast to the action of his father, Isaac, and of his grandfather, Abraham. When these men had experienced famine, they left the place where they were abiding. Abraham went to Egypt, and Isaac went to the border of the land before God stopped him. But by this time Jacob had learned a great lesson. He was not going to leave the land where the house of God was—Bethel. Twice he sent his sons to Egypt to buy food, but he himself refused to leave the land. He had endured all the suffering he could possibly take, and he was not about to leave the land and invite more suffering.

When Simeon was retained in Egypt until the sons would bring their youngest brother, Benjamin, to Egypt, it was almost more than Jacob could bear. Jacob told his sons, "Me have ye bereaved of my children: Joseph is not, and Simeon is not, and ye will take Benjamin away: all these things are against me" (v. 36). The eldest son, Reuben, told his father, "Slay my two sons, if I bring him not to thee: deliver him into my hand, and I will bring him to thee again" (v. 37). However, Jacob was insistent upon not letting Benjamin go to Egypt. He said, "My son shall not go down with you; for his brother is dead, and he is left alone: if mischief befall him by the way in the which ye go, then shall ye bring down my gray hairs with sorrow to the grave" (v. 38).

### Jacob Lets Benjamin Go

Things became worse for Jacob and his family, and it became apparent they would have to go to Egypt if they were to get enough food to live. Jacob's son Judah suggested, "Send the lad [Benjamin] with me, and we will arise and go; that we may live, and not die, both we, and thou, and also our little ones. I will be surety for him; of my hand shalt thou require him: if I bring him not unto thee, and set him before thee, then let me bear the blame for ever" (43:8,9).

Finally, Jacob agreed. The Bible says, "Their father Israel said unto them, If it must be so now, do this; take of the best fruits in the land in your vessels, and carry down the man a present, a little balm, and a little honey, spices, and myrrh, nuts, and almonds: And take double money in your hand; and the money that was brought again in the mouth of your sacks, carry it again in your hand; peradventure it was an oversight: Take also your brother, and arise, go again unto the man: And God Almighty give you mercy before the man, that he may send away your other brother, and Benjamin. If I be bereaved of my children, I am bereaved" (vv. 11-14).

Jacob did not know that Joseph was the ruler in Egypt who had made the demand to see his beloved brother Benjamin. When Jacob agreed to let Benjamin go, the Bible refers to Jacob as "Israel" (v. 11). The Spirit had won out! Death to the self-life finally conquered.

God never leaves believers unrewarded when they totally commit themselves to the Holy Spirit. The reaping is always beyond our highest expectations. This is emphasized in Romans 6:5,8: "For if we have been planted together in the likeness of his [Christ's] death, we shall be also in the likeness of his resurrection. Now if we be dead with Christ, we believe that we shall also live with him."

It is necessary to die to self in order to really live. It is necessary to lose one's life in order to really find it. Jesus said, "Except a corn of wheat fall into the ground and die, it abideth alone: but if it die, it bringeth forth much fruit. He that loveth his life shall lose it, and he that hateth his life in this world shall keep it unto life eternal" (John 12:24,25). No matter how difficult circumstances may seem, nothing can separate us from the love of God, but rather "in all these things we are more than conquerors through him that loved us" (Rom. 8:37).

### Joseph Is Alive!

Jacob discovered the reality of these principles also. Having been willing to give up everything, God returned not only what he had given up—Benjamin—but brought him the further blessing of knowing that Joseph was alive. Even more than that, Jacob and his family were invited to Egypt to feast under Joseph's supervision.

When Jacob's sons returned from Egypt and told him, "Joseph is yet alive, and he is governor over all the land of Egypt" (Gen. 45:26), the Word of God says that "Jacob's heart fainted, for he believed them not." Jacob's sons "told him all the words of Joseph, which he had said unto them: and when he saw the wagons which Joseph had sent to carry him, the spirit of Jacob their father revived: And Israel said, It is enough; Joseph my son is yet alive: I will go and see him before I die" (vv. 27,28). Notice that verse 27 uses the name "Jacob" when it says, "Jacob's spirit revived." However, verse 28 uses the name "Israel" when it says, "And Israel said. . . . "

Israel, not Jacob, now put God first. His aching heart longed for reunion with Joseph, but he did not go to Joseph until he had done something extremely important. "Israel took his journey with all that he had, and came to Beer-sheba, and offered sacrifices unto the God of his father Isaac" (46:1). Jacob did not go to Joseph without first communing with God and seeking His permission. God met Jacob at this time, and this was the seventh and final communication of God with Jacob. "God spake unto Israel in the visions of the night, and said, Jacob, Jacob. And he said, Here am I. And he said, I am God, the God of thy father: fear not to go down into Egypt; for I will there make of thee a great nation: I will go down with thee into Egypt; and I will also surely bring thee up again: and Joseph shall put his hand upon thine eyes" (vv. 2-4). God gave Jacob a fourfold promise. First, God said, "I will there make of thee a great nation" (v. 3). Second, God promised, "I will go down with thee into Egypt" (v. 4). Third, God assured Jacob, "I will also surely bring thee up again" (v. 4). Fourth, God promised Jacob that "Joseph shall put his hand upon thine eyes" (v. 4).

One of God's purposes in permitting Jacob and his people to go to Egypt was so He could make a great people of them there. There was a danger in Canaan that Jacob and his people would mix with the Canaanites and lose their distinction as God's chosen people. There was also a great possibility that Jacob and his people would be destroyed by the Canaanites. In Egypt, however, they would be a separate people, unmolested and allowed to multiply greatly.

### A Separate People

In Egypt, they would remain a distinct people through whom God could work in fulfilling His promises. There was no possibility that the Israelites would be absorbed by the Egyptians because the Israelites were kept completely separate. "Joseph said unto his brethren, and unto his father's house, I will go up, and shew Pharaoh, and say unto him, My brethren, and my father's house, which were in the land of Canaan, are come unto me; And the men are shepherds, for their trade hath been to feed cattle; and they have brought their flocks, and their herds, and all that they have. And it shall come to pass, when Pharaoh shall call you, and shall say, What is your occupation? Then ye shall say, Thy servants' trade hath been about cattle from our youth even until now, both we, and also our fathers: that ye may dwell in the land of Goshen; for every shepherd is an abomination unto the Egyptians" (vv. 31-34). This was part of God's plan to keep the Israelites separate from the Egyptians.

Pharaoh did as Joseph had hoped. He told Joseph, "The land of Egypt is before thee; in the best of the land make thy father and brethren to dwell: in the land of Goshen let them dwell: and if thou knowest any men of activity among them, then make them rulers over my cattle" (47:6). The Israelites needed a place where they could grow as a people and, at the same time, remain separate from the Egyptian people. The attitude of the Egyptians toward shepherds was used of God to make both of these things possible.

Joseph introduced his aged father to Pharaoh: "Joseph brought in Jacob his father, and set him before Pharaoh: and Jacob blessed Pharaoh. And Pharaoh said unto Jacob, How old art thou? And Jacob said unto Pharaoh, The days of the years of my pilgrimage are an hundred and thirty years: few and evil have the days of the years of my life been, and have not attained unto the days of the years of the life of my fathers in the days of their pilgrimage. And Jacob blessed Pharaoh" (vv. 7-10).

Jacob was both bold and spiritually courageous before Pharaoh. Although Pharaoh considered Jacob an outcast because he was a shepherd, Jacob carried himself as a child of God before Pharaoh. After all, Jacob was a son of the King of kings and an ambassador of the Most High. Jacob blessed Pharaoh—"the less [was] blessed of the better" (Heb. 7:7), even as Abraham was blessed by Melchizedek. Jacob realized his true position in God as he stood before Pharaoh.

Jacob also acknowledged his pilgrim status when he referred to the "years of my pilgrimage" (v. 9). Jacob viewed his entire life on earth as a pilgrimage. In this regard, he identified himself with Abraham and Isaac. Hebrews 11:9,10 says, "By faith he sojourned in the land of promise, as in a strange country, dwelling in tabernacles [tents] with Isaac and Jacob, the heirs with him of the same promise: For he looked for a city which hath foundations, whose builder and maker is God."

## Jacob's Request

Genesis 47:27 says, "And Israel dwelt in the land of Egypt, in the country of Goshen; and they had possessions therein, and grew, and multiplied exceedingly." Just as God had promised, there was great enlargement of the nation in Egypt. God was building a nation from Jacob. Of Jacob it is said that he "lived in the land of Egypt seventeen years: so the whole age of Jacob was an hundred forty and seven years" (v. 28).

Jacob was old and about to die, but he did not want to be buried in Egypt. The Scriptures say, "The time drew nigh that Israel must die: and he called his son Joseph, and said unto him, If now I have found grace in thy sight, put, I pray thee, thy hand under my thigh, and deal kindly and truly with me; bury me not, I pray thee, in Egypt: But I will lie with my fathers, and thou shalt carry me out of Egypt, and bury me in their buryingplace. And he said, I will do as thou hast said. And he said, Swear unto me. And he sware unto him. And Israel bowed himself upon the bed's head" (vv. 29-31).

In faith and triumph Jacob looked forward to the time of the resurrection. His desire to be buried with his fathers was not mere sentimentality—it was the embracing of God's promise to possess the land. Jacob's besetting sin of unbelief had now been cast aside and worship in faith was put in its place. Jacob's reason for wanting to be buried in the land was so he could be resurrected from it. Jacob now had an active faith.

## Jacob Blesses Joseph's Sons

Before he died, "Israel said unto Joseph, Behold, I die: but God shall be with you, and bring you again unto the land of your fathers" (48:21). Jacob was confident that all of his descendants would eventually be brought back into the land of his fathers. This act of worship in faith and the blessing of Joseph's two sons mark the climax of Jacob's faith as mentioned in Hebrews 11:21: "By faith Jacob, when he was a dying, blessed both the sons of Joseph; and worshipped, leaning upon the top of his staff."

Before Jacob blessed Joseph's sons, he rehearsed for Joseph God's goodness in promise and fulfillment. Jacob told Joseph how God had said to him, "Behold, I will make thee fruitful, and multiply thee, and I will make of thee a multitude of people; and will give this land to thy seed after thee for an everlasting possession" (Gen. 48:4). Then Jacob claimed Joseph's sons as his own: "And now thy two sons, Ephraim and Manasseh, which were born unto thee in the land of Egypt before I came unto thee unto Egypt, are mine; as Reuben and Simeon, they shall be mine" (v. 5). Having claimed them as his own sons, Jacob told Joseph, "Bring them, I pray thee, unto me, and I will bless them" (v. 9).

The account of Jacob's blessing Joseph's sons is recorded in Genesis 48:10-14: "Now the eyes of Israel were dim for age, so that he could not see. And he brought them near unto him; and he kissed them, and embraced them. And Israel said unto Joseph, I had not thought to see thy face: and, lo, God hath shewed me also thy seed. And Joseph brought them out from between his knees, and he bowed himself with his face to the earth. And Joseph took them both, Ephraim in his right hand toward Israel's left hand, and Manasseh in his left hand toward Israel's right hand, and brought them near unto him. And Israel stretched out his right hand, and laid it upon Ephraim's head, who was the younger, and his left hand upon Manasseh's head, guiding his hands wittingly; for Manasseh was the firstborn."

Joseph objected to what his father was doing: "When Joseph saw that his father laid his right hand upon the head of Ephraim, it displeased him: and he held up his father's hand, to remove it from Ephraim's head unto Manasseh's head" (v. 17). Because Manasseh was the firstborn and would customarily receive the major blessing, Joseph had brought his sons before Jacob in the position for Jacob to lay his right hand on Manasseh's head. But Jacob crossed his arms and did the opposite. Joseph said, "Not so, my father: for this is the firstborn; put thy right hand upon his head" (v. 18).

Jacob refused to do as Joseph suggested. He told Joseph, "I know it, my son, I know it: he also shall become a people, and he also shall be great: but truly his younger brother shall be greater than he, and his seed shall become a multitude of nations" (v. 19).

In this incident we see again God's sovereign choice of the younger son instead of the older one. Seth was chosen instead of Cain; Shem instead of Japheth; Abraham instead of Haran; Isaac instead of Ishmael; Jacob instead of Esau; and now Ephraim instead of Manasseh.

In faith Jacob blessed Joseph's sons. His eyes were weak, but because of faith his vision was strong.

## Jacob Blesses His Sons

The end for Jacob had come. He called all of his sons together for their final blessing. This was a fitting climax which demonstrated the power of God's prevailing grace. One by one Jacob blessed his children.

In all of his earlier life Jacob had been occupied with himself; now he was occupied only with others. In his earlier days he had been mainly concerned about planning for the present; but now he was occupied with only the future. "Jacob called unto his sons, and said, Gather yourselves together, that I may tell you that which shall befall you in the last days" (49:1). As Jacob was blessing his sons, he turned his attention heavenward and said, "I have waited for thy salvation, O Lord" (v. 18). One of the main things Jacob had not been able to do during his lifetime was to wait. But the grace of God had completed a work in his life. What God had begun, He finished. God had enabled Jacob to overcome the sin which had so easily beset him.

Jacob gathered his sons about him to bless them and to foretell the future of their lives and of the tribes who would be their descendants. Jacob said, "Gather yourselves together, and hear, ye sons of Jacob; and hearken unto Israel your father" (v. 2).

They were the "sons of Jacob" in that they were born during his years of carnality when he was a schemer and supplanter. Even though they were the sons of Jacob, he exhorted them to "hearken unto Israel your father." As Israel, he was now speaking the words of God. The predictions given by Jacob in Genesis 49 are some of the most striking predictions found anywhere in the Old Testament. Jacob spoke in love, but he was firm and truthful.

### Reuben

Jacob's attention turned first to his eldest son, Reuben. Jacob said, "Reuben, thou art my firstborn, my might, and the beginning of my strength, the excellency of dignity, and the excellency of power: Unstable as water, thou shalt not excel; because thou wentest up to thy father's bed; then defiledst thou it: he went up to my couch" (vv. 3,4). As the firstborn, the place of excellency and position of dignity belonged to Reuben. However, his place of preeminence was forfeited because of the great sin he had committed earlier. That which was true of Reuben was also to be true of the tribe that would be born from him—"unstable as water, thou shalt not excel."

Because of Reuben's sin, the birthright was taken from him and given to Joseph, the firstborn of Rachel. The birthright involved a double portion of the inheritance and the sceptre which indicated the line of Christ. Whereas the double portion of the birthright went to Joseph, the sceptre went to Judah.

This is also seen from I Chronicles 5:1,2: "Now the sons of Reuben the firstborn of Israel, (for he was the firstborn; but, forasmuch as he defiled his father's bed, his birthright was given unto the sons of Joseph the son of Israel: and the genealogy is not to be reckoned after the birthright. For Judah prevailed above his brethren, and of him came the chief ruler; but the birthright was Joseph's)." The double portion of Reuben's birthright was Joseph's (given to his sons, Ephraim and Manasseh), but the genealogy of Jesus Christ was to be reckoned through Judah.

## Judah

In blessing Judah, Jacob said, "Judah, thou art he whom thy brethren shall praise: thy hand shall be in the neck of thine enemies; thy father's children shall bow down before thee. Judah is a lion's whelp: from the prey, my son, thou art gone up: he stooped down, he couched as a lion, and as an old lion; who shall rouse him up? The sceptre shall not depart from Judah, nor a lawgiver from between his feet, until Shiloh [Jesus Christ] come; and unto him shall the gathering of the people be" (Gen. 49:8-10).

Reuben did not excel, but Judah prevailed above his brethren. From Reuben's tribe came no judges, kings or prophets—those who excelled. However, there were many of the tribe of Judah who excelled, and from this tribe was born the Lord Jesus Christ.

The double portion of the birthright that was given to Joseph was to remain his forever. In Ezekiel 47:13, which gives the borders of the land in the millennial age, God said, "This shall be the border, whereby ye shall inherit the land according to the twelve tribes of Israel: Joseph shall have two portions."

## Simeon and Levi

When Jacob was delineating the characteristics of his sons and of those who would be born from them, he said, "Simeon and Levi are brethren; instruments of cruelty are in their habitations. O my soul, come not thou into their secret; unto their assembly, mine honour, be not thou united: for in their anger they slew a man, and in their selfwill they digged down a wall. Cursed be their anger, for it was fierce; and their wrath, for it was cruel: I will divide them in Jacob, and scatter them in Israel" (Gen. 49:5-7).

These were the two sons who had murdered the men at Shechem after the men had been circumcised. Jacob had told his sons at that time, "Ye have troubled me to make me to stink among the inhabitants of the land" (34:30). Now Jacob said that they would be scattered among their brethren—"I will divide them in Jacob, and scatter them in Israel" (49:7). This was exactly what happened. Simeon did not receive a special portion of the land for himself but had to dwell in the midst of his brethren. Neither did Levi receive a special portion, but he received cities where his tribe was to live. Although Levi had greatly sinned against the Lord, his descendants later took a stand for God that resulted in blessing for their tribe. The incident involved is recorded in Exodus 32. Moses had not returned from the mountaintop as quickly as the Israelites had expected, so they urged Aaron to make gods for them because they did not know what had happened to Moses. Aaron told the people, "Break off the golden earrings, which are in the ears of your wives, of your sons, and of your daughters, and bring them unto me" (v. 2). These were brought to Aaron and "he received them at their hand, and fashioned it with a graving [engraving] tool, after he had made it a molten [melted] calf: and they said, These be thy gods, O Israel, which brought thee up out of the land of Egypt" (v. 4).

When Moses returned from the mountaintop and saw what had taken place, he "stood in the gate of the camp, and said, Who is on the Lord's side? let him come unto me. And all the sons of Levi gathered themselves together unto him. And he said unto them, Thus saith the Lord God of Israel, Put every man his sword by his side, and go in and out from gate to gate throughout the camp, and slay every man his brother, and every man his companion, and every man his neighbour. And the children of Levi did according to the word of Moses" (vv. 26-28).

The sons of Levi did not participate in the sin of making the golden calf. Instead, they were on the Lord's side and did as Moses instructed. In the grace of God, the Levites were chosen for the priesthood and were given cities among all the people, but they were not given separate inheritance of the land.

## Jacob's Final Charge

Jacob gave a special blessing to each of his sons. Genesis 49:28 says, "All these are the twelve tribes of Israel: and this is it that their father spake unto them, and blessed them; every one according to his blessing he blessed them." None was overlooked. Jacob spoke faithfully about the temporal results of the sins of some of them, but each one was blessed with a special blessing.

Having blessed them, Jacob gave them a final charge: "I am to be gathered unto my people: bury me with my fathers in the cave that is in the field of Ephron the Hittite, In the cave that is in the field of Machpelah, which is before Mamre, in the land of Canaan, which Abraham bought with the field of Ephron the Hittite for a possession of a buryingplace. There they buried Abraham and Sarah his wife; there they buried Isaac and Rebekah his wife; and there I buried Leah" (vv. 29-31). Jacob (Israel) realized that Egypt was not to be his final resting place. God had promised that Jacob would return to the land of his fathers. Therefore, Jacob gave instructions to his sons to carry him back to the land where he would wait for the resurrection. He, too, "looked for a city which hath foundations, whose builder and maker is God" (Heb. 11:10).

### Jacob's Death and Burial

"When Jacob had made an end of commanding his sons, he gathered up his feet into the bed, and yielded up the ghost, and was gathered unto his people" (Gen. 49:33). This was the final scene for this man who had become great in the sight of God and in the sight of the world. Everything was now accomplished. The last counsel had been given. The last blessing had been given. The last charge had been laid upon his sons. Then he "yielded up the ghost, and was gathered unto his people." Jacob's death was the death of a believer. He yielded up his spirit to God and was reunited with his own people in the grave.

The funeral procession from Egypt to Canaan was one of the greatest funeral processions of all time. It covered a distance of 200 to 300 miles, depending on which road they took.

Observe the people involved in the funeral procession. Pharaoh gave permission to Joseph, saying, "Go up, and bury thy father, according as he made thee swear. And Joseph went up to bury his father: and with him went up all the servants of Pharaoh, the elders of his house, and all the elders of the land of Egypt, And all the house of Joseph, and his brethren, and his father's house: only their little ones, and their flocks, and their herds, they left in the land of Goshen.

And there went up with him both chariots and horsemen: and it was a very great company" (50:6-9).

It is significant that even "all the servants of Pharaoh" traveled from Egypt to Canaan in the funeral procession. Of this great company of people the Scriptures say, "They came to the threshing-floor of Atad, which is beyond Jordan, and there they mourned with a great and very sore lamentation: and he [Joseph] made a mourning for his father seven days" (v. 10).

What a striking sight this was to the Canaanites! "When the inhabitants of the land, the Canaanites, saw the mourning in the floor of Atad, they said, This is a grievous mourning to the Egyptians: wherefore the name of it was called Abel-mizraim, which is beyond Jordan" (v. 11). This was a climaxing testimony in death that crowned the final faith of God's man, Israel. God had won His man by love, mercy, grace—and the final glory rang throughout the land of his sojourning. The pagans were not without a witness of what God had done and could do.

Abraham, Isaac and Jacob had "looked for a city which hath foundations, whose builder and maker is God." These patriarchs were not satisfied with transitory promises. They were occupied with the thoughts of coming resurrection. Jesus Christ Himself said, "But as touching the resurrection of the dead, have ye not read that which was spoken unto you by God, saying, I am the God of Abraham, and the God of Isaac, and the God of Jacob? God is not the God of the dead, but of the living" (Matt. 22:31,32).

The Christian is inspired by the hope of the resurrection; in fact, the sky, not the grave, is his goal. First Thessalonians 4:16-18 says, "For the Lord himself shall descend from heaven with a shout, with the voice of the archangel, and with the trump of God: and the dead in Christ shall rise first: Then we which are alive and remain shall be caught up together with them in the clouds, to meet the Lord in the air: and so shall we ever be with the Lord. Wherefore comfort one another with these words." This is true dying. On his deathbed, D. L. Moody said, "If this is dying, let me die."

In the Book of the Revelation, the Apostle John wrote: "And I John saw the holy city, new Jerusalem, coming down from God out of heaven, prepared as a bride adorned for her husband. And I heard a great voice out of heaven saying, Behold, the tabernacle of God is with men, and he will dwell with them, and they shall be his people, and God himself shall be with them, and be their God. And God shall wipe away all tears from their eyes; and there shall be no more death, neither sorrow, nor crying, neither shall there be any more pain: for the former things are passed away. And he that sat upon the throne said, Behold, I make all things new. And he said unto me, Write: for these words are true and faithful" (21:2-5).

An all-inclusive invitation is given in Revelation 22:17: "And the Spirit and the bride say, Come. And let him that heareth say, Come. And let him that is athirst come. And whosoever will, let him take the water of life freely." The Apostle John concluded the Book of the Revelation with the words: "He which testifieth these things saith, Surely I come quickly. Amen. Even so, come, Lord Jesus. The grace of our Lord Jesus Christ be with you all. Amen" (vv. 20,21).

If God should call you from this life today, would you be able to say with the Apostle Paul, "I have fought a good fight, I have finished my course, I have kept the faith: Henceforth there is laid up for me a crown of righteousness, which the Lord, the righteous judge, shall give me at that day: and not to me only, but unto all them also that love his appearing" (II Tim. 4:7,8)?

### Jacob in Restrospect

Jacob is probably the most controversial character in the Bible. His weaknesses attract us because they cause him to appear more human. We feel he was more like we are. In Jacob, God's grace and patience resulted in a marvelous demonstration of what God can do with a man because He never wearies or gives up. If you are discouraged or brokenhearted over failure, never forget that God loves you and will not give up working to bring out His best in you. Remember, "the God of Jacob" is your God. He is unchanged, for He is "the same yesterday, and to day, and for ever" (Heb. 13:8).

Through the many tests and trials that God brought into Jacob's life, God brought forth a man who rates in the gallery of the heroes of faith. He calls Himself "the God of Jacob" and He is our God also. Twice in one psalm the psalmist exclaimed, "The Lord of hosts is with us; the God of Jacob is our refuge. Selah" (46:7,11).

## Jacob's Diversified History

Jacob's life may be divided into nine stages during which he was trained and disciplined. First, Jacob's life at home was under his strong-minded and self-willed mother, Rebekah. Her qualities were family characteristics, for Laban was the same way. Jacob also turned out to be a strong-minded, self-willed individual.

Second, Jacob reached a crisis at Bethel where he met God for the first time in a personal way. This seems to have been the time of his conversion and of realizing that God was undertaking for his life—for him personally.

Third, Jacob received training and discipline while he was with his uncle Laban. God used Laban to show Jacob exactly what he himself was like. This stage of Jacob's life lasted 20 years.

Fourth, Jacob's long night at Peniel was a major turning point in his life, for there he began his life of surrender to God's commands. He did not always let God control his life after that time, but he made giant strides in his walk with the Lord because of his attitude of surrender.

Fifth, Jacob's mountaintop experience at Peniel was followed by serious backsliding at Shechem. This backsliding resulted in great sorrow and trials to himself and his family. While living there, his daughter was raped and his sons committed murder in revenge.

Sixth, Jacob finally returned to Bethel and was restored to godly favor and fellowship. From this time on he constantly advanced in spiritual growth and maturity in the faith life.

Seventh, there followed years of deep sorrow and suffering for Jacob which strengthened and mellowed him.

Eighth, there was the restoration of his son Joseph and the restful and fruitful years in Egypt. All of Jacob's life he had had a "restless" faith, but in Egypt he came to the place of a "resting" faith.

Ninth, Jacob's life was climaxed by his final great pronouncement of faith and triumph, by a peaceful death, and by a great testimony even in his burial.

Of these nine periods of Jacob's life, there were three that were especially crucial. His vision at Bethel was crucial in that it was no doubt the time of his regeneration. His struggle at Peniel was crucial in that it was there that he began his life of surrender to God's commands. His return to Bethel was crucial because it was there that he became established in true spiritual warfare for the Lord.

## Jacob's Diversified Character

In Jacob's life there were two completely divergent qualities; yet there was a blending of them. He desired the things of God, but he used carnal means to obtain God's blessing.

In his youth, Jacob had the intense ambition to be the head of the family and to inherit the promises. In his old age, he had a remarkable quietness and gentleness of disposition.

Jacob seemed to have a deep understanding and full appreciation of God's covenant, but there was the sad aspect of his self-seeking disposition which seemed to stop at nothing to gain its ends.

He had a deep love which centered in his mother, wife and two boys, but he was also a cautious, suspicious individual who mistrusted everyone except himself.

Jacob had high aims and worked toward important goals, but he stooped to the most contemptible means of attaining his goals.

Jacob experienced slow progress in allowing the new nature (Israel) to have control over the old nature (Jacob). His old nature was never eradicated, but it was slowly subdued as his life took on more of the characteristics of Israel and less of the characteristics of Jacob. The transforming of Jacob into Israel was a slow process.

From the very first, Jacob's heart was set on the possessions included in the covenant of God which was given to his fathers. He knew that it was of God that he should inherit the possessions. In the closing years of his life, the many years of severe discipline bore abundant fruit and he emerged in strength and glory of character and life. At last he was more concerned about the Giver than about the gifts.

## Jacob's Diversified Training

Jacob passed through *the school of sorrow and suffering.* He reaped what he had sown. His many serious mistakes took their toll on his life. He had deep sorrow because of the loss of his loved ones. There were many severe disappointments in his life. He had worked seven years for Rachel, but his father-in-law cheated him and he had had to work another seven years for her. Then there was Reuben's sin and Simeon and Levi's treacheries. Jacob also experienced much heartache because of Joseph's being sold into slavery in Egypt and because of his sons' demands that Benjamin be sent to Egypt with them during the time of famine.

Jacob also experienced *the school of God's providence.* As God performed His work in him, Jacob became a man of quiet initiative, with abundant resources and a dauntless courage. Slowly but surely God directed Jacob into the path of spiritual usefulness. Jacob's resources were to be used by God and for God, but this was not true early in his life. Through God's constant and firm discipline, He brought Jacob to the place of putting all of his resources at God's disposal. At the end of his life, no one had more courage than Jacob. As Jacob stood before Pharaoh, not even Joseph could supersede him in courage.

Jacob also experienced *the school of divine grace.* This was the greatest and best training ground of Jacob's entire life. God's work in Jacob's life is possibly the outstanding example of God's patience and long-suffering in dealing with His creatures. God's grace in Jacob's life stands out above all else and gives hope to the weakest, lowest and most hopeless believer. God is out to win, and win He will. "He which hath begun a good work in you will perform it unto the day of Jesus Christ" (Phil. 1:6).

God's presence, full of grace and power, never left Jacob from the time of his vision at Bethel to the closing days of his life in Egypt. Jacob may not have always realized it, but God was constantly with him to perform His will through his life. God has said to us also, "I will never leave thee, nor forsake thee" (Heb. 13:5). Thus, we are able to understand why the person who has the God of Jacob for his refuge is blessed. What kind of a God do you have?

Concerning "the God of Jacob," W. H. Griffith Thomas wrote:

"There is scarcely anything more striking in the whole of the Old Testament than the frequency of the title, 'the God of Jacob,' in the Psalms and in Isaiah. We could well understand God being the God of Israel, but to be called the God of Jacob is surely the crowning proof of Divine mercy and grace. What a remarkable point there is in the well-known words, 'The Lord of Hosts is with us; the God of Jacob is our refuge' (Ps. 46:7). 'The Lord of Hosts' is the God of Providence, protecting against foes, overcoming difficulties, and providing for all emergencies, but 'the God of Jacob is our refuge' is very much more than this. It tells of His mercy and grace. The God of Jacob is a God of unwearying love, of unerring wisdom, of unfailing grace. He is our Refuge in spite of our sins, in the face of our failures, in view of our fears. And because He is all this He asks for our unreserved surrender, our unquestioning faith, our unflinching loyalty, our unfailing hope, and whispers in our hearts, 'Fear not thou worm Jacob . . . I will help thee, saith the Lord, and thy Redeemer is the Holy One of Israel.' It is because God is the God of Jacob that we have such unbounded confidence in His mercy and grace, in His love and longsuffering. It tells us what grace can do for even the very worst of us. As a man said to a clergyman not long ago, 'I am cheered when I read the life of Jacob; for if the grace of Almighty God was able to straighten up that man, there must be some hope for me'' (*Genesis, A Devotional Commentary*, pp. 494, 495).

How wonderful it is to know that the God of Jacob is our God also! Claim Him as your own by faith. Rejoice in His love, mercy and grace. Triumph through His almighty power, for He works in you and through you by His indwelling presence. "Christ in you, the hope of glory" (Col. 1:27).